SEMIOTIC INVESTIGATIONS

Semiotic Investigations

TOWARDS AN EFFECTIVE SEMIOTICS

Alec McHoul

University of Nebraska Press

Lincoln & London

Publication of this book was assisted by
grants from the Murdoch University Board of
Research and the School of Humanities
Research Committee.

Acknowledgments for the use of pre-
viously published material appear on page xxiii
© 1996 by the University of Nebraska Press
⊗The paper in this book meets the
minimum requirements of the American
National Standard for Information
Sciences – Permanence of Paper for Printed
Library Materials, ANSI Z39.48-1984.

Library of Congress
Cataloging in Publication Data
McHoul, A. W.
Semiotic investigations: towards an effective
semiotics / Alec McHoul.   p.   cm.
Includes bibliographical references (p.   )
and index.   ISBN 0-8032-3191-1
1. Semiotics – Philosophy. 2. Semiotics –
Methodology.   I. Title.
P99.M397 1996   302.2–dc20
95-43854 CIP

Contents

Preface   vii
Acknowledgments   xxiii

PART ONE
The Limits and Media of Semiosis   1
1 Signifying History   3
2 Framing Photographs   19
3 Culture and Community   41
4 Signs and Not-signs   55
5 Reading Practices   65

PART TWO
From Formalism and Ethnomethodology to Ethics   89
6 Reflexivity, Problems, and Solutions   91
7 Ethnogenealogy: Public Methods for
   Private Practices   101
8 Intelligibility, Actionability, and Historicity   131
9 Indexicality's Horizon of Possibility   137
10 Signing in the Rain   147
11 Closing off Openings   153
12 Gatekeeping Logic   165
13 Converse Communities   173
14 Analytic Ethics   191

Notes   213
Works Cited   231
Index   243

Preface

By 'effective semiotics' I mean the investigation of effective semiosis: the ways signs have meaning by virtue of their actual uses.[1] These uses take place in a number of 'media,' the most important being the medium of history — so important, in fact, that it catches up all the other possible media of semiosis, including everyday life and language, fiction, film, talk, art, mathematics, photography, and so on, as well as the 'communities' that practice these forms. And importantly, this relation of semiosis to history is definitional; for by 'history' I mean the medium-in-general of semiosis. But still the definition is not unproblematic, for there are 'relations' (a number of them) between semiosis and its most general medium — and a discussion of these relations is the central topic of chapter 1.

I begin that chapter with a brief statement about the idea of semiosis as meaning-as-use (as opposed to those formalist views about meaning to be found in linguistic semantics); I then go on to explore a nonlinear and nonteleological view of general history based on Nietzsche. Finally, I turn to Wittgenstein's conception of grammar, since his rather odd use of this term to convey the sense of a grammar-of-use could easily, in itself, form the theoretical base of the present investigations were it not that the idea of history itself is almost absent from Wittgenstein's considerations on this topic.

By connecting Wittgenstein's idea of a use-grammar to Nietzsche's view of history as necessarily undecidable, I establish the major principle of these investigations: that we can never find an absolute answer to the question What is semiosis? For if semiosis is more of a family-resemblance phenomenon and less of a fixed entity, asking about its defining characteristics will be pointless. Instead, we have to ask the question *separately when we begin each new semiotic investigation*. So, as we will see, what semiosis is in the case of, say, human conversation will be a very different question from what it is in the case of (again, for example) comics, films, photographs, logical propositions, or toilet graffiti.

To take one example of this historical process, I turn in chapter 2 to the case of single photograph: a picture of one of the children kept in Barnardo's Homes in the 1880s. What I try to show there is that the meaning of this photograph cannot be either its referent alone (the girl herself) or a fixed set of historical conditions out of which it was produced. Rather, the meaning of the photograph alters and changes (and at times remains stable) depending on the practices inside which it is taken up. Hence the photograph means one thing when used as a form of institutional record keeping and another when used to illustrate a lantern slide lecture, and so on for a very broad range of semiosic technologies. The referent, then, turns out to be a possible thing that may give the photograph its meaning: but only if some particular community treats it this way. The referent is – to use a concept introduced later in the book – only *one* potential 'not-sign' that particular communities use as the outside-the-space-of-the-sign. Other communities might by contrast find, for example, deeper *aesthetic* possibilities in the picture, and hence their use for the referent as a particularly privileged not-sign would be minimal. But what are these communities that seem to be so crucial to the empirical work of effective semiotics? Are they anything like cultures, for example? To ask this question the book moves on, out of a purely historical mode and into the problem of concepts for understanding the meanings (uses) of signs. And the first of these concepts is that of community. This is followed in short order by a discussion of the concept of the not-sign and then of the activity (as opposed to the concept) of reading.

The idea of community is highly problematic. But what I try to show in chapter 3 is that, unlike the concept of culture (or even of *a* culture), the concept of community can be important for the analysis of local semiosic practices. Whereas the concept of culture – particularly in cultural studies – is susceptible to totalization, to coming to be thought of as singular and monolithic, or as a definite substance, the concept of community can be detached from its rather general sense of a consensual grouping of persons who inhabit the same topographical space and time. Recent work on the idea of community (discussed in detail in chapter 3) has shown that it can be used to think of disparate groupings: not just of persons, but also of forms of knowledge with very loose (even barely recognizable) affinities. I refer to this rethinking in terms of communities as 'collections of what happens'; that is, as *effective* loci rather than physical groupings of copresent individuals.

This reconstruction of community allows me to argue in chapter 4 that signs cannot 'mean' by virtue of the existence of *necessary* others (or not-signs) to which they are somehow attached – and such that the work of semiotics cannot be to find the general form of that attachment. Nor – again in principle – can signs ever mean by being completely detached from *any* contingently available not-signs, even though in practice we may find actual communities that do use signs in this way. Rather, the question of 'attachment' or 'detachment' – the question of the not-sign or its absence – is an empirical matter. It varies from sign-use to sign-use, within and between specific communities. If the term 'community' comes to mark, as I argue, a space of difference rather than of pure human presence, then it can be mobilized as the always differential locus of the relations between signs and their locally, contingently, pragmatically, or effectively relevant not-signs. Those relations, however, cannot be specified in their general form or fixed, once and for all, in advance. Rather, they exist neither in the space of the sign-proper nor in the space of its de-signed exterior, but in the frame of effectivity between these supposedly pure and ultimate locations. To this extent the concepts of community and not-sign work hand in hand to destabilize the theoretical idea of the sign-in-general. They point towards the ineluctability of the practical or *effective* space of semiosis and towards an empirical analytics of sign-usage.

To show this in chapter 5, I contrast some theoretical arguments about what it *must* mean for someone to be able to read (as if there were a universal essence of reading) with what it is, within a definite historical locus, to read in a classroom. Here I try to show just how specific a case of reading can actually be, how the criteria for its 'success,' for its bona fide status *as* reading, depend on highly local community relevances. And so we are left with what is, by this stage, a familiar dilemma: historical versus local relevances as the crucial 'framing' space of sign-use.

★

Preface

In part 2, then, I begin to deal with these matters. First, in chapter 6
I attempt to put the question of local versus historical relevances
into a kind of formalism. To be sure, this partly contradicts the
criticisms of formalist semiotics with which I began this series of
investigations; but it is still intriguing to wonder whether the
newer semiotic spaces opened up in part 1 *can* actually be formalized in a way that is responsive to (to name those newer spaces) the
double determinacy/indeterminacy of semiosis and to its double
locality/historicality.

To work this way, I turn to the ethnomethodological concept of
reflexivity, in several of its possible meanings. Ethnomethodology
appears at this point simply on the grounds that it is one contemporary form of discourse analysis that has been highly responsive
to the need to investigate local and particular forms of making
meanings. Yet as with Wittgenstein, ethnomethodology has almost no historical consciousness. In accord with its parents, phenomenological social theory and ordinary language philosophy, it
lives in the here and now of the interactional things-in-themselves
– almost to the point of analyzing the social-situatedness of (for
example) talk in terms of the *physical* space of its occurrence. This
contrasts with the other currently dominant mode of discourse
analysis, Foucauldian archaeology/genealogy. But in this field the
term 'discourse' is used quite differently. It does not mean anything
like communication. In fact the early, archaeological Foucault specifically denies such semiotic concerns: 'What I am analyzing in
the discourse is not the system of its language, nor, in a general
way, the formal rules of its construction: for I am not concerned
about knowing what renders it legitimate or gives it its intelligibility and allows it to serve in communication.' Instead, for Foucault
discourses are formations of knowledge that constrain and enable
the production of types of subjects. They are historical/epistemic
in form rather than ostensibly semiosic. He goes on: 'The question
I ask is not that of codes but of events: the law of existence of the
statements, that which rendered them possible – them and none
other in their place: the conditions of their singular emergence;
their correlation with other previous or simultaneous events, discursive or not.'[2]

Genealogical-archaeological work, then – even though we must
concur with its giving priority to events over codes, and singu-

larities over totalities – still trades in 'laws,' 'conditions,' and 'correlations.' To this extent its version of specificity is incomplete; it can still miss the lived interactional specifics of local forms of semiosis. Can, as I ask in chapter 7, Foucault's concern with discourse-as-history begin to approach ethnomethodology's concern with the present moment? And vice versa, can ethnomethodology's acute sense of the local be given an equally specificist concern with history such as that advocated by Foucault? If so, an effective semiotics may be able to tap into both of those traditions of discourse analysis – albeit in a way unrecognizable to either – in order to generate a third form of that 'discipline' that runs between (or in the space of the frame of) the historical conditions of possibility of semiosis and its everyday instantiations. Again, if this is possible, I ask in chapter 7 whether the resultant analytic form(alism) could be used to investigate (as with learning to read – chapter 5) examples of young persons acquiring a particular material ability – in this case the ability to have sex competently.

The problem of learning sexual competence is a particularly poignant example, for it shows that we cannot deal with semiosis simply in terms of methodic activities *or* in terms of generally available disciplinary formations. Neither ethnomethodology nor Foucault can quite touch on the 'level' at which it happens. It seems to be between the two: at the level of what I call 'socio-logical problems and solutions.' And so I argue in chapter 7 that there is a middle realm – between ethnomethodology's interest in the intelligibility of signs (as methodic practices) and Foucault's interest in discourses (as historically situated formations of knowledge) – where the two may 'meet.'

To sort out these distinctions in chapter 8, I return to the formalist position outlined in chapter 6, mapping ethnomethodological concerns about methodic practices onto the idea of *intelligibility* (semiosic relation, R_1) and Foucauldian concerns with the comparative durability of discursive conditions of possibility onto the idea of *historicity* (semiosic relation R_3), leaving the common intermediate realm of socio-logical problems and solutions (semiosic relation R_2) as the field of *actionability*. These three 'levels' of semiosis then become the main building blocks of effective semiotic theory, such that the site of particular *analyses* is clearly demarcated as the 'middle term,' the realm of problems and solutions, while the main goal of these analyses is to be able to say something about community histories in a nonspeculative and empirically grounded way.

But the idea of 'intelligibility' (R1) – Foucault notwithstanding – needs some attention in its own right before this, since it is the primary 'building block' out of which socio-logical problem-solutions are built. Here the ethnomethodological concept of 'indexicality' ('context-sensitivity') is seen to be crucial for our understanding of intelligibility as a 'property' of practices. However, in chapter 9 I also go on to explore the possibility that indexicality may have effects at all three 'levels' of semiosis. This means shifting the terrain of ethnomethodology slightly, away from the description of signs as (merely) intelligible and towards the idea of a critical understanding of actionability (R2) and historicity (R3).

The shift towards 'critical theory' is made by comparing Derrida's concept of *différance* with Garfinkel's idea of indexicality. These seem to involve a common position: the in-principle instability of the sign. However, whereas ethnomethodology's goal is to show how this instability (as indexicality) is firmed up and all but repaired in practical circumstances of social communication, the goal of Derridean deconstruction appears to be quite the opposite: to show how seemingly 'closed' texts can be reopened to display their necessary dependence on a principle of *différance* (of difference-in-general). Does semiosic instability in principle lead to signs as forms of identity or signs as forms of difference? This question sounds as if it should inaugurate a debate between two opposed general theories of meaning. But what I try to show in chapter 9 is that which of the two happens to be operating in any specific situation is an empirical matter. Signs may be unstable in *principle*, but in *practice* that instability may be augmented or diminished. Different community practices can, that is, open up the 'indexical potential' of signs, or else they can close it down, to use a shorthand. Whichever happens is whichever happens – empirically. This is therefore one of the matters that effective semiotics sets out to investigate.

Apropos of this, in chapter 10 I look at a particular case of a community that reads the indexical potential of its 'own' signs in such a way as to open up that potential towards indefiniteness (rather than 'fixity' or 'repair'). The community in question is exemplified by a cinephilic reading of a song-and-dance sequence from the musical film *Singin' in the Rain*. What I try to show is that such readings actually *require* certain objects within the film text's diegetic space to be movable, unstable in time and space, and therefore 'illogical' according to any professional or common-sense version of topography and geometry. While being geometrically nonsensical, for the community that routinely uses them (that is, reads or views them) these filmic elements are *expectably* unstable and illogical. The point is simply to show that indexical particulars can be as much exploited for their indeterminacy as they can (on other occasions, in other communities) be 'repaired' or brought to practical semiosic *ends*; and that that 'exploitation' is a routine part of 'life as usual' for such communities rather than something special, rare, or disturbing.

However, this 'life-as-usual' character of sign-usage can be slightly different in other communities. In chapter 11 I look at fans of the comic book *Batman* to see how they are prepared to go so far and no further in opening up the indexical potential of the texts they read. What I am after here is the limit point: the threshold beyond which semiosic polyvalency cannot go, beyond which a reading ceases to be 'competent' within that community's relevances. 'Theoretical' readings of *Batman*, especially in cultural studies, have argued that popular texts (such as comics) are highly polyvalent, subjectable to multiplicities of reading practices, highly unstable in terms of their readability.[3] Further, some forms of cultural studies have argued that this instability constitutes a form of resistance by active consumers of popular textual materials. What I try to show in chapter 11, against this rather voluntaristic version of things, is that actual communities of readers do have limits. It *may* be that they can exploit the indexical potential of the words and graphic images to be found on the pages of *Batman* comics – and it *may* be that such 'exploitation' works counter to, or in the face of, the design strategies of the cultural industries that produce them. But this does not mean that, as a competent reading, anything goes. On the contrary, my investigation in chapter 11 shows not only that there is considerable consumer-producer codesign (through, for example, the letter pages in *Batman*) within the historical development of this comic form, but also that limits to semiosic polyvalency are in order for Batfans. My question is, in the case of a particular issue of the comic that approaches those limits: Where do the limits lie, and what are the socio-logical problems and solutions community members use in making them happen? Hence what a community *is* is highly imbricated in the methods it has available for making texts intelligible (R1); the socio-logical problem-solutions (R2) it uses to find the limits of intelligibility; and the ways these problem-solutions come to be historically embedded as generally available community methods for reading (R3).

This is all very well in the case of intracommunity communications. But what happens when different communities with quite different interests and relevances come into contestation (or potential contestation) over how particular signs are to be used? Intracommunity semiosis is the topic of chapters 12 and 13. In the first of these investigations I look at how 'gatekeeping' occurs in popular accounts of science. These texts have something of a contradiction built into them: they often want to show that scientific concepts, ideas, formulas, constants, and so on, have quite specific values and positions inside a conceptual whole (a discipline or a discourse) and that misunderstandings of them can lead to false conclusions or sheer bad science. But at the same time, by popularizing science, they are making complex ideas available to the 'laity,' to readers from nonscientific communities. In fact they are specifically designed to do this. How can both of these aims hold in the same textual space? For popular science writers, this is a sociological problem that has to be managed by definite rhetorical strategies. But in the case under investigation here (Roger Penrose's *The Emperor's New Mind*), we can see that the rhetoric does not always come off. That is, the rhetoric itself (in this case an argument for mathematical realism) is also interpretable by nonscientists. Adopting a counterrealist position (known in mathematics as 'intuitionism'), I try to show how Penrose's defense remains contradictory in his own terms. At root his faith in mathematical realism turns out to be just that – a faith – and one that can be countered by adopting an antithetical belief structure.

If scientific forms of semiosis are fragile enough to be contestable from without, if the methodic activities they are built on are challengeable *in principle* from the standpoint of alternative community relevances, then can we find actual cases of such contestation in everyday life? How do these operate? Surely in such cases we are coming to the very limits of communication.

But if we assume this, we are relying on the idea that communication arises out of common grounds or forms of consensus – principles that appear to be 'agreed,' as it were, before entering into semiosic exchange. What I try to show in chapter 13, by an investigation of a set of conversational transcripts, is that communication (as community membership) does not necessarily have to rest on such grounds. At the supposedly 'deep' level of consensus and agreement, we can find such things as conflict, contestation, contradiction, discord, disharmony, and friction. But this does not mean that notions of community have disappeared. On the contrary, my investigation of intercommunity semiosic conflict is designed to show the very opposite: that community positionings, relevances, and interests often become clearer and more obvious when put into contestation with one another. Intracommunity forms of life as usual (as ethnomethodology has shown us) are unremarkable. They rely upon a seen-but-unnoticed background of common relevances and expectancies (to use Garfinkel's terms). But intercommunity exchanges can, in some cases at least, bring fundamental differences between such 'backgrounds' to the fore. So again, it would be simple to say in such cases that 'communication' is not taking place. I want to show otherwise: that communication itself may have dissensus and dissonance at its very core. Happiness may be a *result* of communication in some circumstances, but it is not a prerequisite.

By this stage we will have seen a variety of different communities and communications at work – in science, in conversation, in photography, comics, and film (among others). But this neglects a crucial self-reflection. What kind of community is semiotic analysis itself? How does it relate to its 'object' communities? This raises the question of the ethics of analysis. Can an effective semiotics have anything to say on this question? Can it 'help itself' by an analysis of the ethical? This is the final question of the book.

To delineate this limited analytic ethics, however, it is necessary to look at what philosophical ethics, specifically in its so-called 'postmodern' varieties, has to offer us. And further, to see how contemporary ethics arrives at what turn out to be a series of paradoxes and problems, it is also necessary to situate it in terms of its subjectivist and objectivist opponents. The ultraparadoxical nature of 'postmodern' ethics turns out to have valuable lessons for the more limited analytic ethics I finally propose: an ethics that is different from postethics in terms of its positivity as well as its unashamedly empirical basis.

★

But after (or before) all this, what is the point? Why *do* semiotics at all, let alone the unconventional version of it I am trying to establish in these pages? As I argue at the very end of this book, semiotic analysis *may* be of no use to anyone but the analyst. It may be no more than an exercise in (and of) the self: a way of coming to understand the world and one's own position in it differently through an understanding of how different communities of sign-users understand themselves and their positionings. Again, as I claim there, this may not be a completely useless end in itself. It may be the limits of an empiricist ethics.

But at the same time there is always a possibility (no more than a possibility, for we are now in the realm of the unpredictable effects of a text and its uptake) that effective semiotic analyses of the intelligibility, actionability, and historicality of sign-uses will themselves have effects on both the various other analytic communities they draw on (general semiotics, linguistics, discourse analysis, ethnomethodology, archaeology/genealogy, critical theory, and postmodernism in particular) and the communities they investigate (including comics readers, users of photographs, cinephiles, mathematicians, and so on). That is, they may come to be incorporated into the activities (methodic practices, socio-logical problem-solutions) actually used in those communities as historically embedded and available forms of action. At the limit, they may even constitute – in cases of social injustice marked by Lyotard's concept of the *différend* – counterarchives of means by which resistances to (and transgressions of) injustices can be brought off in quite practical and effective ways. But this always remains a hope – something out of my hands and dependent on so many factors outside the aims of this book, aims that remain almost completely *methodological.*

So why then look for a new *method* of semiotic analysis? A passage that immediately caught my attention when starting this project comes from Saussure's letter to Meillet of 1874. Saussure writes:

But I am heartily sick of it all and of the general difficulty of writing even ten lines of common sense on linguistic matters. For a long time I have been particularly concerned with classifying linguistic facts and the viewpoints from which we treat them. And I am more and more aware both of the enormous amount of work necessary to show the linguist *what he is doing*, by reducing each operation to its appropriate category, and of the ultimate futility of what can be accomplished in linguistics.

Ultimately, the only aspect of a language that interests me is its picturesque or quasi-ethnographic side – what distinguishes it from others as the property of a particular people with certain origins. But I have lost the pleasure of unreservedly devoting myself to such study and appreciating a particular fact pertaining to a particular milieu.[4]

At this point in the letter Saussure proposes to undertake the investigations reported in his *Course in General Linguistics*.[5] 'Only then' – that is, after the *Course* is complete – 'I confess, shall I be able to resume my work where I left off.' That work (Saussure's central interest) is presumably the investigation of language's 'picturesque or quasi-ethnographic side.' Yet unfortunately that work was never taken up again. His quasi-ethnographic semiotics was abandoned in favor of a formal investigation of the system of *langue*.[6] But imagine this abandonment had not occurred! Then we should perhaps have had something like an effective semiotics from Saussure himself. My question is simply, What could such a semiotics look like?

Traditionally, semiotics has asked, What is the relation between an expression (signifier) and what it expresses (signified) – and the latter is usually thought of as something akin to a mental state. What I ask instead is, What is the relation between an expression and its effect? Here the concept of effect is always thought of as quite concrete and material (but does not therefore preclude the mind, since it too can be considered materially). This is what I think semiosis is: something effective, what works, is *wirkliche*. Again, because expressions are *acts* (of expressing), they too are material practices. The whole of semiosis is material, not a separation of thing and mind, self and world, subject and object. It is fundamentally *not* binaristic. Expression-effect is one material thing.

Yet in offering these bare outlines of what I mean by effectivity, I don't pretend that my work would be anything like what Saussure proposed and abandoned. Nevertheless it does constitute one possible way of taking up that challenge. Here we should note previous 'social semiotic' attempts to restore this missing (quasi-ethnographic) dimension to Saussure's machinery.[7] Their project was to *attach* a social geometry to a preexisting Saussurian linguistic geometry – producing an always divided theory rarely able to cope with the fundamental idea that semiosis is never *not* social. It is social (practical, historical and political) from the ground up. And since this happens specifically, 'eventally,' at local sites, no formal geometry will capture its operations. In place of anything like a 'geometry,' then, I want to propose, in the first instance, a description of actual practices of how semiosic figures are made. Then it might be possible to think of scrapping the Saussurian machinery, plus the recent renovations and additions that have made it a very ugly vehicle indeed, and so build anew, as it were, from the beginning. But where *is* the beginning?

Each investigation in this book sets out *as* a new beginning. The chapters are not linear or sequential. As each begins, the question is asked anew: How can we construct an effective semiotics? Thus the question may have different answers for each of the empirical and theoretical objects it inquires about: one semiotic method for analyzing conversations, another for analytic ethics, still another for comics, and so on. Yet the reader may discern among these investigations (each striving to begin anew) a loose and implicit continuity. The struggle to begin afresh each time inevitably fails; some terminology, for example, persists despite my best efforts to repress that persistence.

The inevitable looseness and lack of linear continuity this produces in the book will be a hindrance to some readers' understandings of it. But as Nietzsche writes, 'One does not want only to be understood when one writes but just as surely *not* to be understood.'[8] A book that is merely understood adds nothing, leaves no puzzles and no interesting ways for readers to solve those puzzles. Understanding (semiosic closure) and not-understanding (semiosic openness) are always *both in play* when one writes or reads, teaches or learns, and thus neither is ever complete. So to simply be understood would be to put oneself outside the domain of semiosis itself and into an unthinkable space of pure knowledge. If a book were only ever understood, it would have a single reading – it could never be read otherwise. But it is a condition of history that any event is always open to being otherwise, at least in principle. It is therefore also a condition of meaning. An impossibly *complete* understanding would mean that a book had no history, no semiosic potential. It would be a kind of tautology: always true, adding nothing. To add something is, on the contrary, to risk contradiction. This is what might be meant by the term 'paralogics,' where 'para-' would point to the double ideas of being alongside or beside logic and being false or contradictory.[9] A paralogic position would be the position of one who walks beside, prompting, arguing, contradicting, creating a puzzle or problem with what is said. And this is precisely the position I want to adopt in relation to both formal and social semiotics.

Instead of assuming, then, that a book has a merely linear and singular effect, we might turn to Foucault's account of writing:

> A book is produced, a minute event, a small handy object. From that moment on it is caught up in an endless play of repetitions; its doubles begin to swarm around it and far from it; each reading gives it an impalpable and unique body for an instant; fragments of itself are made to stand for it, are taken to almost entirely contain it, and sometimes serve as refuge for it; it is doubled with commentaries, those other discourses in which it should finally appear as it is, confessing what it had refused to say, freeing itself from what it so loudly pretended to be.[10]

As I argue later in this book, some disciplines (especially the sciences) are predicated on the idea that the semiosic materials they 'own' should be kept from interpretation, whereas others (which we might call 'poetic') deliberately open up their 'own' materials to alternative readings and versions. In the face of Foucault's writing conditions, this means either 'policing' a book's possible repetitions or else encouraging them. Effective semiotics, as I conceive it, takes the latter course. It situates itself as a poetics rather than as a science of semiosis. Many disciplines – not just this one – are in a constant state of starting afresh. One way, then, to mark such a fresh departure is to pluralize it from the start: to offer an initial way into it; then, instead of pushing on, going back to the start again and heading into a new space – avoiding mastery and any claim to definiteness. In this connection my model here and elsewhere has always been Harold Garfinkel's *Studies in Ethnomethodology*, albeit one whose clarity, economy, and importance I could never hope to attain.[11] Let me offer, then, a further outline of the principles on which I have begun my semiotic investigations (against traditional semiotics, but in a direction suggested by Saussure's abandoned project):

1   Meaning is a practice or practices – not an inherent property of linguistic materials (Saussure's 'sickness' with formal linguistics).

2   Inquiries into meaning are necessarily investigations of specific local practices (Saussure's idea of a 'quasi-ethnographic' semiotics).

3   Which practices are pertinent to meaning in any local circumstance is a matter specific to the community operating in that circumstance (Saussure's 'particular people with certain origins').

4   How meaning is produced depends on the piecemeal application of the methods routinely available to a particular community (Saussure's skepticism about the very possibility of a general linguistics).

5   Although the 'objects' about which meaning is made by communities are semiosically indeterminate 'in themselves,' a semiotic analyst cannot say in advance whether meaning will be produced by resolving that indeterminacy, leaving it as it is, *or* amplifying it (One community – as with 'scientific' linguistics itself – may crave fixed and logical conditions, while another may prefer Saussure's 'picturesque' version of its semiosic positioning).

6   Communities do not have to be copresent. They can be, but they may be consocial strangers. For example, they may be 'audiences' (Saussure's wish to investigate a 'particular milieu').

7   Because the analysis of meaning is dependent on the in-principle indeterminacy of objects' meanings and the local communitarian workings of that indeterminacy, there are no definite methods of semiotic analysis that are generic or

omnirelevant. Instead, each inquiry must ask afresh what semi-osis *is*, every time it starts.

I would like to think these basic assumptions would mean that the 'linguistic' and the 'cultural' can never be entirely separate matters – though later in this book I will have cause to move away from the idea of semiotics as in any sense purely linguistic and cast some doubt on the analytic utility of the concept of culture. Nevertheless, many of the forms of 'cultural analysis' available today do 'jump off' one form or another of linguistic analysis, especially when they attempt to ask questions about how communication is realized. If effective semiotics is one such form of cultural analysis, it is a form that offers a relatively unusual version of how communication is possible (insofar as it *is* possible). That version is: For any community, the means of producing a semiosic object are *identical* with the means of recognizing it. That is, I can under-stand you when I would do as you do if I were to be saying what you say. Interestingly enough, as I show in chapter 13, none of this presumes or necessitates the idea that consensus is what underpins or defines communities.

Meaning is not a matter of similarities or identities between signs and objects, or signs and mental acts, but a matter of *how* signs are made from one occasion to another. This 'how made' *can be* (but need not be) expressed as rules. Rules are an analytic con-venience for expressing this 'how made' after the fact. And they have the drawback – which is expressly against my intentions here – of leading analysis to assume that consensus is the key to com-munication.

This is most clearly seen in the *learning* of the use of signs of all sorts. I have taught someone the use of a sign when she or he goes on to use it just as I would in those situations.[12] Here I am teaching not simply the use of signs but also, at the same time, membership in a community. Hence the emphasis in many of my investigations on young persons and their training.[13]

★

These, then, are what count for me as 'reasons' for trying to do ef-fective semiotics. But – to shift the terrain to more biographical matters – I have not been alone in my work. Anne Freadman, John Frow, and Ian Hunter offered me many helpful suggestions during several trips to Brisbane. Along with them, a more local community of friends and colleagues has been beside me throughout – sometimes in agreement and sometimes not, but always giving aid and comfort. Among these have been Claire Colebrook, Niall Lucy, Tom O'Regan, Toby Miller, Horst Ruthrof, Bob Hodge, and Garry Gillard. Each read the manuscript in different draft forms, and they all had their own important effects on my attempts to think the effective.

Last – yet historically prior to all this – this book came out of a meeting I had in Amsterdam in July 1991 with my friend, colleague, and teacher Rod Watson. In his characteristically Yorkshire way, he asked me why I had criticized so many positions without adopting one myself. This book is my answer – *for Rod* – though I don't doubt he'll disagree with, and I hope criticize, almost everything in it.

Acknowledgments

S ome data and analyses used in this book have appeared in earlier versions in a number of journals – though they are all substantially reworked and rewritten in their current versions. I thank the editors of the following journals for allowing me to return to those materials: *Continuum: The Australian Journal of Media & Culture* (chapter 2); *Theory, Culture and Society* (chapters 7 and 9); *Southern Review* and my coauthor there, Tom O'Regan (chapter 11). Chapter 5 is a substantial reworking of a piece that appeared in Carolyn D. Baker and Allan Luke, eds., *Towards a Critical Sociology of Reading Pedagogy: Papers of the XII World Congress on Reading* (Amsterdam: John Benjamins, 1991). While I was still working on it, Herman Parret asked me to contribute chapter 13 (again in a modified version) for publication in his edited collection *Pretending to Communicate* (Berlin: de Gruyter, 1993). My thanks to those editors and publishers.

SEMIOTIC INVESTIGATIONS

PART I   The Limits and Media of Semiosis

1. Signifying History

Hardly anyone today will dispute the claim that meaning is not – as formal semantics would have it – an intrinsic property of signs but rather an aspect of their use. But what does this mean? To put the question another way: How can we sensibly *use* the idea of semiosis, the idea of meaning as the use of signs? In what 'medium,' we might ask, does semiosis have its being? And this will inevitably lead us, once the apparent 'clarity' of formal semantics has been cleared away, to questions of history.

There was once great comfort to be had from formal semantics. That is, if we think of meanings as inhering in signs themselves, then we can comfortably leave aside all historical, social, and political questions. We can do semantics, as it were, at home. Given the signs and given a previously reliable set of semantic rules, all that remains is to apply the latter to the former. It is the same comfort that derives from pure mathematics. The analyst in both cases is involved in no more than an algorithmic manipulation: setting the parts of the machine in order and seeing what they generate. This is an almost entirely self-contained enterprise. It is self-contained precisely to the degree that it is systematic: and in being systematic, it forgets the very medium of history in which signs play, move, shift, change, alter, develop, appear and disappear. So it is not merely that formal semantics neglects the 'diachronic' dimension of semiosis. Rather, in leaving history unproblematic, it neglects semiosis *itself* as an always already historical formation of human practice.

If formal semantic models are rejected, however, the question of method becomes more hazardous, less *heimlich*. Something from outside the tiny, self-contained world of algorithmic manipulation has to intrude. If we can no longer make up sentences in line with the analyses to be performed on them, there is a very basic question of what we should be working on at all. From parsimony we move into a complex historical plenitude that can overwhelm us:

the manifold and varied world of everyday language use. The shift from formal semantics to semiotics is therefore a radical one: rejecting what is, a priori, one particular and limited domain of 'doing' sign manipulations and moving to the analysis of any sign manipulations whatever.

Quite clearly, then, there can be no simple solutions here. For our investigation will be the very opposite of the one undertaken by Descartes. Just as Descartes wished to strip away his learned, social, commonsense attire in order to see what remained, for him, as an essential relation between himself and the world, we are now faced with the question of how to put on the very clothing he discarded. We have to re-dress the body of semiosis rendered naked by Cartesian linguistics, which stripped it of the historical, the everyday, the contingent, the effective.

And just as Descartes arrived at nothing but a disguised tautology, a myth of the autonomous individual standing naked in relation to nature but connected to it by a thin filament of 'thought,' we must now face the opposite possibility: that we *are* nothing but the contingency of everyday signs, the bundle of rags hung on that stark Cartesian frame. If the king of philosophers had no clothes, we subjects of today may be nothing more than our garb. If no pure cognition underpins and guarantees social knowledge – or rather, if the complex myth of pure knowledge is just another vestment – then what are we to go looking for?

Later in this book there will be a series of alternative answers to this question: in 'community,' in everyday culture, in film, and in human conversation, to name only a few. But the first and most obvious semiotic principle is a historical one: that we use signs inherited from the past and under specific conditions. For this reason, and perhaps for many others, we cannot just do as we please with them. But what it is we have inherited is not so definite.[1] Otherwise there would be no investigation to make. Our legacy is, in each of its aspects, composed of coins of indefinite value. And this is the paradox. Any idea we might have of the limits and conditions of semiosis must always be given by and through the very kinds of signs we are trying thereby to understand. So, because it seems we must somehow pull ourselves up by our own bootstraps, it looks as if anything goes. If there is nothing outside the text (the ensemble of signs), as some believe, then we can invent any histories or conditions that appear to fit. And we can be as playful as we like in making them fit.[2] But this quickly transgresses the historical principle I have just mentioned: the conditions of semiosis become so fluid that we lose all sense of their specificity.

This paradox is not new. In one form or another it has plagued the so-called human sciences from their inception. The pre-Socratics wondered how each name could name one thing alone and how, conversely, each thing had one and only one name, when the worldly balance between things and names was manifestly out of equilibrium. Yet how else could definite meanings be achieved? On one side a dogmatic principle; on the other a baffling array of complexity. If you begin to state the conditions under which signs have meaning, the statement you end up with always seems to look out of kilter with all the other things you could reasonably say. It is as if the ideal solution would be to step outside language in order to describe it – to say what you see, just as (according to traditional Cartesian ideas about science) language is supposed to step outside nature and say what it sees. But in describing language itself, of course, nothing could then be described, since description is just one linguistic practice among many. One is always left with a remainder, a fragment of the 'object' (language) that can never completely describe itself. It seems that in this case any ultimately scientific move would have to involve an utterly impossible form of transcendence.

Do we really know, then, that there are conditions and histories to semiosis, to our uses of signs? Here the paradox is that without this idea we end up with yet another kind of idealism. If there are no conditions, we think, then any sign can say anything. But this, in any specific and particular event we care to think of, is nonsense. And so our sense of the limits of semiosis does not, and cannot, stem from transcending those limits – something imposed from outside the domain of history, of human social practice. Rather, the limits must themselves be constructed historically, in and by human social practice. For all this, however, they *are* limits, like any others, just as the exact regularities of Lorenz's waterwheel in full flow cannot be predicted before the first drop falls, but from a certain point we can begin to see their formation so that we can say with confidence, 'It is now turning clockwise with such a force that there will be no sudden reversal in the next two seconds.' This fact is arbitrary, to be sure. Given slightly different initial conditions – small variations in the timing and direction of the first two or three drops of water – things could easily have been very different. But in practice, as we look, they are not.[3]

This is a further paradox, then, for any effective semiotics. The conditions of semiosis appear irrevocable, intractable. We appear condemned to write, to paint, to speak, to film, and so on in precise ways, according to precise codes. Yet at the same time these ways and codes are historically contingent: they guide human practice, but equally they arise out of the very practices they guide, control, or even determine. In turning to apparently fixed laws, we neglect the everyday medium of their continuing construction and reconstruction.[4] On the other hand, however, in turning merely to an inspection of the (apparently free) vicissitudes of everyday life alone, as it were, we miss any idea of the conditions that make them possible.

Again, this situation is not unique to semiotics or even to the humanities. It appears wherever questions of historical necessity and contingency arise. Evolutionary biologists, for example, now recognize that evolution is not some grand teleological design, moving from the most primitive to the most developed (even though the term 'evolution' has become almost synonymous with 'development'). In fact, given the most basic initial bacteriological conditions we currently have evidence about, the chances of their producing anything even vaguely like human beings are infinitesimal, as Stephen Jay Gould has pointed out.[5] Once a species has occurred, we can see – that is, we can describe – how it came about. But we cannot find a necessary reason for its existence. This is exactly like attempting to account for the use of a particular sign or utterance on a particular occasion. To remedy the situation, it seems that an effective semiotics would have to be able to account for *both* the apparent fixity of the limits of semiosis *and* the historical plasticity those limits always attempt – unsuccessfully – to fix.

In the history of ideas, no figure has been more important than Nietzsche for our contemporary sense that 'things were not as necessary as all that,' to quote Foucault's apt phrase.[6] Nietzsche has been responsible, in this sense, for a wholesale modalization of our historical sense – by which I mean our sense that 'X was not, but *could have been*, otherwise' – a form of thought that has only recently come to contest ideas of necessity and causality in science (for example, as we have seen, in evolutionary biology). To this extent it would be helpful to pay some attention to Nietzsche's idea of 'effective history' (*wirkliche Geschichte*) to see if it can provide us with the beginnings of a history of semiosis – or rather, since Nietzsche is the least likely source for any type of totalizing history, to see if his ideas can offer a way of understanding how semiosis is both historically located but, for all that, also 'outside' strict historical *necessity*.

Nietzsche, especially in *The Use and Abuse of History*, makes strong arguments against Hegel, whom he considers the philosopher par excellence of the rational telos. For Hegel the present moment gets its meaning, truth, and authenticity from being directly descended from the past – as though it were but the latest offspring of a long family tree. The present is, accordingly, like the most recent syntactic element (for example, the word one is currently reading in a sentence). Like that element, the present is supposed to be guaranteed by the grammar of history (the Spirit). However, moving towards a more Nietzschean position, just as the meaning of a word cannot be guaranteed simply by its location in a sentence, neither can the meaning of the present historical moment be guaranteed by the abstract Spirit or necessary grammar of history. For Nietzsche, both history and language are contingent. To think history in this Nietzschean mode is to avoid a metaphysical conception of history based on the identity and presence of each event with respect to an underlying and necessary structure, system, telos, Spirit, or grammar. It is, to invoke Derrida, to think history without a particular center – which is to say, a history with many candidate centers.[7]

Into Hegel's faith in the identity and presence of each event, Nietzsche inserts difference: the particularity and contingency of the event. And in terms of method this means each event must be dealt with piecemeal. Foucault calls this procedure 'eventalization,'[8] and he allies it with the Nietzschean idea of a 'general history' as opposed to a 'total description.'[9] So Nietzschean history is a history of the difference of the present, not a history for which the present is totally explicable as a necessary next stage, a mere effect of the past – its slave. Nietzsche even goes so far as to suggest that Hegel's history is an *effect* of the language that describes it –

the language of necessity that haunts scientism's false will to predict and control nature, for example, or the future. This apparent mastery of history gives history its necessity, turning it into the true master. And so the language that does so is always in excess of history itself (if one can speak in such terms), since it always adds to it the supplement of necessity or, in other words, the gloss (an extra layer) of its own language. At the same time, Hegelian language is always less than history itself, for it misses the difference and uniqueness of the event by subsuming that difference into its own totalizing gloss. In this case Hegelian language needs, as *part* of Nietzschean history (or 'genealogy'), to be problematized. To this extent, then, one of the initial connections between semiotics and history involves a realization of the very semiosic forms by which history comes to be written and is therefore made to appear in the first place. History – as the condition and medium of semiosis – is not so much something that is to be described and explained. Rather, it is something for which the writer must take ethical *responsibility*, as I will argue in the final chapter of this book. Part of the effective engagement between the *disciplines* of semiotics and history, then, has to do more with responsibility than with formal methods for the correct description or explanation of signs.

Returning once more to Nietzsche: to be in history, to be a historical subject, is to be in a space of contradiction rather than of certainty; it is to be in the differential space of the present event. Under the historical umbrella of Hegelian certainty, progress and the future are guaranteed by their necessary extension or projection along the lines of a singular, given, and fixed past. But to be in contradiction is to be in the space between what language and thought *produce* as the real and the always unknowable constraints of 'the real' (life) itself. This is as true of Hegelian language as it is of any other: there is no guarantee that any next event will be an exact derivation from all the previous ones. If history is like a syntax in any way at all, it is like the syntax of poetry rather than that of logic.[10] There is always the space of ill definition, contradiction, and uncertainty over what being a historical subject *is*. Any philosophy or theory must therefore always be able to call itself into question. It is always potentially more, less, *and* different from what it would ideally explain or describe. It is always a self-questioning fiction, construction, or creation (*poesis*). To refuse this calling-into-question leaves us with a closure, to be sure, but not a logical one: rather, it is a metaphysical closure. In closing the meaning of an event, once and for all, we risk being overpurposive, overefficient in our language. We risk missing the irremediable openness for which the conditions of history and semiosis provide.

At the same time, if the historian cannot accept a space of total free play, total anarchy or antimethod, then this is not because something *utterly real* constrains the inquiry – rather, it is because of the power of dominant metaphysical discourses, particularly that of scientism. It is the discourse of a certain dogmatic realism that constrains more than 'the real' itself. To struggle against this metaphysics is to search for proliferation, difference, and dispersion among theoretic discourses: to approach the anomic whose frequent avatar in Nietzsche is the animal, the beast who is languageless, truthless, nonconscious, historyless. This struggle for the polymorphous, the diverse, replaces and goes beyond metaphysical notions of morality (good and evil) that attempt to fix those qualities into timeless and unitary forms. The struggle is also an affirmation of the undecidable present – and of the undecidability of presence. For semiotics, it means we must always ask What is semiosis? afresh on each occasion.

This is no more and no less than the discovery that the indefiniteness of meaning *in principle* (or as I shall later call it, 'indexicality') itself means that actual semiosic effects must always be produced *in practice*. Any sign (as with any present event) will have meaning only insofar as it *is* a practice (its own practice, its being identical with a practice). It is not as if one had the sign here and the practice there, so that the analyst's job was to connect up the two. That would assume the sign could have a *definite* meaning *in principle* (a telos), as it were, already trammeled up in it, ready to go, awaiting only the arrival of the practice (from where?) in order to unleash it. Instead of thinking of 'a sign,' we should think instead of 'signing' in Derrida's sense.[11] In this way 'sign' (like 'event') is always already an activity, a practice, an action, in play, a carrying through or a living out. It is never, to use Wittgenstein's phrase, 'on holiday' or merely 'idling.'[12] So from here on we should use the word 'sign' accordingly: not as inert 'matter' (statics) but as active power or 'energy' (dynamics). Without this version of things, the sign is nothing but a kind of dead script from which life must be 'performed'; but this is not how we actually speak or write, for example.

For traditional linear history, on the other hand, the present is no more than a gap between the origin (the real past and its necessary principle) and the fulfillment of its purpose: the end (the future). It looks, in this case, like an infinitesimal textual gap, a tiny unfilled point in a grand syntagmatic chain. To assert the importance of this gap, as Nietzsche does, against the metaphysics of linearity is to make a preposterous move in traditional terms – as if silence were affirmed, difference, negativity, nonbeing. And hence the continual charges of nihilism against Nietzsche. But as it turns out, this *gap* is not nullity, it is the historically discontinuous space in which we find ourselves: constituted by the yet-to-be, the undecidable, the unforeseeable, the unplannable, the aleatory. And it is precisely this dimension of history (its distinction from the planned and the plannable) that no semiotics has yet fully embraced. The very idea of a *system* of signs always points in the opposite direction, towards certainty and the hope of definite interpretations.

Paradoxically for some, the natural scientists today are scarcely so confident. A few physicists have even suggested (against scientism) that physics involves a constantly unsatisfied interrogation of nature ('reality') whose results cannot be known in advance. Nature does not easily conform to the requirements of uniformity, consistency, and necessity that we may insist on from time to time. To quote one popular account of John Wheeler's views on this matter:

> Wheeler evokes what he calls the 'surprise' version of the old game of 20 questions. In the normal version of the game, person A thinks of an object – animal, vegetable or mineral – and person B tries to guess it with a series of yes-or-no questions. In surprise 20 questions, A only decides what the object is *after* B asks the first question. A can then keep choosing a new object, as long as it is compatible with his previous answers. In the same way, Wheeler suggests, reality is defined by the questions we put to it.[13]

The view *may* be controversial in physics, but in semiotics it ought to be practically a truism. Putting questions to the semiohistorical world, that is, will always be an event in that world, altering it in some way, no matter how small. 'Surprise 20 questions' reminds us that semiosis (everyday sociohistorical action) cannot be fixed, cumulative, or linear; and this 'nonlinearity means that the act of playing the game has a way of changing the rules.'[14] Physics may therefore have realized what semiotics still needs to know: that there can be no strict separation between any analyzing discourse and the object it would (ideally) analyze.

Nietzsche's continuing struggle was to work against having his positive affirmation of discontinuity (eventalism) recuperated or rehabilitated back into metaphysics. To see this, we must follow Nietzsche's idea that the closed metaphysics (against which he moves) is not in fact a theory of time at all. Hegel's, for example, is a history *without* time: for to acknowledge time would mean acknowledging temporality, accidence, contingency, and open-endedness. Hegel tries instead to free history *from* the contingencies of time and to provide a blueprint for an eternal history. By contrast, Nietzsche tries to return us to that contingency (against what he saw as the dominant 'common sense' of his time, progressivism): to see that an event in the past did not *have to* happen as it did. Reality is not foreclosed by virtue of some principle of determination ('identity') but can always be otherwise – or at least, to repeat Foucault's phrase, can always *have been* otherwise.

One of Nietzsche's tactics (or methods) for maintaining a differentialist view of history is that of remembering/forgetting. Perfectly describing the relation of semiotics to history, he writes: 'We must know the right time to forget as well as the right time to remember, and instinctively see when it is necessary to feel historically and when unhistorically. . . . [T]he unhistorical and the historical are equally necessary to the health of an individual, a community, and a system of culture.'[15] In this sense, as I noted above, if Nietzsche is right there is no point in debating the importance of synchrony over diachrony or vice versa. Any attempt at a totally diachronic study will always be situated in its own present, as its own synchronic event. It will not simply deliver us a given and fixed history but will always take part in the field it would ideally describe. By the same token, a purely synchronic analysis will always have its own relation to history (even if it is one of denial). What I take Nietzsche to be saying in the passage above is this: The 'pure forms' of the synchronic and the diachronic are never practically available to us; yet we can calculate the balance, work on tactics – and indeed intuitions – for when to work synchronically (forgetting) and when diachronically (remembering). And those tactics will always have to do with what it is we want to achieve, our responsibility as writers of history, how we want to construct a future, albeit locally. And this has to do not with 'what we know *is*' but with 'what we want *to be*.' The method, in semiotics/history, is always given ethically (not purely epistemologically or ontologically).

The ethical needs of the present determine (if anything) how the past is to be read – not vice versa. The present does as it must (not as it 'likes') with the past, but it cannot completely forget it (pure synchrony) or totally describe its 'truth' (pure diachrony). There must always be some element of remembering, of the diachronic – especially of the past as itself once contingent (as a former synchrony). Remembering may indeed be to condemn: there is nothing to say whether the past should be treated with celebration or with violence. And forgetting is always forgetting something in particular (it is a synchrony of 'just this'); it is not an aimless refusal to remember at all, not a cutting off of the past or an a priori limitation of one's investigation to the present for its own sake. This, it seems to me, is what Nietzsche means by 'effective history'; and hence my goal in these investigations happens to be called 'effective semiotics.'

Much of what I want to say, here and elsewhere, is also informed by a Wittgensteinian view of language. But to any reader, history is Wittgenstein's weak suit. Indeed, my interest is not in rehashing the Wittgenstein of the *Philosophical Investigations* for an already given semiotics. This has already been worked through, with limited results.[16] Instead, what I'm doing here could be seen as a critical dialogue with Wittgenstein's earlier (so-called transitional) text, the *Philosophical Grammar*. In this text the 'life' of the sign, its 'use,' and so on are seen to reside in its grammar. But this term 'grammar' cannot be taken in its current, formal linguistic sense.

To illustrate this, we can turn to Wittgenstein's lectures from 1930–32 where he was discussing many of the ideas to appear in the *Grammar* (written between 1932 and 1934). Ray Monk gives the following succinct account:

What replaces theory is *grammar*. During this series of lectures Moore made a spirited attempt to insist that Wittgenstein was using the word 'grammar' in a rather odd sense. He presented to Wittgenstein's class a paper distinguishing what he took to be the usual meaning from Wittgenstein's use. Thus, he argued, the sentence: 'Three men was working' is incontrovertibly a misuse of grammar, but it is not clear that: 'Different colours cannot be in the same place in a visual field at the same time' commits a similar transgression. If this latter is also called a misuse of grammar, then 'grammar' must mean something different in each case. No, replied Wittgenstein, 'The right expression is "It does not have any sense to say . . ."' Both kinds of rules were rules in the same sense. 'It is just that some have been the subject of philosophical discussion and some have not.'[17]

Monk then goes on to quote from the relevant lecture:

> Grammatical rules are all of the same kind, but it is not the same mistake if a man breaks one as if he breaks another. If he uses 'was' instead of 'were' it causes no confusion; but in the other example the analogy with physical space (cf. two people in the *same* chair) does cause confusion. When we say we can't think of two colours in the same place, we make the mistake of thinking that this is a proposition, though it is not; and we would never try to say it if we were not misled by an analogy. It is misleading to use the word 'can't' because it suggests a wrong analogy. We should say, 'It has no sense to say. . . .'[18]

Thus grammar is not merely a linguistic calculus, it is also a calculus in the domain of 'sense'; that is, as we now say, in the semiosic domain. Hence, throughout the *Grammar* (by contrast, to some extent, with the better-known views of the *Investigations*), Wittgenstein refers to grammar in terms of the whole *system* of an expression's use: 'The role of a sentence in the calculus is its sense.' 'A proposition is a sign in a system of signs. It is *one* combination of signs among a number of possible ones, and as opposed to other possible ones.'[19] It is an uncharacteristically Saussurian moment in Wittgenstein's thought, and with it come both a rejection of and a mistake about history.

In the *Grammar*, Wittgenstein uses 'history' and 'cause' almost synonymously. In rejecting the importance of the 'cause' of a sign, an utterance, or a proposition coming to be used in a certain way, he also rejects its 'history.' Or else Wittgenstein writes of the 'mere history' of a sign's use, something inessential to its meaning. Hence:

> Isn't it like this? First of all, people use an explanation, a chart, by looking it up; later they as it were look it up in the head (by calling it before the inner eye, or the like) and finally they work without the chart, as if it had never existed. In this last case they are playing a different game. For isn't it as if the chart is still in the background, to fall back on; it is excluded from our game, and if I 'fall back on it' I am like a blinded man falling back on the sense of touch. An explanation provides a chart and when I no longer use the chart it becomes mere history.[20]

Instead, as we have seen: 'What interests *us* in the sign, the meaning which matters for us is what is embodied in the grammar of the sign.'[21] But note that Wittgenstein refers here to 'the' (I want to say 'particular') 'meaning which matters for us.' As though there were others; such that there might be another 'meaning' that *was* historical, that did have to do with the fact that a certain practice once involved the use of a look-up chart (though it no longer does today). And quite simply, who is to say that a contemporary instance will be definitely, irrevocably, shorn of its connections with previous 'technologies'?

Moreover, following Nietzsche, history cannot simply be confined to causes. Wittgenstein is no doubt rejecting a Hegelian and scientist conception of history as cause, and that is well and good. But this is only one version of history. If, contrary to this version, history is more like the sense of the temporality of the sign (that is, of the practice), then things start to look very different. Strategically, it means that remembering/forgetting (diachrony/synchrony) is crucial to the analyst, even one who is not interested in 'causes' and is confined to 'the grammar' of the sign. The sign's temporality cannot be so simply detached from its grammar; instead, it would be a crucial component of it. Perhaps what this shows is that if grammar is to be distinct from history, then the *former* term is the more problematic of the two.

How far, then, are we to go along the Nietzschean track? Above all else, Nietzsche alerts us to what might be called the modal sphere in the history of semiosis ('It could have been like this . . .'). But this may only have one purpose: to point out its own self-evidence. And it can seem almost malicious when used in any other way – for example, to make us *doubt*, *unreasonably*, that certain conditions now prevail. A history without 'causes' and, more especially, without an underlying historical principle – guiding it from above history itself, like a sublime Newtonian equation, working itself out with one and only one possible solution – is still a history for all that. Objections here are like those of a builder who refuses to build on granite because at one time it was molten as hell. Our concepts are fluid, their boundaries blurred. There are times and places when, indeed, they are so fluid and blurred – when nothing, moreover, seems clearly to occupy their centers – that the world looks like nothing more than a lattice of fuzzy boundaries, a fragile honeycomb with no occupants, ready to fall to dust with the next gust of wind. But there are, equally, times and places when the boundaries are sharp and firm and the specific contents are clear and distinct.

Allow me to speculate. Semiosis shifts historically, to be sure. Any etymologist or lexicographer could tell us that. But what is more radical is the realization that the *conditions* of semiosis can shift. And since, after Nietzsche, there can be no universal principle guaranteeing such shifts and no necessary pattern to them, we must conclude that they occur and are constructed relatively locally and piecemeal. The locus or agency of this process I shall call, for want of a better word and with deep reservations, 'a community.' More radically still, communities may be what they are, in their distinctness (in what is sometimes called their 'cultures') because of the specific ways in which, historically, they produce, reproduce, and replace their semiosic conditions.

To put this another way, semioses (the ways a sign is used) will be both historically and locally specific. The practices and actions that produce this specificity can be thought of as varieties of local technology – methods or ways of doing things that are relatively peculiar to those who do them. It is this specificity that I want to mark by the term 'community.' To be sure, the term has an unfortunate connotation for some: it seems to invoke a sense of harmony and singularity of purpose. In fact it seems to presuppose,

from the outset, a consensus model of society-in-general. However, the notion of community that I offer here should not be
thought to contain, by necessity, any such elements. If meanings
are constructed in (or as) social uses, this does not mean they have
to be consensual or to produce agreement or semiotic unity – as we
shall see many times later on, on the contrary. All it means is that
semiosis, including semiotic *contestation*, occurs in the form of
methodic activities. A 'community' is simply a name for whoever,
locally and contingently, carries out or materially embodies such
methodic activities. In this usage the term bears comparison with
Wittgenstein's notion of a 'form of life.' Community is an empirical concept in this sense: it means 'whatever' or 'whoever' (in the
plural). Community, then, is a semiohistorical *locale*.

To exemplify this, I shall mount, in the next investigation, some
initial attempts to show what an effective semiotics (in the Nietzschean sense) would look like in analytic practice. When it comes
down to analytic practice, is it so easy just to follow Nietzsche into
– or out of – history? Can his theoretical rejection of historical origins and geneses be followed in the course of an empirical analysis? Or is it rather that their pure forms are unavailable to the analyst who must nevertheless make do with reference to their local
remainders? Can we simply reject historical and semiotic realism
in favor of a politicist relativism that, in extremis, would argue
that signs and events can mean whatever a political system would
want them to mean? As we will see, the question is particularly
acute in the case of visual signs. And indeed, for some time social
semiotics has been moving away from the analysis of purely verbal
objects and towards the inclusion of visual texts.[22] In order, then,
to contrast the idea of an effective semiotics with other forms of
analysis – and in particular the fashionable view that semiotics is
or should be 'political' merely by virtue of a kind of antirealism[23] –
my focus is a collection of photographs taken in the last quarter of
the nineteenth century for Dr. Barnardo, founder of the well-
known British institutions for orphans and street children. In particular I examine, as historical and political texts, the individual
portraits of the children he 'rescued' from street middens. A paradigmatic case is looked at in some detail, a photograph taken by
Thomas Barnes or Roderick Johnstone on 5 January 1883 of a
young girl called Sarah Burge.

Photograph of Sarah Burge, by Thomas Barnes
or Roderick Johntone, 5 January 1883. Courtesy
Barnados Publicity Services, Ilford, Essex

2. Framing Photographs

Here is a sign — a picture of girl, taken over a hundred years ago. Our question in this chapter will be: What can a semiotics based on the idea of an effective history tell us about this sign? For now, I will not be able to say exactly what the answer is; but I think I can show it, display it, give an example. To do this I want, first of all, to clear up some currently fashionable notions about photography — and in particular I shall work against the idea that photographs are necessarily 'political' because they *don't* simply and unproblematically act in a 'realistic' way. That is, I want to be able to say that there is a relation between a photograph and 'what it is a picture of,' but that that relation has to do with effective historical elements rather than with the necessary properties of any given photographic sign. Now, this is not to say that we can analyze photographs in terms of a simple realism, by connecting the photographic sign to its referent or referents; nor is it to say that the best method of reading photographs is to tie them to the historical context in which they were produced. That is, photographs cannot be analyzed just from *within* their frames (concentrating on, for example, the 'syntax' of their composition) or just from *outside* those frames (concentrating, in this second case, on their 'contexts'). Instead, I want to show that an effective semiotics would look at the frame or framing itself — at its 'parergon,' to borrow Derrida's term.[1] 'Parergon' means literally 'with the work'; and accordingly, my investigation will ask what goes with the 'work' of the photograph, with the term 'work' taken in two senses: as in 'artwork' (photographic text) and as in the 'work' of photographing. These two collide, as it were, in the space of the frame, the border region between fixed context and historically mobile sign.

How does the sign flicker between fixed and mobile meanings? How does it remain tied to the conditions, technologies, and institutions of its production and yet also have new and unpredictable meanings in different times and places? By turning to these questions, I presage an important theme of this book concerning the question of meaning in general: meaning is neither fixed nor fluid. Which of these it is, how it comes to be so, and in what specific ways, all depend crucially on the work practices (semioses) performed on signs by specific communities. Hence, in this investigation we will not be concerned with realism or antirealism ('textualism,' perhaps) as general theories of meaning for the understanding of photographs; rather we will examine how the communities that made this photograph, used it, circulated it, and read and consumed it effectively gave it different (though sometimes related) sorts of meaning by taking it up as part of their everyday lives. So to begin with, then, we must surmount the limitations of the fashionable binary of the 'real' versus the 'political' as moments for understanding the meaning of photographic signs.

Despite my reservations, it's practically a commonplace today that photographs are political. Side by side with a reconsideration of the photograph as a form of semiosis and despite – for example, Roland Barthes's own reaffirmation of his lifelong devotion to 'realism'[2] – almost no one today claims that photography is a mere window on the world, a neutral mechanism for snapping reality within a four-sided, two-dimensional frame.[3] This shift in epistemic ground is apparently the basis for its politicization. If the real is not available, so the story goes, what must move into the ground it once occupied is something called 'the political.' But why? How does the political, a *moral* category (as in the term 'the moral sciences'), simply come to replace realism, an ontological and/or epistemic category? Are they not different matters entirely? For it remains that various communities – not only families, historians, business corporations, and so on but also philosophers, semioticians, and critical photoanalysts themselves – continue to cite and reproduce photographs in order to refer to, or make visible, not just the texts of those photographs themselves but also what those texts ostensibly show: their 'objects.'

The relation between a photograph and its object, then, continues to be problematic in ways that generalized social-semiotic references to 'the political' cannot easily solve. The most dogmatic relativist will not say that a Polaroid snapshot I take of him is *not* him but someone else. In removing all possibility and consideration of a realist problematic, we run the risk of embracing a kind of naive and uncritical relativism (or 'textualism,' as it is sometimes called). Instead, we could begin to ask what a tactics for bringing off an effective or piecemeal political-historical analysis of photographs – including the politics and history of the referent – would look like. This would have its own risks, for to subvert realism we would first have to install it; to contest it we would first have to inscribe it. This tactics would acknowledge that there is no pure challenge without some incorporation of the theories being challenged.

And this is one of the consequences of turning to the parergonal, to the frame or framing of the sign. We can put it in the following rather simplistic terms: Realism wants to find a sign's meaning in its referent, or a historical event's meaning in its origin. By contrast, what we might call 'politicism' interprets signs and events in terms of the social and institutional systems they are part of, including (especially) their economic and historical systems of determination. But these positions are not exclusive. They come together in the space of the frame. For the frame is the space of difference *between* the sign and its referent or origin and also *between* the sign and its social-institutional 'context.' It is neither inside nor outside in any pure sense: it shows at once the necessity of referring signs to their origins/referents and to their institutions of production and consumption, along with the necessary 'impurity' of such analytic endeavors. Or rather, there are two impurities. That is, with politicism and against realism, I want to say that there can be no pure origins or referents onto which we can simply map signs; but with realism and against politicism, I want to say that the space of the political 'determination' of signs is itself open to a certain kind of empirical inquiry. There can then be a politics of the referent: but one that makes the whole idea of reference historically and politically problematic. And there can be (what I shall call) a limited realism pertaining to sociohistorical 'contexts' of sign production, but one that reads these 'contexts' in terms of their specifically local actuality or effectivity. Meaning is a matter neither of genesis (realism) nor of structure (politicism), in any pure and singular sense.[4] It partakes of both, in their necessarily impure and plural senses, as *questions of possibility* only. The effective *is* the space of the frame, of *possible* geneses and structures, *possible* referents and institutions, *possible* origins and reinterpretations.

And so what we need to ask is, In what specific *ways* are photographs political/historical? And depending utterly on the particular circumstance, this may *or may not* lead to asking how their relations with their objects play a part in those specific ways. To ask the text-object question in this way also opens up the possibility of multiple relations between photographs and their 'others' (their possible 'not-signs' as I will call them later), one that does not especially privilege the referent or object as a specifically central other, even by negation. More generally for semiotics, this means that the sign may have multiple others (or not-signs) such that one analytic problem would be to disclose what some of these *other* political others can be and how they become situationally relevant. Productional loci would then be just one – not necessarily privileged – instance of these others. And as I have said, I want to look at relations between the text (in this case a photograph) and its historical locus of production, at its concrete and practical uses as a form of communication between the institution that produced it and other institutions and, later, at its generic position in terms of current modes of pictorial consumption and distribution.

As we saw to some extent in chapter 1, formal or traditional semiotic analysis by and large treats the sign (for example, the photographic image) synchronically. What this neglects is the ways a photograph can carry, either explicitly or implicitly, the *traces* of its initial historical locus of production. To say this is – again – not to privilege a historical 'origin' as the categorical meaning or ultimate truth of the picture as would a 'total' history: rather, it is *to remember*, in Nietzsche's sense of a 'general' history, a sense in which (as we have seen) history is put at the service of a critical philosophy of the present rather than celebrated as an ultimate and fixed point of reference.[5]

So when Sarah Burge had her photograph taken by a relatively new process in which halftone blocks could be made cheaply and reproduced en masse in the form of albumen prints, she and her image were caught up in a whole range of quite new institutional and technical apparatuses.[6] This type of 'writing,' the easily disseminable photo-graph, now made a new phenomenon available for mass consumption: the ordinary person. It is, then, effectively from the 1880s that members of mass populations could 'consume' one another as material images; it is from then that they could have something that today we take for granted: pictorial images of themselves. This possibility – especially as it coincides with the extension of the franchise, the introduction of mass schooling, and major developments in sanitation, welfare, housing, and working conditions – sounds emancipatory.[7]

However, the new ready availability of the cheap snapshot meant new loci of institutional control surrounding the distribution of both photographic equipment (the popular Kodak camera, for example) and its products. As Noel Sanders has argued, when Victorian families began to take and distribute their 'own' portraits at this time, it was more often than not a woman who posed, along with some simple props, and a man (father or husband) who hid under the black cloth to snap her.[8] Either this or one went to a photographic gallery where a woman and/or her family were also subject to a photographic practice controlled by men.[9] At a time of empire and colonization, men could send back to their families at home likenesses of their possessions, including wives and children. In an old photograph I have in my postcard collection, a group of women pose within an enclosure like a boxing ring. A sign distinguishing them and 'their' technology is pinned to the ropes, reading 'EUROPEAN LADIES.' Popular photography was, then, definitely a European and possibly a masculine form of representation, and what it did, among other things, was to capture women. Even when men were photographed, they were thereby at least partly feminized: as Sanders shows, they 'camped it up' in front of the camera, coming to be scrutinized for the first time in a way that had previously been reserved for women; they could now be seen to be seen as opposed to just looking. This began to map out a series of relations of control of (and by) the photograph in general. To be photographed, since then, has meant to be 'taken.' The allegedly non-European belief that photography can capture the soul may not be all that mystical a construction. And a similar notion appears to have been entertained by Wittgenstein in a characteristically materialist moment: 'The human body,' he wrote, 'is the best picture of the human soul.'[10] So the political history of photography might begin with the initial question: Who is taken, by whom, and with what?

What we know of the Barnardo photographs suggests an entirely typical set of nineteenth-century pictorial relations – though it's true that Barnardo inaugurated a few members of the set. He does not take the photographs himself; his work is cut out in more overtly practical tasks than that of mere representation, which always carries the connotation of pleasure. That work is therefore passed on to a particular agent within the institutional division of labor. Nevertheless, Barnardo is the one who literally captures the subjects, the children. According to his own rather romantic reconstruction of his eponymous Children's Homes origins, the Irish missionary in training T. J. Barnardo was taken one night in the late 1860s, by one of the London 'street Arabs' he taught, to a 'lay' where boys slept in bundles beside a rotting wharf. It was 'a spectacle to angels and to men enough to break any heart of love,' as he later put it.[11]

Barnardo began to literally collect these boys, these 'Arabs,' who were utterly and completely other to him and to the charitable middle classes of the time on whom he came to depend for funds. The discourses that pervade Barnardo's accounts construct this radical otherness as if the children were another race or even another species, one to be both helped on its way and scientifically understood in the manner of nineteenth-century evolutionary biology and colonialist ethnology. Barnardo had indeed wanted to go as a missionary to China. Now the oriental other was available to him practically on his own doorstep, no farther east than the Isle of Dogs.

To convince official political sources that a social problem of substantial homelessness even existed in London, Barnardo was forced, again according to his own account, to lead Lord Shaftesbury himself to a lay, 'Queen's Shades' near Billingsgate. As the official photo-catalog account puts it, 'There he found the largest "lay" he was ever to see: seventy-three boys came stumbling out from under a huge tarpaulin, shivering in the bitter night air. With the powerful support of Lord Shaftesbury and his friends his deep longing to help destitute children came a step nearer fulfilment.'[12] The key to this early success was a decisive *empirical* victory: a practical demonstration. Shaftesbury literally saw the problem with his own eyes. Barnardo's mission, as much as to run destitute children to ground, was to have as many people as possible undergo Shaftesbury's and his own visual experience of those specimens. And hence the utterly critical role of photography for Barnardo. The practice of photography acted as a problem-solution – and on a number of fronts. This is a crucial aspect of one of its local (historically specific) meanings.

Photography, however, was only one – though perhaps the most singularly effective one – of a battery of writing forms Barnardo had available. His own sermons and speeches were legendary for moving audiences to give. His technique is the prototype of the monetary evangelist in this respect. But closest to his conception of himself as the central organizer of orphan charities in Britain – with a colossal export business to the colonies of Canada and Australia[13] – was the practice of keeping official records. As we shall see, photography was a technique that could span both sides of this double strategy. It could work to illustrate sermons and lectures and other public appeals as well as to bolster Barnardo's claim that he kept meticulous internal records. On the latter score, Barnardo became an obsessive record keeper, perhaps since the more traditionally philanthropic Charity Organization Society had accused him publicly of not being 'scientific.' His journal *Day and Night* was subtitled *A Monthly Record of Christian Missions and Practical Philanthropy*. This monthly record was in itself a doubly useful tool; it took toll of the problem he faced (as a quantitative empirical phenomenon), and it also recorded his success at controlling it. It was both spectacular and demographic. That is, keeping records in this kind of detail – with a portrait photograph the main part of each personal history – meant that Barnardo's edge over competing institutions could be publicly visible in documentary form while, at the same time, it also worked internally to the nascent organization itself as a mode of regimenting, ranking, and categorizing the vast and disparate array of young people brought in during the weekly culls. In this way they could be most efficiently routed and deployed in large numbers through the various quasi-domestic and labor departments of Barnardo's: from the Babies Castle and the Tinies Home to the Weaving and Tailors Shops and the Wood Chopping Brigade. As noted, central to this record keeping was the photograph: a means with a double end. It recorded each child's unique features, and at the same time it homogenized the children as a whole, making them specifically Barnardo boys and girls.

The year 1874 saw the establishment of a separate department at Barnardo's for photographic records of this kind. Initially Thomas Barnes, a photographer with a shop close to Barnardo's in Mile End Road, was employed to run this department. His approach is an interesting one generically, since his subjects largely fill the frame of the photograph and are often posed with props such as tables and chairs clearly visible. In this sense they have all the characteristics of Victorian portraiture: technical masculine control of the apparatus on behalf of an institution and its interests; feminized and romanticized subjects acting compliantly and complicitly in their own representational subjection. On the other hand, the pictures can be stark, especially from the point at which Roderick Johnstone took over the section, possibly as early as 1883. From 1885 onwards, at least, the portraits offer less pleasure; they become more technical and officially institutional, and they begin to have names and dates etched on their surfaces. The 'homely' props are more spartan from this point on. It is as if the mode of publicity was giving way to that of bureaucracy. Sarah Burge appears to be caught squarely in the middle of this barely perceptible switch of idioms. She is at once a person (in the style of nineteenth-century portraiture) and a part of an institutional record. We can equally imagine her both illustrating a lecture and glued into a clinical case folder.

In this respect, as Tagg and Wagner and Lloyd have noticed, there is a growing influence at Barnardo's from the seminal work of Hugh Diamond, psychiatrist, superintendent of the Female Department of the Surrey County Lunatic Asylum, and founder of the Royal Photographic Society. The conjuncture is an interesting and perhaps disturbing one, for Diamond's interest in photography is predicated on his Galtonian theory of insane types and a correspondingly eugenicist paranoia over protecting the English population from their spread. Photographic evidence, he believed, could prove the existence of these contaminating types, and from this impulse emerges the 'mug shot' in both mental hospital and police station. One could speculate on whether Barnardo had a

similar taxonomic interest in street children and some corresponding theory of their proper treatment and management.

Nevertheless, Sarah Burge's photograph was taken during a medial period. Occasional police photographs were taken then, but
the London police had no photography department of their own
until as late as 1901, and what seems to be a model for Barnardo –
the passport photograph – did not emerge until another thirteen
years later with the outbreak of the First World War.[14] In this sense
the Barnes-Johnstone jobs at Barnardo's took as much a part in developing the generic categories as in following them. That is, they
almost precisely capture the double function of their institution.

It was a 'home' and so substituted for the families of the children
it took in. Like the bourgeois family of the time, on which it was
modeled in spirit if not materially, it was a site of portraiture. Photographic portraiture was a way of keeping its history as a family,
a kind of practical genealogical record, a line of descent. It was a
means of creating ancestors for those yet to come as Barnardo boys
and girls. Barnardo kept his photographs in albums, and they were
available for inspection as in any family. At the same time, Barnardo's was also a growing welfare agency with a function utterly
different from that of the family. It had an emergent bureaucratic
problem of keeping records and accounts of its activities, of inscribing its own raison d'être in an increasingly instrumentalist
public world. Thus the photographs were pasted onto 'personal
histories' that noted age, height, hair and eye colors, complexion,
bodily marks, and vaccination points as well as date of admission
and attendance at reformatory or industrial school. In this second
sense, then, the photographs were a technical form of writing, severed from the interest and pleasure of the familial gaze and closer
to the genre of hospital and police records.

The photographs work in two ways: they *give* these children
who are severed from the institution of the family real biographies
in terms of an alternative institutional structure; they also *take* any
identity they may have had outside the confines of Barnardo's,
merging them into a common ID. A double use of the photographs
corresponds to these joint techniques of individualization and normalization. Below I shall continue with this idea of a double use
(hence, double meaning) of the Barnardo photographs. However,

as we shall see, this double meaning soon fractures and suggests a very broad proliferation of photographic uses and meanings.

It's hard to imagine, looking at Sarah Burge, that some unique individual was not being treated and cared for in an utterly personal way, at the moment this photograph was taken, in the way the bourgeois father was then supposed to care in loving detail for his daughter. A narrative of this kind would almost fit the picture except for some details (the clothes, for example, and the wild hair). And in one sense this is exactly the effect photographs such as this were supposed to have strategically – just as today we can send our charitable donations to aid a particular named child or family like, but also unlike, ourselves. But as with today's charities, we know that in all probability there is a vast official network operating and that the personalist approach, both to subscriber and on behalf of the apparent recipient, is another (quite legitimate) mode of sale. The personal charity picture is in this sense no more and no less personal than the group of 'friends' on the beach in a cigarette commercial. But what is important is the effect or *function* of the 'real person.'

Against that uniqueness, and indeed beauty, of Sarah Burge stands a stark fact. Between 1874 and 1905 the Barnardo photography department took over fifty-five thousand photographs. As Wagner and Lloyd put it, the photographs were 'mostly taken systematically when the children were admitted.'[15] One barely needs the vast Foucauldian historical-critical apparatus that Tagg, for example, brings to bear on these matters and that writers such as Donald have followed up in terms of the great educational and welfare changes that swept through Europe in the last two decades of the nineteenth-century.[16] Suddenly the ordinary person was visible as more than a constituent of a mass. She or he had connections with macroinstitutions where names, numbers, and histories were inscribed. Historical existence, of a kind, became available outside the commission of outrageous acts. Public records began to count heads rather than hearths,[17] and though many a humanist critic saw this as the period when people became mere ciphers, it is often forgotten that it is also precisely the time they became anything at all. Beforehand they had not been even this distinct in anyone's terms but their own. A number in a particular institutional locale is unique; it constitutes individualization and is also part of a system of numbering and accounting, but it is still unique. To normalize and homogenize, in this specific late nineteenth-century sense, *is* to individualize and personalize. There is no technical paradox here. And this we can take to be one of the main discoveries of such seminal works as Foucault's *Discipline and Punish*.[18]

However, Foucauld*ians* such as Tagg tend very strongly towards one side in this matter. Both Tagg and Donald quote Barnardo, through Wagner and Lloyd, to the effect that the photographic record had a central and dominant surveillance function. It apparently existed

> to make the recognition easy of boys and girls guilty of criminal acts, such as theft, burglary or arson, and who may, under false pretenses, gain admission to our Homes. Many such instances have occurred in which the possession of these photographs has enabled us to communicate with the police, or with former employees, and thus led to the discovery of offenders. By means of these likenesses children absconding from our Homes are often recovered and brought back, and in not a few instances, juveniles who have been stolen from their parents or guardians or were tempted by evil companions to leave home, and at last, after wandering for a while on the streets, found their way to our Institution, have been recognized by parents or friends and finally restored to their care.[19]

The point can be taken, and I would be the last to deny either the general or the specific policing function of the Barnardo photographs. Their sheer number, their generic connections, their material uses in connected bureaucratic practices of control all speak too loudly against any other interpretation. But isn't the Barnardo text a rather peculiar one? Why does he seem to protest too much — to lay on very thickly and openly the meshing between his photographic practices and the official authorities of law and order? Is he perhaps writing a kind of defense here? Has some accusation been made as to the propriety of Barnardo's interest in photographing so many young people in such detail?

The obvious pornographic possibilities can be quickly mentioned. For example, the penultimate figure in the official Barnardo exhibition catalog is from as late as 1892. It shows double images of a teenage girl, naked but for her knee-length stockings, garters, and leather boots. A cloak is draped across her left shoulder, but the picture is taken from her right. The two pictures are a 'before' and an 'after' shot. What the photographs are designed to show, however, is not the improving effect of some treatment for her physical deformity, but rather how the photographer's art can cover it up. The catalog caption reads: 'Two photographs taken at the same time in 1892 showing a girl with severe lordosis. The one on the left showing the worst aspect, and the other disguising the symptoms almost completely by careful arrangement of the girl and her cloak.'[20] The arrangement of the figure as a means of making the white flesh against the black cloak more appealing to a viewer, as well as the other details, cannot but remind one of pornography. Could this be the kind of problem Wagner and Lloyd refer to guardedly as 'unpleasant rumours' about Barnardo?[21] Why was this photograph taken, then? Why demonstrate that the camera can lie by turning a cripple into a more 'normal' object for the male sexual gaze? The answer has perhaps rather more to do with the micropolitics of advertising's very careful attitude towards naturalistic representation and other realist *practices* than with pseudopsychoanalytic speculations about the repression of the reality *principle*.

Barnardo was charged with a number of counts of misconduct in the late 1870s. A Baptist minister accused him, in blunt terms, of faking his records.[22] He wrote:

> The system of taking, and making capital of, the children's photographs is not only dishonest, but has a tendency to destroy the better feelings of the children. Barnardo's method is to take the children as they are supposed to enter the Home, and then after they have been in the Home some time. He is not satisfied with taking them as they really are, but he tears their clothes, so as to make them appear worse than they really are. They are also taken in purely fictitious positions. A lad named Fletcher is taken with a shoeblack's box upon his back, although he never was a shoeblack.[23]

Gillian Wagner has Barnardo 'fully acquitted . . . on the gravest of the original charges,' and yet Valerie Lloyd notes a change in photographic methods 'after the Arbitration Court had ruled against Barnardo on one of the published photographs as being "artistic fiction." '[24] Henceforth a more strictly documentary type of photograph took over in any case, though this was never a thorough change, as the lordosis example shows, and Barnardo's photography department appears to have had a continued interest in manipulating its subject matter 'to aid in advocating the claims of [the] Institution.'[25]

Barnardo's impulse, especially in the 1870s, seemed to be very closely tied to such matters of publicity. He used his then predominant 'before and after' mode of picture taking to raise subscriptions. His problem was to turn every potential subscriber, no matter how poor and uninfluential, into a Lord Shaftesbury. He had to lead them to 'lays' ('before') and show them the improvements their subscriptions were buying ('after'). The model of cause and effect, disease and diagnosis, means and ends, is a classic nineteenth-century one. This was *the* available discourse on proof. It furnished what counted as truth.

But the photographs played a different (though related) role vis-à-vis the subscribers. As the British sociologist John Lee has argued, acts of charity confer on the donor certain rights and privileges with respect to the recipient.[26] Lee cites an example from the late Harvey Sacks, who, at a seminar in Manchester in the 1970s, analyzed the following example. A man had given an old coat to a boy begging in the street and later remarked to a friend in casual conversation, 'I gave this young lad a coat and you know he was so grateful that he wore it all the time, day and night – I wouldn't be surprised if he wore it to bed.' In this sense the material object, the coat, is 'exchanged' for rights to ascribe to the recipient what that recipient can normally only avow on his own behalf ('*I* was so grateful,' etc.). It could be seen, perhaps, as conferring a formal right to condescend. Or more strictly, it should be seen as the right to *represent* the recipient. Barnardo's problem, as the organizer of one of the first mass charities and therefore as 'mediator' between a large population of recipients and an even larger population of donors, was simply this: how to deliver to donors their traditional rights of representation. The technology of the photograph, its 'realism,' and its mass reproducibility, as a highly literal form of representation, solved the problem. In return for their monetary donations, subscribers were sent picture cards showing the recipients in the streets or in better conditions following their 'rescue,' or both. These could in turn be shown to friends as evidence of good work done. They are the pictorial equivalent of utterances like 'he was so grateful . . .' And in a very literal sense they can be read as techniques for allowing donors to *represent* recipients.

At this time in Britain, three types of photographs circulated on cards, often collected in decks or, with the obvious exception, mailed through the new penny postal system as the recto of that correspondingly new generic form the postcard. The three forms were family portraits, pornographic poses, and Barnardo-type charity photographs. The subscriber's investments in the corresponding spheres of semiprivate familial interest, the forbidden-private-become-public, and the overt sphere of public welfare were measured by the amounts spent on the cards. Barnardo's East End Juvenile Mission put out sets of paired cards. The first of the pair would show a boy in rags, supposedly as he was discovered on the streets. The second would show him spruced up in gainful labor: 'Once a little vagrant,' 'Now a little workman.' But as the official catalog has it, 'in fact the two pictures were taken on the same day.'[27] The cards' versos carried an emotional message to subscribers, but one that also played, no doubt, on their scopophilic curiosity:

> These Photographs are sent forth at the request of many kind friends, who had already obtained one or two single copies in a more private manner, but desiring a collection of them, suggested the publication of the present series. We earnestly hope that the view of the bright, or, it may be, the sad faces of our young protégés will lead the friends who purchase the Photographs to sympathize very truly with us in our happy but sometimes deeply trying labours.[28]

The cards, then, positioned themselves exactly between the other two popular forms of photograph card. Barnardo had calculated the limits of transgression with precision.[29] From pornography they took the desire to collect representations of the experience of the 'other' in a way that makes such curiosity appear natural and even wholesome. From the family portrait they took the notion of direct personal interest in kin, albeit extended: a specifically kinless kin joined to the viewer through some new humanistic notion that becomes 'the family of man' – a frequent topic of photograph collections and exhibitions since the turn of the century.

Barnardo's art was specifically this well-calculated form of sale, and his need for funds appears to have been desperate. Not only were Baptist ministers and the Charity Organisation Society breathing down his neck, perhaps because he had cornered the 'good works' market, but a whole range of powerful and influential counter-charities were competing directly for his funds. He had no choice, effectively, but to go for what his more conservative peers and competitors saw as lurid methods, targeted much further down the market than the traditional philanthropists. The risk, of course, was to have his motives questioned.

This is why, I suggest, in the passage cited above (and routinely quoted as evidence of his purely panoptic interest in photography), Barnardo comes on so strongly as a conservative authority figure. His problem was indeed one of retaining his moral respectability in the midst of rumors about his almost scandalous quantitative success, both with the children and in his methods of attracting capital. It is with Barnardo that the capitalized base of charity moves away from a few rich philanthropists towards a mass of widows' mites that count for very little in themselves but amount to a great deal when calculated en masse. And this is itself an ur-form of the methods that would eventually emerge in twentieth-century consumer capitalism. Whereas the classical capitalism Barnardo grew up with made its profits from monopolizing major life necessities, the later consumer capitalism realized there were greater hedges against falling rates of profit to be had from the conviction industry – from selling images of what was *available* rather than simply from selling what was manifestly *needed*, image or no image. In this sense consumer capitalism created its own needs and markets rather than simply plugging into and satisfying preexisting ones.

Barnardo sold nonmaterial goods along the same lines: he sold moral righteousness on the same broad canvas to those who previously could not afford it. His was perhaps the first genuine 'people's' charity. Those who had so suddenly acquired personal identities now felt, with Barnardo's skillful prompting, that they should provide financially for this possibility to be extended to all the newly emergent 'humanity' of which they now felt themselves

a part. The new secular 'sin' was anonymity. The photograph
marked two points in this: the point of public conviction (the advertising cards) and the point of its fulfillment (the 'familization'
and 'deanonymization' of orphans through the internal 'Home'
portrait).[30] 'Of course,' a subscriber could believe, 'the children
are being cared for – they're being *photographed*!' Where does this
leave us, then, in terms of the politics of realism and the referent
with which we began our investigation of the Barnardo photographs?

Perhaps the answer to the question of realism has been staring us
in the face. 'Realism' – after this long detour – may be the term that
applies precisely to the neat and tidy closings of moral-political circles exemplified by Barnardo's photo *practices*. Realism would
then be the double philosophy of representation that both compels
a particular reading and also *proves* that same compulsion to be
empirically warranted, in the same move. This is why it is so effective and why neither philosophers nor photo analysts can easily
confine its ingrained presence to the convenient oubliette of naive
relativism.

Putting the question another way, and also opening another detour, can we possibly know what photography *meant* in the nineteenth-century? Perhaps we can only arrive at the barest outline.
At least it is a paradox that what seems to us the very signifier of
age, the sepia photograph, was in its own day the very picture of
modern technology. Thus it carried with it a notion almost of vulgarity, of the mechanistic and of antiart: a revulsion barely reserved these days even for laser images and computer simulations.
Writing of childhood in the period when Barnardo was at work,
Proust makes it clear that the provincial bourgeois family of his
main character, Marcel, held photography in high contempt. His
grandmother, for example, 'would have liked me to have in my
room photographs of the finest buildings and most beautiful land-
scapes. But when it came to the actual business of buying a photograph, even though she recognized that the subject of it retained its
aesthetic value, she would think of the mechanical process by
which the picture had been produced and was instantly put off by
the vulgarity and uselessness of photography.'[31]

What seemed to shock much less in those days – and hence its
use as a means of appealing to educated, refined, and less mani-

festly prurient tastes – was the much older and more respectable
technology of the lantern slide show. It retained, interestingly, the
connotations of art and magic and notions of being a fit medium
for visual education and the reproduction of great paintings. Thus
Marcel's family has no such doubts about allowing him access to
this technology as they have about photographs. The magic lantern 'fitted over the top of the lamp' in the young Marcel's room. It
was a fixture, part of the fabric, more like a television than a photo
album in its presence: 'After the manner of the first Gothic archi-
tects and master glass-artists, it turned my opaque walls into intangible rainbows and preternatural images in all sorts of colours,
depicting old legends in a sort of tremulous and transitory stained-
glass window.'[32] The lantern figures in Marcel's childhood therefore resemble the windows of the local church much more than
they do the newfangled X-ray pictures that barely anyone can understand.[33]

Barnardo was not slow to recognize all this: especially that to be
respectable meant bringing pictures to subscribers as directly as
possible without allowing the interpretation that they might have
ignoble interests – so far and no further. All the better, then, if
these could be reinforced by the real presence of an informed and
knowledgeable voice, preferably Barnardo's own. Thus the Photographic Department at Barnardo's became, by at least 1890, the
'Photography and Lantern Slide Department,' and Barnardo, as it
were, began to slip back into the older, more respectable mode of
the illustrated slide lecture.[34] At this time, to quote Wagner and
Lloyd, 'Sequences of slides with moral themes were sold in great
numbers to a public enthusiastic for almost any kind of knowledge.'[35] To maintain correct and standard commentaries, the war-
dens of Barnardo's Young Helpers League also roamed throughout Britain, drumming up subscriptions with slide-based lectures.

What this shows is something unique to the way the nineteenth-
century viewed the photographic image. Although its subject, as
Marcel's ur-Benjaminite grandmother knew, preserved its aesthetic dimensions in the photograph, what was lacking from the
print form was not only color but also light. The photograph
counted only as an *almost* naturalistic representation, then, complete but for its stubborn opacity to light. It was poor pigment, not
quality luminescence – more on the side of the plain printed text

than that of the oil painting. One could not see through to its proper subject, and this, by contrast with the well-known lantern slide, always reminded nineteenth-century viewers of its technical aspects – though no doubt there were others who thought this unintentional alienation technique a virtue.

All of this remains entirely foreign for us today. On the contrary, we see a series of paradoxes in the photograph of Sarah Burge: a young girl in an old picture; someone long dead illustrating an appeal for children with their lives still ahead of them; a street urchin in ragged clothes who remains picturesque and who, these days, would have to be costumed to look this way as if for a scene in a stage musical.[36] The paradoxes are, almost literally, matters of life and death. This is what we see in all sufficiently old photographs.

Writing of this same set of relations between temporal distance, death and representation, Roland Barthes raises the case of Alexander Gardner's photograph of the condemned boy Lewis Payne, who attempted to assassinate the U.S. secretary of state almost twenty years before the Sarah Burge photograph: 'The *punctum* is: *he is going to die*. I read at the same time: *This will be* and *this has been*. . . . What *pricks* me is the discovery of an equivalence.' Then, turning to the image he most wants to understand, 'In front of the photograph of my mother as a child, I tell myself: she is going to die: I shudder . . . *over a catastrophe which has already occurred*. Whether or not the subject is already dead, every photograph is this catastrophe.'[37] In Sarah Burge we see a 'rescue' or a 'capture' that has already occurred. She has been taken . . . from the street. The photograph, by its very existence, *means* this. But she also stands synechdocally for all those who never were; she stands for the eternally unknowable because unrecuperated others. She reminds us of the oblivion of unwritten history, of our deepest reason for writing and being written and, at the same time, of its failures. And she too is dead. Her presence for us continually fades and returns, depending on how we look. It flickers. There she is, at one moment, in black and white, her photograph infinitely more important than herself. It has now passed into the genre of late twentieth-century disposable bourgeois art. Recherché bookshops from Covent Garden to Fremantle sell postcards of Sarah Burge alongside designer gift wrap and hardbound copies of *The Rustle of Language*. She is reproduced in 'art' catalogs and in aca-

demic studies of photography and portraiture. She appears in
Screen Education, John Berger's popular book and television series *Ways of Seeing*, and now in this book.[38] She may even lapse
over into being identified with the late 1980s – and therefore passé
– trend for teenage girl models.

But amid this vitality, life, future, and hope in the apparent
énoncé, the *énonciation* always returns this infant to death. The
dark, determined, but still forlorn eyes stare out from a corpse as
much as from a living girl. The chiaroscuro effect of the black and
white is almost sinister and recalls for us the clichés of film noir.
This is Barthes's 'catastrophe.' We want to ask, 'Who *is* she?' (forgetting; synchrony). But the question is always blocked by, 'She is
dead, where did she go?' (remembering; diachrony).

This double that now takes over the print from the equally but
differently realist doubles of its nineteenth-century loci is a paradox, a puzzle. What has become a black-and-white art photograph keeps disappearing as we view it and turning into something
else: something lost and gone that fashionable relativism can
barely grasp, since its stance towards history amounts at worst to
either nostalgia or denial and at best to parody.[39] This 'something
else' is the historical other (the trace perhaps) that inhabits the
frame upon a certain kind of viewing. We can glimpse it only occasionally through the opaque surface of the print, but it insists –
precisely as a discursive effect and in no other way – on having its
subliminal presence. For us the text of the photograph has at least
two others, then: one dominant and the other marginalized. The
first connects with 'art' and the retrospective romanticization of
poverty. The second is the lingering doubt and possibility of a real
empirical person who presumably never figured anywhere but
here – Sarah Burge. The first always suggests what Brecht continually condemned as 'tui'; the second suggests the utterly unattainable. However a contemporary viewer looks at this picture, it will
keep slipping away into meaninglessness. We can barely *make* an
interpretation of it. The most common reaction is that it shows
and says nothing special. And this is achieved, perhaps, through
the mutual cancellation of its two others, the almost total embrace
of 'tui' art and the near impossibility of authentic history. The
punctum here, as it were, is not 'She *is* dead' (history) but 'How
can she be dead?' (ethics).

This points to a set of limits, a crisis for contemporary realism, for it demands two incommensurate readings of at least some pictures. First there is a kind of technical – almost ethnological – realism through which the shot of Sarah Burge can begin to unfold a case history, for example. What this realism sees is an *as-yet-alive* Sarah Burge (magic realism!) situated in a particular time and space that are the objects of its inquiry. It is a realism parallel to that of the ethnographic film or the nature documentary. For it the photograph acts as evidence for a particular conjuncture of 'human life,' just as much as the historical evidence around it 'situates' the photo-text.

But then there is a further realism, as we have seen, a kind of 'facing of facts' whereby the monochrome sepia trace speaks of everything but Sarah Burge's presence. Realism produces both an 'it is' and a contradictory 'it was.' And this is crucial to our understanding of its political effect – the effect that expunges the very temporal contradiction it rests on. 'Realistically' a photograph can never be timeless or universal, yet realism always perversely demands that it be read that way. However philosophers may use the term 'realism,' the *practice* or *activity* of realism – a technology of pictorial production and consumption – collects up the contradictory double of the fleeting empirical moment in all its particularity along with notions of timeless essence. Somehow, and this is still the mystery of it, the two are supposed to coexist. And so theoretical realism, along with many a metaphysical discourse, can say only one thing in practice: accept . . . ask no questions . . . assimilate the text to the overwhelmingly ordinary, the stream of quotidian affairs as you find them, and do it without making those affairs problematic. Realism is quietism. Perhaps this should be its acknowledged position in our studies of photographic images. Yet the debate on realism is shaping in quite other directions.

Eagleton, for example, with his own kind of nostalgia, wants to know what happened to 'the referent or real historical world.'[40] Huyssen, less wistfully, condemns the postmodern relativist idea that 'history does not exist except as text.'[41] And Hutcheon defends that stance by saying, 'Within a positivist frame of reference, photographs could be accepted as neutral representations, as windows on the world. In . . . postmodernist photos . . . they still represent (for they cannot avoid reference), but what they represent is self-consciously shown to be highly filtered by the discursive and aesthetic assumptions of the camera holder.'[42] Neither side of the debate has much news for traditional or contemporary realism – nothing that cannot be incorporated by them. Eagleton's nostalgia for the firm and solid 'real historical world' is something realism recovered from almost as soon as it became modern (let alone, if it ever did, postmodern). And on the other side, the idea that images are 'filtered' by discourse and aesthetics is entirely compatible with realist readings of technology and human psychology. It can all be too easily accounted for within the very discourse that is being contested; and this state of affairs suggests that historical and political investigations of the image still have some way to go.

Why does it appear that some theories always want to *close down* the potential range of meanings (uses) a sign can have, whereas other theories always want to *open it up*? Why do we think that all signs in all situations must mean either by being narrowly confined to some particular not-sign (for example, a referent) or by indefinitely proliferating their points of contact with a potentially endless series of other signs (for example, texts)? Why isn't this ever an empirical question? Surely these two theoretical positions merely represent two empirical possibilities? Signs *can* mean (can be used) in either of these two ways; moreover, there seems to be no reason they could not be used in ways that are between the two extremes (represented here by Eagleton's realist Marxism and Hutcheon's relativist postmodernism).

Unlike certain versions of postmodernism, I would want to retain realism: but precisely as an analy*zed* rather than an analy*tic* category; that is, as an empirical category, something to be investigated, as one set of means a particular community may have for making sense, as one semiosic technology among others. Realism requires at least some kind of archaeological treatment. As we have seen, its paradoxical reading effects have changed their valences in the past century of photography, but they still remain no less strong and active as modes of producing and consuming pictures. Just as author functions will not simply vanish by theoretical fiat upon the announcement of the author's death by avant-garde critics, neither will practical realist forms of interpretation.[43] This is especially so with regard to the photo-text's multiple others, the multiple and even contradictory 'reals' ('others,' 'referents,' 'not-signs') with which we often cannot help but read it.

And so our initial historical investigation suggests we must move on to examine a number of other theoretical concepts in terms of their practical applications. This takes us, first of all, to the central concept of community. Is the concept merely a substitute for that of culture? Or does it offer a less totalizing and more effective way of dealing with who (or what) makes sense of signs? Then we are led to a further question: What is outside the space of the sign itself? What are the candidate not-signs I have mentioned briefly in this chapter as part of our limited realism? And more important, how do actual communities use them in practice – in their practices of making sense, their semioses? These concepts, community and not-sign, are therefore the central topics of the next two chapters. They lead us into an investigation of the process of reading itself (chapter 5) and eventually to the idea (in chapter 6) that – despite our earlier deep reservations about formalism – there might be a counterformalism inside effective semiotics itself that can adequately capture the unpredictability and occasion-specific nature of actual, everyday, communities' ways of working with signs. This counterformalism is designed specifically to allow for the possibility that meaning is neither fixed and closed nor indefinite and open, except purely in principle, outside the space of the effective. In practice, in effectivity, it can be either of these, or else somewhere between, depending precisely on what semiosic communities do. What are these communities?

3. Culture and Community

In the previous investigation we saw that it can be useful to look at the frame of a text, at the parergonal space where signs and their many possible not-signs connect and disconnect in order to mean, in order to be used in locally specific ways. But once again, is there an all-embracing term for this space immediately surrounding (or still further 'outside') the sign? Is there a general ensemble of sign-to-not-sign relations? And if so, what is its name? We have already seen in chapter 1 that the idea of a total history is unavailable to any effective semiotic investigation. 'History,' in the Hegelian sense, then, cannot be the name of a general sign-context. Instead, we have seen that history needs to be thought of as a local and piecemeal positioning of semiosic techniques undertaken by and for particular communities, in and as particular forms of everyday life. To use Maurice Natanson's distinction, there is no 'big history' ('the history of Hegel, Spengler and Toynbee') – or rather, 'big history' is always only an idea, always an ideal effect of particular and practical 'little histories,' the histories of 'ordinary people in the everyday, working world, living their lives, involved in the daily web of obscure projects and minor skirmishes, the history of the unknown, the unsung, and the easily forgotten.'[1] That is, there is history in the space of the effective: the history of Sarah Burge, for example. Once history is detotalized in this and other ways, can we then move on to a more appropriate general 'medium' for semiosis? Could we just call it 'the popular' and leave it at that, thus allowing some version of cultural studies to move into semiotics? Does culture, as a concept, really work in any definite way?

In recent times, and at least since the ascendancy of cultural studies, it has become increasingly tempting to invoke the term 'culture' as a kind of benign proxy for the more problematic term 'history.' 'Culture' has at least had the advantage that it can stand in for the kind of contextual-explanatory work that is strictly not available to formalist semiotics. It is as though we could 'flesh out' the extralinguistic (or perhaps extrasemiotic) aspects of a sign or

text with a single concept, 'culture,' that would provide us with a
new englobing context and an immanent 'spirit' for it. What I have
in mind here, then, is that the idea of 'culture' may be (as 'history'
was before it) far too general to do the work of analyzing signs – or
saying how particular signs mean (how they are used). And I think
the problem remains even if we refer a sign to a *particular* culture
rather than to culture in some very general sense. Used in either
sense, the analytic concept of culture seems to betray what Wittgenstein called our 'craving for generality,' our 'contemptuous attitude towards the particular case.'[2]

One possible recent exception to this overtotalizing version of
culture would be Stephen Greenblatt's 'cultural poetics,' a continuing argument about the *boundaries* of specific cultural objects
and their *negotiability*.[3] Greenblatt rejects general theories of the
relation (in his case) between 'art' and 'society,' particularly those
of Jameson and Lyotard. Whereas Jameson, he argues, reads (capitalist) society as closing down the possibilities of aesthetic meanings, Lyotard characterizes it as proliferating meanings, almost to
the point of meaning*lessness*. Greenblatt, against both, argues that
capitalism involves a dizzying oscillation between the two. But can
semiosic closure and openness (separately or in oscillation) be the
basis of a general theory of social signs? Isn't their specific operation in situ a more appropriate object of analysis – without any
necessary and a priori condition of proliferation, monologism, or
oscillation? (Which is not to say that any of these three might not
be part of some actual community's semiosic 'tactics.') And why,
after his critique of Jameson and Lyotard, does Greenblatt want to
hold on to the centrality of capitalism as the marker of the social?
In these instances we can see that contemporary relativist positions, such as the 'New Historicism,' still hold on to the remnants
of a totalizing version of the relation between history, society, and
culture on the one hand and signs, texts, and artworks on the
other.[4]

However we study the vast and indeterminate area known as
'culture,' there is, as I have suggested, a possibility that the term
'cultural studies' will come to be the descriptor for the ensuing investigations.[5] The problem here is that 'cultural studies' is also a
name with a very specific history, having by and large to do with
events and ideas in Birmingham (England) in the 1970s. Origi-

nally, the Birmingham Centre for Contemporary Cultural Studies
(CCCS) had a fairly straightforward conception of the problem:
how to take cultural affairs out of the hands of English departments, appreciationism, and aestheticism and resituate them on a
Marxist (or perhaps even semiotic) terrain.[6] If one looks at the
work of Stuart Hall, for example, it's easy to see him beginning
with a radical economism and moving towards a position whereby
the domain of culture is not just produced (by material economic
forces) but productive in its own right. Nevertheless, even at its
most 'culturalist' moment (and this seems to be the central problem), Birmingham Cultural Studies has always wanted to theorize
at least some kind of *relation* between economy and culture, as if
one already possessed the firm dockside (economy) and the un-
predictably bobbing ship (culture), so that all one needed was the
rope. This, of course, raises many questions. The one that concerns me most is the idea of having to find a relation *of any sort*.
And we can approach this problem by looking at the 'noncultural'
partner in this uneasy marriage: economy.

Why economy? The answer has to do, I think, with the central
position of something called 'the economy' within 1970s Marxism
– even though a conglomerated concept of 'the economy' is nowhere to be found in the writings of Marx. (It does not appear until Keynes and does not arrive in popular English idioms until the
1960s – before this, 'economy' meant 'economizing.')[7] The upshot
of this is that 'economy' and 'culture' become reifying terms: gloss-
ing over specific, local, and particular social practices in an effort
to produce an idea or a 'theory.' (And it is to this extent that 'culture' has become something rather like Natanson's 'big history.')
In fact, all that is produced is a kind of theoreticist game with large
blocks of hazy conceptual entities whose 'relations' are supposed
to be investigated. The struggle is almost always for a ghostly
'third term' ('reflection,' 'refraction,' 'semiautonomy,' and so on)
that will make the connection. But there is no good reason for separating the two in the first place – especially when both are so neb-
ulous that they can quite easily contain each other's features (as
Raymond Williams has so aptly shown).[8]

And so if one wanted to study some domain called 'culture,' it
seems it would be necessary, nowadays, to imagine – *per impossible* – a discipline called 'culturics' (on the model of the terms 'pol-

itics' and 'economics') that would try to specify a *positive* domain of analysis rather than an epiphenomenon of some other. And that bizarre problematic, so far as I know, is not currently being pursued. When culture is always the central object and always, at the same time, secondary to something equally unspecific, the concept seems very unsatisfactory and of very little use in the analysis of fine, local, and specific uses of signs.

But after all this, has there been no 'culturics'? One of the recent upshots of Birmingham-style thinking – perhaps by virtue of the problems raised above – has been its more libertarian wing. What I have in mind here is those research programs that have taken the question of cultural 'autonomy' so seriously as to turn it into what was previously (for Marxism) a kind of 'material base' in its own right, so that now cultural structures and systems are supposed to explain other things outside them ('everyday life,' for example). Now we hear that readers, audiences, 'consumers,' and so on have complete autonomy over what it is they do, in and as cultural practices, such that any and every reading can be made, and such that these readings are 'resistive' and 'transgressive' – with the consequence that the traditional Marxist domain of 'production' can be forgotten altogether. Reading, it seems, no longer has limits; it no longer comes to an end anywhere but is, rather, all-encompassing, a means by which persons create their lives and meanings just as they wish – as though they were to pull themselves up by their own hair.

Curiously, the effect of this movement has been to reinscribe 'culture' into the domain of the aesthetic: cultural analysis and cultural practice (or intervention) become indistinguishable. Instead of an analysis of signs, we get a kind of creative writing. The value of 'culture' now, it seems, is just as it was for F. R. Leavis: neither dogmatically working class nor decadently aristocratic but, for example, ethnically, racially, genderedly, and so on 'authentic.' Analyzing signs in terms of their cultural locations means, effectively, returning them to their 'authenticity,' which then takes on the position of another essence or center.

The concept of 'culture' can be so broad, then, that almost anything can be placed within it. And this includes the use of signs, so that only the most general references to 'semiosis' or 'discourse' need be invoked. Returning to Stuart Hall, we find him writing, for example, of 'discourses' in the most general way and yet appearing to say something profound about a particular historical and political situation: 'Anyone who is genuinely interested in the production and mechanisms of ideology must be concerned with the question of the production of subjects and the unconscious categories that enable definite forms of subjectivity to arise. It is clear that the discourses of the New Right have been engaged precisely in this work of the production of new subject positions and the transformation of subjectivities.'[9] I have no doubt that Hall is referring here to a very significant problem: any semiotics that is to get beyond a purely formalist manipulation of signs for its own sake is going to have to come to terms with questions of the subject and subjectivity. But to do it in this way, as if one were manipulating large blocks of material called 'ideology,' 'discourse(s),' 'the subject,' 'the unconscious,' and so on, will miss precisely the level of specificity to which an attention to the use of particular signs is directed. In fact, cultural analysis of this kind constitutes another kind of formalism in its own right: a formalism of abstract sociopolitical categories that, as it were, stand proxy for actual investigations. Simply because semiotic concepts (such as 'discourse') *can* become all-embracing, or can be subsumed under even more general categories such as 'culture,' does not mean they must or indeed that they should.

'Culture,' whatever its pseudoexplanatory power as a concept, is a sign in its own right, and it is a fairly recent one. It dates roughly from the Enlightenment, though (so to speak) certain urforms of it can be found from the very beginnings of political investigations of human practices *as* specifically human practices (that is, where those practices are accounted for in terms of collective human volition rather than divine or extrahuman forces). Although one could return to Aristotle here, the notable turning point for English-speaking people is the intervention of Hobbes. From Hobbes to the Enlightenment, there is a concerted attempt to find what it is that's 'behind' human affairs – if you like, a replacement for an absent God, a quasi-causal locus that would go towards explaining how it is that people sometimes seem to act in perspicuously regular ways when in relatively close association (so that one comes to need a name for the groupings that do act in those ways, as opposed to others who act in differently regular ways). But the national and local practices that need to be conflated by such a concept are so diverse that whatever concept is used to collect them will be virtually meaningless in terms of any of those specific practices. Ur-terms such as *Weltanschauung, Zeitgeist, lingua mentalis*, and so on all share this problem, as do contemporary forms of reductionist structuralism. They want to do everything at once: to provide the name of a secular god and its church, a common 'membership,' 'institution,' and 'purpose' behind incommensurate and disparate practices. The Enlightenment concept of 'culture' fitted the bill perfectly, to the point where it is now almost impossible to imagine a practice that is not 'cultural' and does not *itself* have a concept of (or like) 'culture.'

And so there is a problem for us in attempting to use the concept of culture to do studies of how signs are used that are answerable to the *specificity* of those usages. For the use of the concept of culture is going to completely detract from those ends. 'Culture' is like a nostrum.[10] Saying that something is 'cultural' makes us feel better. It might make us feel as if we have located our proper objects in a specific intellectual domain. But in fact the 'fitting' is always illusory. All we have done by saying, for example, that specific uses of signs are 'cultural' is to make them vaguer, more like each other, less differentiable.

'Culture' is like the quasi-scientific terms philosophers use to categorize specific events into more general types that the later Wittgenstein sought to criticize on the grounds that they provided a whole range of illegitimate questions (such as those concerning the 'relations' between the types). In his practical work with Grant and Reeve on patients suffering from (what was routinely referred to as) 'battle shock' or simply 'shock,' Wittgenstein sought to remove the same kinds of 'fog' from diagnostic practice – not simply because it was 'philosophically' wrong, but also because it did no good for the patients themselves. A passage in Grant and Reeve's final report may possibly, argues his biographer, have been written by Wittgenstein himself:

> In practice we found that the diagnosis of shock seemed to depend on the personal views of the individual making it rather than on generally accepted criteria. Unless we were acquainted with these views we did not know what to expect when called to

the bedside. The label alone did not indicate what signs and symptoms the patient displayed, how ill he was or what treatment he required. The only common ground for diagnosis that we could detect was that the patient seemed *ill*. We were led, therefore, to discard the word 'shock' in its varying definitions. We have not since found it to be of any value in the study of injury; it has rather been a hindrance to unbiased observation and a cause of misunderstanding.[11]

Ditto the concept of culture in the study of how signs are used.

To overcome this problem, throughout its long history, the term 'culture' has come to be defined, therefore, not just in terms of massive generality and englobement but also in terms of what it is *not*, in terms of its noncultural 'other.' Naturally the two tendencies do not sit easily together, so that the candidates for the title of 'other' have been so mixed and variable that, depending on preferences – like the preferences of those who diagnose shock – they can be either included (as 'cultural') or excluded (as 'other') almost at will. Sometimes culture is opposed to society; at other times it is included within it; or else society is included within culture. The same goes for language, utility, science, nature, economy, politics, history, discourse, reality, nation, government, morality, community, everyday life . . . and so on. Eventually everything is cultural or (depending on preference) almost nothing is.

One disturbing aspect of this is that the term 'culture' is not (and has not been) simply used as an analytic concept, or even a descriptive one. At each phase it has also had a strong element of normativity about it, such that it not only appears to *account for* human practices (as it were, after the fact) but also, perhaps inevitably, is used to control and prescribe those practices. Jon Stratton argues that, for example (and here we must cut a very long story short), mainstream sociological conceptions of culture emerged alongside and within the industrial bourgeoisie in the nineteenth century, to provide an abstract 'spiritual' schema to legitimate its privileged social position in the absence of obvious traditional or religious grounds for that privilege.[12] The refined version that emerges later, with Talcott Parsons, Stratton argues, is no more nor less than an identification of society's 'cultural function' with middle-class forms of correct conduct (such that, for example, one has a built-in theory of deviance in terms of divergences from it). Even the more libertarian attempts to identify 'deviant sub-cultures' on their own terms (and thus to explain their 'antilan-guages') seem to require at least some division of this sort. In short, the act of *choosing* a circumscription of the domain of culture, from the long list of available circumscriptions, always involves a political-ethical choice that has consequences for the judgment (as well as the analysis) of human practices. It is not that this prescrip-tive domain can be eliminated in order to provide a kind of neutral science – in semiotics or elsewhere. On the contrary, factual claims, especially in the humanities and social sciences, insofar as they are always interpretable by the 'objects' about which they are made (persons, groups, cultures, and so on), will always carry value. This is not the point. The point is that the concept of culture seems to want to do double duty in this field: to cover everything (the totality of facts and values 'purely' from outside those facts and values) *and* to discriminate, to value this or that as – factually – 'cultural' or 'other-than-cultural,' for example, as 'economic' or 'natural.' And this would mean that if culture is to be a central con-cept of any investigation, it is always already duplicitous.

And so, perhaps against the grain of current trends in the hu-manities and social sciences, I think there is much more to be said for a concept that is designed to refer to the local specificity of me-thodic activities (signs) than for a concept that elides this level of investigation. There is no currently available term for the former type – hence the rather awkward term 'community,' which I bor-row to some extent from the history of science. Although Kuhn's conception of a 'scientific community' has strong vestiges of neces-sary consensus, contract, and agreement worked into it, the recon-struction of that concept by Latour does not.[13] In fact, Latour makes an empirical object of how it is that scientific communities struggle to maintain semiotic unity (that is fixity or noninterpreta-bility) for the signs in their domains of interest. This struggle sug-gests that the kinds of agreement Kuhn relies on are themselves predicated on the possibility of contestation over meanings. And again, for Latour, a 'community' is an empirical locus rather than an arrangement of abstract and general ideas into a consensual paradigm.

The idea of a community as a topographical entity – a group of persons who are physically copresent to each other and who, in some rather abstract way, agree or contract to act together in concert – is no longer its central sense in philosophy or the social sciences. For example, Johannes Fabian has argued that anthropology relies on a version of the communities that make up its 'object' such that they are seen as occupying different times and spaces from anthropological communities.[14] He shows, then (even if he bemoans the fact), that communities need not be, to use his term, 'coeval.' They do not have to be bound by synchronicity, contemporaneity, or concurrence; rather, they may be dispersed in time and space. Instead, communities can be connected by looser social structures and forms of knowledge. To extend this notion, we could think of communities as any collectivities that assemble (physically or by other means) for relatively common (including dissensual) semiosic activities. A community *may* be a traditional grouping such as a particular group of religious practitioners who meet regularly for common worship. But it may also be a looser group connected by relatively tenuous affinities, such as the '/Trekkers' (or 'Slash-Trekkers') – fans of the television and movie series *Star Trek* – who communicate through a diversity of means, mainly through the circulation (in magazines and on electronic bulletin boards) of fan stories in which the *Star Trek* characters are radically altered from their more expectable sexual identities.

Other communities may be much less specific, bound by the most general of ties. At the limit, they may barely be able to be described as communicational entities at all. An example here is Derrida's 'New International,' a community that hardly exists but may be brought about at some later date. This New International will, Derrida claims, comprise an ensemble of men, women, and children who all are suffering despite or because of the international spread of so-called liberal democracy. In today's supposedly egalitarian 'new world order,' the apparent goal is the deletion of violence, famine, economic oppression, and so on. Yet for Derrida the claims are false – particular and local forms of suffering are manifest everywhere, in every country, at every crossroads. Derrida's new International announces a bringing together of these local points that have (specters of Weber?) lines of *affinity* rather than a common party, doctrine, or ideology. The point of this is, in the end, a new deconstruction outside its narrow philosophicoan-

alytic confines: the irruption of a new form of justice whose name
is 'deconstruction.'[15]

The example is an extreme one, but it does have alignments with
some recent philosophical thinking about the idea of community.
Following the later work of Heidegger, Jean-Luc Nancy, for example, argues that the concept of history is no longer available in its
total form:

> Our time is no longer the time of history, and therefore, history
> itself appears to have become part of history. Our time is the
> time, or a time . . . of the *suspense* or *suspension* of history – in
> the sense of both a certain rhythm and of uneasy expectation.
> History is suspended, without movement, and we can anticipate
> only with uncertainty or with anxiety what will happen if it
> moves forward again (if it is still possible to imagine something
> like a 'forward movement'), or if it does not move at all.[16]

Paradoxically, this Heideggerian-Nietzschean version of history
has itself a particular historical locus that happens to be now – and
no doubt it has a specific geographical locus too, which Nancy
fails to mention. However – and important for us – if for Nancy a
total history, a grand narrative of history, is no longer available,
we still have to understand what our specific history is: we have to
understand what takes its place. And his answer is just this: 'History – if we can remove this word from its metaphysical, and therefore historical, determination – does not belong primarily to time,
nor to succession, nor to causality, but to *community, or to being-
in-common*.'[17] 'Community,' that is, is Nancy's term for the state
of history after (total) history; yet his 'being-in-common' does not
return us to an unduly *Gemeinschaft*, organicist, folksy, or just
plain jolly sense of community as a 'common being.'[18] Instead of
this irenics, Nancy's being-in-common points to what *happens*; it
points precisely to the domain of the effective, the in-process:

> And this is so because community itself is something historical.
> Which means that it is not a substance, nor a subject; it is not a
> common being, which could be the goal or culmination of a pro-
> gressive process. It is rather a being-*in*-common which only *hap-
> pens*, or which is happening, an event, more than a '*being*.' I

shall attempt to present this happening of being itself, the noninfinity of its own existence, as *finite history*.[19]

Communities, on this reading, would then be collections of what happens – documentably. And since happening is never available in its purity (as a pure event-object), it is always a happening-in-semiosis, an activity that for 'us' (those doing it) is more or less methodic. Methodicity indicates a common way, particularly a common way of doing things. This commonality is therefore not an object like 'common sense' that can be analyzed for its regular properties. Rather, we (even those of us 'doing it') may be surprised by the next turn of events. This is precisely because we have no sense of what a fixed history, or fixed rules, may bring. A community, then, is whoever (collectively) copes – methodically – together with what happens, which may conform to what we think are collective expectations but also may not. This is the possibility of otherness – even of otherness-from-us. 'Finite history is the occurrence of existence, in common, for it is the "togetherness of otherness." This also means that it is the occurrence of freedom and decision to exist.'[20]

Another way, then, of expressing this revisionist concept of community would be to say that communities are collections of members. But here we would have to think of membership in its early ethnomethodological sense. Here 'member' does not refer to a person: rather, 'it means a course of activity, recognizable for its directionality, its origins, its motivated character, by a procedure for demonstrating that that is what is going on. . . . Do not think a member is a person. Think of "member" as an ongoing course of activity locatable as a feature of an organized course of activities in its course.'[21] And with a possible caveat about the term 'origins' (above), this idea of members as courses of activity seems to fit well with Nancy's idea of communities as 'what happens.'

But on a different reading, it may simply be that empirically, today, communities are just not 'cultural' or grounded in any traditional sense. Community may no longer imply the stifling but secure sense of 'culture.' The 'freedom and decision to exist' outside that space may be a function of its sheer nonavailability. This is what Edward Said conjectures, somewhat autobiographically, and following in the wake of Giles Deleuze and Félix Guattari's nomadology:

> It is no exaggeration to say that liberation as an intellectual mission, born in the resistance and opposition to the confinements and ravages of imperialism, has now shifted from the settled, established, and domesticated dynamics of culture to its unhoused, decentred, and exilic energies, energies whose incarnation today is the migrant, and whose consciousness is that of the intellectual and artist in exile, the political figure between domains, between forms, between homes, and between languages. From this perspective then all things are counter-original, spare, strange.[22]

Community, after Kuhn, Latour, Derrida, and Nancy (and perhaps after Said) may be the concept with which an effective semiotics could handle the space around the sign, its framing. And in this sense it would be my preferred option – if there needs to be an option. But this still leaves open an important question: What are the relations between any given sign (or signs) and its possible others (its not-signs)? This does not look as if it will be easily resolved by a single overarching theory or concept, even if the concept of community is the front-runner. Is there any way we can account for the potential dispersal and difference of this domain, or indeed for its potential closure (for we know that there are actual communities that work this way), each depending on particular circumstances? Is there, that is, any way of accounting for the *specificity* of relations between sign and not-sign and still having something like a general theory of semiosis? Perhaps it is not exactly a theory that's required here so much as a method or analytic mentality that allows for a highly piecemeal, or nomadic, understanding of semiosis. This is the direction of the investigation in the next chapter.

The idea of a 'not-sign' (of an outside-the-sign) is obviously something it would be better for any respectably theoretical semiotics to do without. It sounds, to use the Kantian term, noumenal: a thing-in-itself that is (at least potentially) knowable and to which the sign can be fastened. In its ultimate, absolute, and pure sense, everything so far points away from this and nothing towards it. But what if there are communities who actually work this way, who act (dare we say 'as if'?) on the basis of existents outside the signs they use, and in order to make those signs work? And to continue the hypothetical point, it may be that any given 'not-sign,' for any given community, may not be (as some philosophers have always hoped) a thing-as-such. Instead it might be any number of available others. So this is what our investigation of the not-sign will always remember: What is taken to be outside the sign, as its point of contact with some meaning-for-now, is not an object for philosophical scrutiny. Rather, it is what a particular community is using, here and now, as part of the practical management of its everyday affairs. This is where effective semiotics parts company with philosophy.

4. Signs and Not-signs

Why have the various forms of semiotics tended to neglect the problems and complexities I have proposed? A simple answer would be that most types of semiotics have been unashamedly ahistorical; they have concentrated on the 'synchronic' aspects of language and other 'sign systems.' In this formulation of the problem, the synchronic is opposed, in a binary way, with the diachronic (the study of signs in terms of their historical development). But surely, we could argue, this binary is at least problematic, if not false. In the case of any given, empirical use of a sign, the synchronic is always and necessarily bisected by the diachronic. In terms of the idea of meaning as use, it makes no sense to carve up a particular use into two separate lines of development (syntactic and historical). It is only for the purpose of a highly theoreticist investigation that the difference can be made in the first place – not to mention that, after the bisection, only one aspect will tend to be taken into account.

But there may be another answer to the question. This answer will involve a paradox – a paradox concerning how I write what is to follow. That is, to show the dehistoricization involved in previous forms of semiotics, I will have to use their own terms and assumptions, which, if I am right, will necessarily be dehistoricized ones. But this is a risk I must take. And it is one that displays my point: I cannot simply undo the history of semiotics itself, as a discipline. Its own signs are *historically* situated, albeit in an imaginary space of the ahistorical. This cannot simply be transgressed by an act of will, so any semiotic critique of ahistoricism in semiotics *must* be an immanent or inhabitational critique.

My answer to the question of semiotics' neglect of historical differences and complexities has to do with its most basic assumption. Almost by definition, every type of semiotic investigation has begun with the following idea: *For a sign to mean, it must bear a relation to something else.* We might be tempted to think that this 'something else,' this thing-outside-the-sign, would be something like a context. Then this notion of context, it seems, could easily slip into notions of history, sociopolitical complexity, local specificity, and so on. But this has not been the case. The thing-outside-the-sign (which I will henceforth call the 'not-sign') has by and large been thought of by semioticians as being an object or a referent. At least this is the starting point for many semiotic theories, even if they later proceed to bracket questions of object and referent by concentrating on the internal structure(s) of the sign. So we could simply say that the mistake in semiotics to date has been the misconstrual of the not-sign as being an object or something very like an object: something autonomous and fixed, rather like the objects that preoccupy physical scientists.

But this would leave out of account some more recent developments in semiotics. For example, it would not apply to those semioticians who have argued that a sign, if it refers at all, can refer only to another sign. The idea begins with Charles Sanders Peirce, perhaps – though he also believed that the highly relativistic consequences of this view (the not-sign as other-sign) could be solved by saying that the endless chain of sign-to-sign reference exists only in principle – while in practice what a sign is *for*, its temporary end (or 'telos'), will effectively close off the chain. On the Peircean account a sign's meaning may not be like an initial or antecedent cause, but it is something like a *final* cause, or a point where it happens, empirically, to close. The meaning does not make the sign happen; it does not propel it into existence from some imaginary root point firmly fixed in ultimate reality. But it at least finishes its happening; it pulls it along, *from* an end point (a function), *to* that end point.

The consequences are shocking. Either (1) we maintain a simple semiotic view where the meaning of a sign is its objectlike referent, or (2) we think of the not-sign as only arriving ultimately at the functional telos of the sign-to-sign chain, or (3) we suppose that sign-to-sign reference goes on endlessly beyond any not-sign, or (4), using a weak version of position 3, we say that we can never know where the chain may end, that it's *potentially* indefinite. None of these positions seems to me very satisfactory. Each seems to maintain at least a vestige of the not-sign as a kind of object. The argument is clear in case 1. In case 2 the teleological terminus at least suggests a kind of meeting between sign and object – especially if we allow the word 'object' to mean 'goal.' In the third and fourth cases the argument is much less clear. Here it seems as if these theorists could think of the not-sign as only ever being *possibly* an object, and (being relativists) they have wanted to do away with all fixed objects – so they have tried to do away with all not-signs. And this, in a peculiar and perverse way, valorizes the idea of the not-sign as object. Whether one values it (case 1, and possibly case 2) or whether one rejects it (cases 3 and 4), the same underlying position holds: if there *is* a not-sign (though there may not be), then it's an object.

All I would suggest is this: We can keep the not-sign (to continue with the shorthand) but we must think of it radically, as something other than an object.[1] In short, it's the idea of the object that blocks the path to a dynamic, historical, and complex idea of the sign. Instead, I want to begin to think of the not-sign itself as a relation or connection – but a complex one, quite unlike the kinds of relation or connection to be found in cultural studies (for example, the connection between culture and economy) that we examined in chapter 3.

There is a reason for this approach. In the tradition of Saussure, especially as he is read by the early Barthes, the sign-object relation is introduced and quickly forgotten. The notion of object or referent is assumed to be in place and, quite quickly, a different kind of medi(t)ation is put in place – though this is much less true of Anglo-American semioticians such as Peirce or Ogden and Richards, influenced by the logicist tradition of Frege and Russell. According to the Saussurean position, the semiotician is supposed to forget the referent and turn instead to the internality of the sign. The sign is accordingly split into two parts: the signifier and the signified. The signifier is usually held to be the material vehicle of the sign: a sound or an imprint on paper, for example. The signified is, by definition, not an object or referent. Rather, it is an *idea*: what the signifier calls to mind, its mental (rather than objective) equivalent. So this too is a forgetting of the domain 'outside the sign' – at least in its initial state. Though we should be fair to Barthes in particular here, noting that his complexification of the sign, whereby it expands into metasigns and connotations, at least allows for the possibility of a kind of 'contextual' build-up. But no matter how far this goes, it goes on within the domain of the sign (or, because of Barthes's expansion, the sign system) itself. Eventually all questions of the relation between the sign and the not-sign become irrelevant. All of the contextual action, as it were, takes place on the side of the sign. Yet the referent remains as a necessary, if vestigial, part of the theory. It remains repressed. And like all repressions, it threatens to return at any moment.

But within the larger picture that's emerging here, we can notice a certain possibility: that a sign has both internal and external relations, relations that seem never to arise alone in their purity but that instead, as we saw in the case of photography, infect one another in the space of the frame or parergon. This is so even if we look beyond the particular split into signifier and signified (as the primary internal relation) or the split into sign and object (as the primary external relation). To explore this question, I shall simply focus on these two relations in the abstract for the present, without naming them or fixing them in a specific way. So for the sake of making a beginning only, let us say that *for anything to mean it must bear a relation to itself (R1) and also a relation to something else (R2).*

Now, there's a certain absurdity here – a breach of grammar even. For we can see how the second relation (R2) *is* a relation in a quite straightforward sense. But in the first one (R1) the word 'relation' could be used only in an overtly metaphorical way. The phrase 'a thing's relation to itself' is prima facie nonsensical, as Wittgenstein well knew, since it made him laugh. But in another sense we know that some things can have relations to themselves. Human beings are typical examples: we have self-images, self-esteem, self-worth, self-loathing, and so on.[2] The idea of a relation to oneself appears to be a feature of the things we call 'conscious.' So, within my metaphor, I would want to say that R1 marks the 'consciousness' of the sign, the practice: its consciousness to (or of) itself.

Lest I be thought to be indulging in the grossest kind of metaphysics here, I want to clear this up. I am taking the term 'consciousness' from its early use by Giambattista Vico. In his *New Science*, Vico separated *coscienza* from *scienza*.[3] *Coscienza* is a form of knowledge – it is knowledge of *il certo* (roughly, the certain). But this 'certain,' for Vico, is like our use of the term when we say 'certain men,' 'certain houses,' and so forth. It does not mean definite knowledge but has more the idea of particularity: particular events, customs, laws, institutions. *Coscienza* is the domain of the observable: what we can see around us as rather specific things. Its opposite, *scienza*, is also a form of knowledge: knowledge of what Vico calls *il vero*, the true. This truth consists of universal and eternal principles. It is a Platonic domain of underlying sempiternal structures that pervade all times and places. *Scienza* claims to know ideality, that which is not historically specific, and is the sort of thing Wittgenstein refers to when (as we saw in chapter 3) he writes of 'the craving for generality' and 'the contemptuous attitude towards the particular case.'[4] The opposite is true for *coscienza*. So when I refer to a sign's relation to itself (R1), I want to refer to its here-and-now specificity: this sign in this place at this time doing this job, and so on. (This is what *might* be meant by the term 'the materiality of consciousness.') To locate a sign's internal relation as deriving from *coscienza*, from its particular materiality, means that an effective semiotics can avoid the problem of wanting to find, in and as that relation, a sign's 'primitive,' 'original,' or 'pure' meaning. That is, it retains for the sign a very definite *empirical* particularism that steers between the ideas of both singular immanent meanings and meanings-in-general.

So we can see at once that this 'internal' relation of the sign is by no means a calculable or algorithmic one. It is not fixed and stable. It is therefore unlike the necessary structural relation of signifier to signified (for Vico that relation would be very strongly associated with *scienza* and *il vero*). In traditional semiotic terms, R1 is the point of intersection of the synchronic axis of the sign with its diachronic axis: the point the specific sign occupies, what it does just here and now, as a specific practice of a specific community (synchrony), as opposed to there and then (diachrony). If a sign's internal relation were to be a point (if we could somehow conceive of it as a point) within an event, within 'what happens' (to return to Nancy), that point itself would never be an infinitely small one; it would still occupy a space. No points are spaceless – all points point, or make points within and as part of a field. In short, R1 consists of everything that is specific to a particular sign as it is used (and such that it is never *not* used). This relation, R1, to take the simplest of cases, would not be identical in the case of the sign '!' as it is used just there and as it is used just here! And even this simplest of cases could produce, I suspect, a complex analysis.[5]

By contrast, the relation R2 would connect the specific sign to all and any possible not-signs. It might therefore connect one sign to another, since one sign may be another's not-sign. It might, depending on the circumstances, connect the first exclamation point (above) with the second. One has to say 'might' here, because *specific circumstances* and relevances that cannot be known in advance will always determine the relevant connections and relations – and 'specific circumstances' must refer to what a community is using a sign for. Thus, even with two uses of (perhaps) 'the same' sign, we can see that the relation R1 will necessarily produce differences while the relation R2 may (or may not, depending on the circumstances) account for the relation between those differences – or else it might, for example, constitute a relation between one of the signs and some totally different not-sign. Hence the not-sign is always and necessarily what is not *just-and-specifically-this-sign*. Hence, to restate the case, it *can* be another sign, though it is not *necessarily* so. R2 will be formed wherever and whenever one sign connects with something else in whatever way it happens to do so by virtue of the practices of a specific community of sign-users. The not-sign, to use Schutz's distinction, is always a concept of the second order: it is not available to analysis (and still less for 'theory' to decide as a general matter) before its construction, first of all, in and by a community's practical (that is, effective) activities.[6] The point of an effective semiotics would be – among other things – a descriptive investigation of whatever a community might or might not use in this way. The not-sign, then, is always an empirical (rather than an in-principle) matter, such that any empirical investigation may find it to be absent in any specific case.

So we can already see that a sharp division between 'internal' and 'external' relations is becoming difficult to sustain. R1 has simply to do with the fact that nothing is atomic, that things are always complex, and therefore opens up the question of the relations between parts. But these parts may not necessarily be contained within its borders. For as we have already seen in the case of the two exclamation points, the 'particular' differences that mark off one from the other are literally that: they mark off one from the other. They are not intrinsic properties in any ultimate sense. Hence both R_1 and R_2 are only stresses, tensions, or modalities.

The first mistake in semiotics is to assume that either R_1 or R_2 will furnish 'the meaning' of the sign. On a referentialist view, R_2 is thought to provide the exclusive meaning of the sign. Vice versa for sign-internal theories in the tradition of Saussure and the early Barthes.

The second mistake in semiotics is to assume that either of these relations must have definite and universal structural forms. There is no reason to think that R_2 must be a sign-object relation. It is simply whatever relation exists – as a matter of use – between just-this-sign and its relevant not-signs (including, again, other signs). Equally, there is no reason to think that R_1 *must* consist of the relation between signifier and signified. It is whatever is specific to, and pertinently different from, just-this-sign, and hence it cannot be totally divorced from the sign's R_2.

So I would say – if I had to state my position in such formal terms – that the meaning of a sign is the relation (or exists in the possible space of the relation) between R_1 and R_2. Let us call *this* R_3, which should be recognizable now as the space of a sign's community-historical framing. And since neither R_1 nor R_2 can be fixed or given in advance, neither is the meaning R_3. This meaning we are calling R_3 is something like the solidus (or any other mark, or space) that we must write when separating or connecting R_1 *and* R_2 to form a whole, albeit a split one: R_1/R_2. In this sense, being split and whole, being an unprespecifiable effect of two unprespecifiable relations, it is not unlike what Derrida, throughout his work, calls the *mise en abyme*. However, according to the position I have outlined here, because we are never talking of signs in general (for example, we would not necessarily want to be discussing exclamation points in general, just the two in question), the *abyme* can never reach infinity – for there is no *effective* infinity. Like other abysses, it has a bottom: though where this is can never be known in advance of falling – falling into communication, perhaps. The bottom is not necessarily Peirce's teleology: for the 'function' of a sign in motion may be an effect of its motion. Neither is it necessarily an object: for an object is only one kind of not-this-sign (and on some theories, not a particularly unified matter at all).

Although all this indeterminacy will be of little comfort to formalist semioticians, it appears to me to be the only way of bringing the radical idea of meaning-as-use into semiotics. If meaning is use, this does not mean that only R2 will be affected. Use is not merely a gloss for something external to whatever has meaning, a kind of separate context, outside the frame of the sign. It pervades the 'internal' and 'external' relations of the sign (and hence the frame itself, the relation between those relations), finally making their borders and boundaries indistinct. If the concept of 'use' provides the idea of a frame, this is not an inert boundary that simply exists to make some kind of pure separation; it is a frame in which work can be done, (a) framework. Yes, we can say, such-and-such is definitely outside and beyond the sign in question: an innumerable amount of pertinent and impertinent 'others' can then be pointed to. And yes, such-and-such is definitely a part of it: look, for example, at the bar across the top of that letter *T*. But for a whole range of features, they exist on, in, and as the framework. They *do* framing work. And how they do so is never going to depend on pure, analyzable, abstractable 'properties' of signs in general, or upon an utterly signless and fixed reality outside them. How they do so is going to depend on how they are worked in specific communities. This answers, perhaps, the theoretical questions of semiotics – too formally and neatly maybe – with a very firm indeterminacy. But it leaves all the work still to be done. A chaotic object of this kind is much more difficult to grasp than a linear one.

I began this investigation by taking a risk: employing a more-or-less standard semiotic vocabulary to try to unpick traditional semiotics itself. Another way of naming this risk would be to say that my 'preservation' of *any* form of not-sign retains a too strongly realist possibility; that not-signs seem to be stipulated by the very duality I attack; that they are ultimately noumena in disguise.[7] What can be said to try to remove such lingering doubts – as much my own as anyone else's?

Like every dog, every sign has its day – or hour, minute, or second. What it is very specifically *not* at that time *may* (or may not) be pertinent to how it is used, how it works, how it means. And here 'pertinent' must always mean 'pertinent for a specific community.' Then, after all this, there is a tendency for theorists to take this possibility – and it is only a possibility, even locally (for there may pertinently be no not-sign in play) – and turn it into a universal principle, or a principle of universal availability. When this happens, we get an obsessive insistence on binarity, so that someone could say, 'If x is a sign, y will be the (only) not-sign that (always) *gives* it its meaning.' Then y is turned into a fixed entity, an object beyond doubt, the pure external presence that x properly names. It comes to occupy the space of 'the primitive meaning, the original, and always sensory and material, figure.'[8] This is how it comes to look noumenal. Why do we do this? Why crave this generality?

On the other hand, if any not-sign is just as local as 'its' sign, this mistake cannot be made. We can no longer find a proper, permanent, or singular not-sign for every sign. The double mistake in semiotics is precisely this: to think of all not-signs as proper, permanent, or singular, *or else* to give up the whole business of them. It is this *methodological* binary (much more than that between sign and not-sign) that I object to. If we discover a community that clearly requires particular (locally constructed) not-signs as part and parcel of its use of signs, then it is going to be just as problematic to ignore this (perhaps by telling them they are wrong and there can be no noumena) as it is to fix this particular and local usage into a universal scheme.

The space outside a sign is always there – for a sign never covers the entirety of the universe – and so some part of this space is always *potentially* part of its use, its framing. That potential may or may not be put into practice by a community: but if it is, a very particular not-sign is made pertinent to the case. Yet any particular item that is subsequently found in that space (and is held to be relevant to it by some community of users) should not be assumed to be always and immutably its opposite and therefore its 'meaning.' It should certainly not be assumed to be its equivalent in the ultimately real world – the noumenon to the sign-as-phenomenon, for example, or its transcendental signified.

What we find as relevant to a particular sign depends on local circumstances. The local circumstances may (or indeed may not) include what we (as analysts or 'members') see as absent from them. This is all the concept of the not-sign proposes: that what is absent from, as well as what is present in, particular circumstances may be relevant to how a sign is used. No more than that, and with no a priori ideas as to what may constitute presence or absence in general.

Let me rephrase this in terms of a theoretical paradox. If there *are* not-signs, we (analysts) risk their becoming fixed, not-signs-in-general. They become the absence (or other potential presence) from which the supposed presence of the sign is guaranteed its meaning. They become, for example, noumenal. But if there are *no* not-signs (a position some theorists have adopted because of the problem just mentioned), the sign itself seems, as I have said, without limit. It becomes a plenum; it fills up the space of presence all on its own, existing without boundary, frame, or limits. Neither of these positions is satisfactory in terms of an effective semiotics. Any theory that fixes not-signs into universals *as well as* any theory without any conception of not-signs will be incomplete. This is why it is essential to rethink the not-sign as (1) a movable and flexible absence (when it is, empirically, in place; when it happens to be *made* pertinent to a specific community practice) and (2) not *necessarily* in place at all on some occasions, even as an absence. The concept of the not-sign is the mark of the possibility, in practice, of an other-than-just-this-sign-here that is practically pertinent to it.[9]

The onus is on us now, therefore, to begin to depart from wondering (or wandering) about the general forms of semiosis and return to a particular case. So in the next chapter I will examine the case of reading as a practical activity, as a means of localized semiosis (by explicit contrast with theoretical accounts of its essence or general form). What counts as reading on any specific occasion will, as we shall see, depend on whether it is thought of as even *having* a 'not-reading' and – if it *is* thought of this way – on which specific not-reading, from a broad range of candidates, happens to be in place or to be invoked as pertinent for quite practical purposes: for example, the purposes of teaching a class of schoolchildren to read.

5. Reading Practices

In this chapter I attempt to show that there is no unified, prespecifiable thing or practice that counts always and only as reading. Put another way, the word 'reading' has no single meaning. Or, it is always possible to defeat the idea of a definite, distinct, and universal boundary between a practice or thing called reading and its opposite, *not*-reading. This position was discussed in chapter 4, at least as a principle of analysis. Here I want to see what this absence of a definite distinction looks like in practice. But the position I adopt does not mean that everything is reading and nothing isn't: that kind of radical relativism – a sort of 'freebase semiosis' – has already been ruled out. Rather, it means that in general, in the domain of *theories* of reading, almost everything *can* be reading, and that when it happens that something is (or isn't) reading depends on unprespecifiably local matters. Needless to say then, a consequence of my position is that there cannot be a precise pedagogic science of reading that covers every possible instance.

A related consequence is that those who have a professional interest in teaching reading – or one of its contemporary euphemisms, 'enhancing reading,' 'fostering reading,' and so on – must face the fact that no one can give them either precise descriptions of what it is they are teaching or, a fortiori, exact recipes for how they should go about it. It seems to me that there can be no 'programs' of reading instruction, no sets and lists of 'skills,' and no developmental 'stages' in the acquisition of reading. For to believe there can be such things is to believe that reading is a universal quantity or state.

Another thing this investigation sets out to do is to take, from the extremely wide band of things and practices that might be readings, the particular things and practices that have counted as 'reading-in-a-classroom.' In this neck of the woods (pedagogy), the theories of reading have tended to be mentalistic in orientation. More specifically, they have tended to think of reading as a particular mental state or set of mental states belonging to already formed and autonomous human subjects. I do not want to prove this 'wrong,' but only to show where its limits lie.

In addition, I want to show that if we are to have anything approximating a study of readings – even a study that is limited to the classroom – the approach must be wider and broader than these currently dominant mentalistic ones. In fact, it should be an effective semiotic approach. However it may be formulated, those who prefer the narrow confines of psychologistic readings of readings will read my effective semiotic approach as dealing with something like 'reading contexts.' They will tend to read me as providing a theory of the mere *situations* in which the 'real' (mental) process of reading takes place. But if we can see that psychologism's particular selection from the domain of readings is arbitrary, if we can problematize that particular theory, it should then be possible to see the alternative (semiotic) approach as actually being a theory of readings-as-such and not one simply of an epiphenomenal 'context.'

After our discussion of the idea of culture (chapter 3), we ought to be duly skeptical of the term 'context.' It is, for many theories, the prime candidate for being 'not-reading.' Here the reading, there the context. Here the real mental process, there the mere material space and time 'in' which it takes place. But by what criteria do we make this division? I have no idea how one could be so definite, just as contemporary physics no longer considers the universe to be composed of matter 'in' a 'context' of space and time but thinks instead of a space-time-matter continuum. So when I write of reading-in-a-classroom, I am referring to reading, there, as such, not to a separate 'context' that happens to be a mere vehicle for a universal process. In this sense I am asking what it is to read in a classroom and so what it is to be produced as the kind of human *subject* who does this. And so, in a paradoxical way, I do seek to make a contribution to the idea of reading-as-subjectivity – but in the sense that the production of subjects and subjectivity is always through-and-through a material, social, political, and historical practice. To this extent I agree with James Donald when he says, 'How the curriculum embodies a particular ordering of the symbolic, and how this then plays into the ordering of subjectivity, remain perhaps the most tantalisingly underexplored question[s] in the study of education.'[1]

So there are three things to argue: reading has no essence; psychologistic approaches to reading have arbitrarily cut down the
meaning of the term so that it can refer only to mental predicates;
we can approach particular 'genres' of reading, such as reading in
a classroom, an observatory, an office, a library, a tarot reader's
tent, and so on and provide alternative semiotic analyses of the
readings, there, themselves, over and above questions of mere
'context' and with a view to examining the work of subject production they entail.[2]

Again, my initial arguments rely broadly on the work of the later
Wittgenstein, particularly as he has been interpreted by Staten and
other roughly poststructuralist readers.[3] Between sections 156 and
171 of the *Philosophical Investigations*, Wittgenstein takes apart
the idea that reading is a 'particular process' – especially the popular idea that this process is a purely mental one. He asks how it
could be that '*one* particular process takes place' when we read.[4]
We might read a sentence in print and then read it in Morse code,
to give his example. In such a case, is the (supposedly psychological) process the same? I expect that most of us will think not. But
Wittgenstein is not dogmatic about this. He wants to know, I
think, why we *come to think* of the process as a singular one. And
the tentative answer he gives is that we are perhaps fooled by the
uniformity of 'the experience of reading a page of print.' He continues: 'The mere look of a printed line is itself extremely characteristic – it presents, that is, a quite special appearance, the letters
all roughly the same size, akin in shape too, and always recurring;
most of the words constantly repeated and enormously familiar to
us, like well-known faces.'[5] This is why we feel uneasy about tin-
kering with these familiar faces – moves to legislate for spelling reform, for example.[6]

But the uniformity of a page of print and the repetition effect we
get in scanning it, for all that they point to a surface definiteness
and specifiability, do not mean that reading is a single and undifferentiated process. Instead, a brief inspection throws up a whole
range of differences and distinctions regarding what the concept of
reading might cover. Staten speculates that one candidate for the
'soul' of reading might be to specify it as being the *derivation* of
repetitions from an original. And this again is one of the directions
in which computer metaphors of reading have tended to take us.

But then we also have to ask: What is to count as deriving? The problem simply shifts to another terrain. Perhaps, Staten goes on, we should always refer to the 'systematic' derivation of, for example, sounds from marks. But we all know it is possible to derive the wrong sounds. If we do that, are we reading? Again, we could say that the essence (or *Merkmal*) of reading was the presence of a certain kind of inner experience rather than a derivation. But we may, and do, have this experience while we are asleep or affected by drugs. Are we to say that then we are reading?

Instead of looking for a definite and singular characteristic of reading, Wittgenstein suggests we look on reading as an 'assemblage of characteristics.' Moreover, according to Staten, these characteristics will 'in each separate case of reading . . . be variously reconstituted, and in these different reassemblings there will always be the infection of characteristics of what does not correspond to what we want to think of as really, essentially, *reading*. . . . It is as though these characteristics had dual membership in two mutually exclusive sets.'[7] First, then, we cannot prespecify the characteristics that go to make up reading. Second, if we could, we would always find them in new and varied combinations in any actual case of reading. Third, we will always find, in among them, characteristics we should not want to associate with reading as such but that are crucial to that case. Reading is like soup or slime. And so we would be mistaken if we tried to specify its essence according to a neat digital calculus: not that it has no soul as such — rather, it has a multiplicity and 'any one of them could at some stage take over and guide the sequence in its own direction.'[8] It is because of, not despite, their pleomorphism that we recognize cases of reading.

Staten's argument convinces me there are no general rules for reading, though we might find some specific semiosic *regularities* operating in particular circumstances that we could easily confuse with deep-seated and general rules. This would mean that reading could not be identical with 'knowing rules.' Rather, it is knowing, if there are any rules, what they are rules *for*. For instance, when a child in a classroom 'goes wrong' in reading, this is like a wrong move in chess. A wrong move in chess is not usually a case of, say, moving one's pawn as if it were a bishop. Instead, it is poor strategy, like putting one's queen in danger of being taken. Reading, then, is not a set of formal properties like the constitutive rules of chess but is much more like knowing how to play with texts strategically. It arises not when we know the formal characteristics of reading, but rather when we enact certain differences – differences between readings and other sorts of events. And which other sorts of events these *are* will depend, precisely, on the scene of enactment. 'Enacting' here means going through the process of inscribing a certain cultural *practice*, *P*, such that it is visibly not not-*P*. To read in the classroom therefore means to separate the reading off from other things, very specific and occasioned not-readings. Teachers and students do these things together. In enacting reading, they are inscribing what they are doing as a definite case of just-this-thing, for these purposes. And so on. Because this work is inscriptional; because it is left as a trace on a memory, a community, a classroom wall (perhaps, in the form of a timetable for reading); because it is inscribed in, for example, education manuals and in administrative procedures; because it is historically inscribed; and because this inscription is always predicated on difference rather than identity – on its relation to what it is *not* rather than its relation to its own internal essence or presence-to-itself – it is not a contradiction to call reading a form of writing-in-general after Derrida.[9]

Having come this far, it is strange to look back and find this plurality of reading*s* – this inchoate soup of tactics for delimiting the field of writing-in-general – arbitrarily reduced and confined by some theorists to a particular ghostly process, a particular mental state, activity, or experience. As Coulter has pointed out, Chomsky's well-known ideas about reading are a case in point.[10] Unlike Wittgenstein, Staten, or Coulter, Chomsky believed that reading could be reduced to a set of specific rules; rules mapping onto particular mental states, as it were, inside readers' heads as they read. He believed as follows: If the rules can be shown to be in place, so too can the corresponding mental states, and so one can say that one has a genuine case of a reader reading; but if the rules turn out not to be in place, then neither are the mental states, and so 'competent' reading is *not* taking place. For Chomsky, reading always and only has one form of definitional *not*-reading: the absence of a mental state of a particular kind. He writes that he, in his guise as the ideal-reader-cum-ideal-analyst, has 'a (no doubt in part uncon-

scious) theory involving the postulated mental acts of humans per-
forming certain acts such as reading, etc., which is related to my
(also unconscious) system of linguistic rules in such a way that I assert that A is reading when I believe him to be in such a mental
state, and my assertion is correct if my belief is correct.'[11]

Chomsky's concept of 'rule' here is an instance of what Coulter
calls the 'rule-regularity conflation.' By this Coulter means that
even though a description of actions or behaviors can work with
utter empirical reliability and predictability – for example, a grammar might account for all the well-formed utterances of (a limited
set of) a language – this (of itself) nevertheless does not provide an
argument for transferring such general properties 'to the mind.'
The actional regularities do not, ipso facto, translate into mental
rules. Even if the toaster always provides perfectly browned slices,
this does not mean that it 'knows' when the toast is done.[12]

In place of this Coulter uses one of the central devices of Wittgensteinian analysis – family resemblance. He shows how the concept of reading always glosses a nondeterminate, only relatively
precise family of cases. The members of this family are not held together by some defining characteristic that is 'essentially' reading.
Moreover, that single characteristic, even if it were analytically acceptable, could never be something like a feeling, an experience, or
a mental state of any kind. If reading were an inner process we
could not argue with someone who simply closed his eyes, claimed
to be having that experience, and therefore insisted on being
deemed one who could read. This would certainly not pass in a
school reading lesson or in an immigration literacy test.[13] In fact, it
would not pass in any social formation – no matter how mystical.

In place of defining characteristics, Wittgenstein argues instead
that *criteria* of application hold together concepts or *families of
practices* such as reading. Although we may want to argue from
entailment and so be able to say, 'If x is in place, then y is occurring,' no such definite characteristics can always be found. Criteria, for Wittgenstein, *replace* the logician's goal of strict entailment:

> For Wittgenstein, the notion of a 'criterion' *replaces* the notion
> of truth conditions in semantics. A criterial relationship be-
> tween an assertion and its evidences is weaker than classical en-

tailment but stronger than inductive evidence. If q is a criterion for p, then it is part of the meaning of p that q is a conventionally fixed evidence for the truth of p. However a criterion is not decisive evidence in itself, for additional circumstantial evidences can defeat the criterial support for an assertion. And yet, *undefeated criterial evidence constitutes the correctness of an assertion.*[14]

So the application of a concept (like reading) cannot depend on entailment of the form 'if the mental state, then the reading,' or vice versa. Instead it depends on a relation of 'conventionally fixed evidence,' the 'soupy' details of Staten's argument. To understand reading is to understand the conventions and ingredients that may come to make it up, that can surround it, that can come into and out of play in particular cases. For educators this would mean looking to the conventions and traditions of reading in the classroom; to what Anne Freadman calls its 'ceremonies.'[15] This almost calls for a 'philology' of classroom reading – a history of its texts and textual practices. Accordingly, what would the genre of reading we call 'reading-in-the-classroom' look like under such a description? What are its subgenres, for example? And what practices lie in the fields adjacent to it? Even my sketch of an answer may be surprising to some, for it is an answer that has more to do with sewage systems than semantic systems; more to do with public health than private experience.

If this were to indicate simply a social semiotics of reading, then the work of Halliday would surely be relevant. But is there really very much in the concepts of field, tenor, and mode, for example, that is going to be to the point here?[16] Isn't this in effect only another version of back- and foregrounding, one that ultimately begs to be read as 'text and context' as soon as it is thought sociopolitically? Freadman's distinction between 'game and ceremony' is perhaps more to the point for our purposes, if only because, for Freadman, where one begins and the other ends is so unclear that there cannot be an analysis whose goal is to 'clear up' the distinction. To put it another way, the *framing* of the game/ceremony distinction is not clear. Along with the playing of the game, as such (whatever 'as such' may mean here) there are also 'the preparations, the choice of partners, occasion and venue. There is the warm-up, the toss, and, at the end, the declaration of the winner and the closing-down rituals – showers, presentations, or the drink at the bar.'[17] Who is to say that these ceremonial elements are not elements of the game of tennis? Tennis could barely even *be* tennis without them, and yet they are not what are commonly known as 'the essential ingredients.'

We can make the same mistakes about reading. We sometimes think only of the reader scanning the pages, deriving sounds from print images, having mental experiences of a certain sort, and so on. And this is equivalent to serving, lobbing at the net, scoring a point, and so on in tennis. But there are also the ceremonies of reading without which, I want to add, it is equally just not reading. When we think of 'reading' we think too much of a particular genre of it called 'reading off,' including subgenres like 'deriving' and 'scanning.' But what are these other possibilities, these ceremonies? How do they differ from games without being not-games *exactly*? Freadman goes on:

> Ceremonies are games that situate other games: they are the rules for the setting of a game, for constituting participants as players in the game, for placing and timing it in relation to other places and times. *They are the rules for the playing of a game, but they are not the rules of the game.* Games, then, are rules for the production of certain acts in those 'places.' To the extent that the grammatical rules of my language permit me to make this distinction, I could say that, where ceremonies are rules for playing, games are rules of play. That there is 'play' at both these levels is important: knowing the rules is knowing what would break the rules, but being a skilled player is knowing how much play the rules allow and how to play with them.[18]

In some 'professional' circumstances – say, coaching tennis or teaching reading – it is very easy to teach the game (the rules of play) and not the ceremonies (the rules for that playing or playing out). Seeing how much the formal rules can be subject to free play, we think, comes later, after 'the skill.' One almost wants to limit the field or the court to those kinds of technical considerations. Still, of course, to be fully professional one is necessarily interested at the same time in the individuality and uniqueness of the (perhaps young) player(s) one is coaching. As we shall see, this humane interest does not rule out a purely technical limitation of reading to the mere game, the game that does not stand on ceremony. On the contrary, the two can be seen as equal parts in the tactics of the reading coach, of the model player.

My approach to reading seems to boil down to this: What would it be to turn one's attention to the ceremonies, not *instead* of the game but *as well as* the game – ceremonies Freadman reads as constituted by 'moments, phases, stages, or "places"' where each of these, moreover, can be called 'a genre'?[19] For the category of 'ceremonies,' in effect, subsumes the game. My own preferred tactic here would be to look at precisely the place or genre of reading closest to the hearts, minds, and bodies of the educators: the place or genre of reading-in-a-classroom. In particular I want to consider the subgenre or microplace of beginning-reading-in-a-classroom. The beginning of reading, as we shall see, is not utterly distinct from the beginning of the modern classroom in the political and historical sense; just as (as we saw in chapter 1) the beginning of the modern personal photo portrait is not utterly distinct from the beginning of the institutions of confinement.

The point of the speculations that follow is to show that these ceremonial places *are* readings. A reading is never not-framed, and there is never any simple distinction, as with Möbius strips, between the 'inside' and the 'outside' of the frame. The distinction, to be made at all, needs to be an utterly fuzzy one. The fuzziness is not a fault but a prerequisite of framing, of parergonality. The indistinct picture, to quote Wittgenstein's phrase, is 'often exactly what we need.'[20] The framing itself – always there but never specifiable without indefiniteness – consists of what a text 'does to situate itself in relation to its social, formal, and material surrounding.'[21] This is much more of a candidate for the title 'what reading is' than any ghostly internal process. Moreover, it is this reading-as-always-already-enframed that teachers and students actually orient to in deciding whether it takes place, as a purely practical matter.[22] They simply do not have available, as part of the frame itself, inside it, or outside it, any pure mental process or experience separate from the reading with which to compare the reading. What they do have is material social practices.

Here then are my speculations about the practices of classroom reading, my minimalist descriptions of it. They ask how reading is administered, almost in a medicinal sense, and what it administers to readers. Each remark or paragraph could be read as being prefaced by a phrase like 'in the classroom . . .' Together they constitute a quite particular and possibly 'personal' version of reading-in-the-classroom.

★

We read together, sometimes aloud, sometimes silently. There are places and times for each. We learn these, and sometimes they are marked on the wall in other texts that we must know how to read. To know the subgenres of 'aloud' and 'silent,' there is something we must already be able to read: a timetable, a movement of the teacher's finger, the volume of noise in the room, and so forth.

We are compared in our reading together, aloud and silently. The moments and times come around when we are to go up or sit quite still for this comparison. There are winners and losers in this, whether or not their names are spoken in public. We are separated – for example, the fast from the slow – by relative degrees. We are given our orders as to how we should proceed in our reading; the advance and the retard are sounded for us collectively and individually. These changes of routine are no more and no less than markers of the school day, like bells for recess and home time on a smaller scale.

We are put into competition in our readings. Sometimes there are ladders and tables with names and stars on the walls of the room. These represent, they map onto such things as 'where we are up to' – book 6 or book 7. It's no good being able to read if you can't read these.

Sometimes we do not know whether this is a private or a public space. Sometimes the reading is in our heads, private like our thoughts and a refuge from other things in the classroom. Then we feel like autonomous souls with thoughts of our own. Sometimes, on the contrary, the reading is a matter of public rhetoric. Reading in and reading out: both of these can come into play. They can be in play at the same time. And they can commingle with reading aloud and reading silently. Sometimes it's your innermost thoughts that are up there in the space of public rhetoric. Other times it's a big and impersonal public historical voice that's playing through your own head.

There are serious consequences for either being low on the reading scale or not taking the scale seriously: playing badly or not playing seriously. The reading we do is controlled: we can't just read any way we like. Sometimes the control is word by word, as when the teacher points to words on the board. Sometimes it's paragraph by paragraph or book by book, and so on. We learn to see parallels between textual levels by learning their similarity in terms of their control. We can feel that these things are 'meted out' to us in controlled doses. Someone somewhere knows how much each can take and also the techniques of feeding us by the rules of those precise quanta. The teacher is the closest someone who knows this, but there are probably others. The schemes of reading, the regimes of reading books, must come from *somewhere*. There is some design to this, for it is so definitely controlled. It is within this space of control that the free play of our reading must take place – that we must show ourselves as we 'really are.'[23]

Although we are to find connections and derivations word by word, occasionally sentence by sentence (at least for now), we are rarely asked to make them book by book. The area of our own particular mastery is delimited to specific amounts of text. We are not asked, for example, what a whole book means, what it says – at least not yet. And when enough is meted out so we can be tested on our judgment of whole books, there will no doubt be some greater unity that is kept from our personal judgment and mastery. How far can this go?

Although we are always massified in our reading, as a class, what we read is the smallest units, sometimes even individual sounds or letters of print. Somehow there is an association between our individual smallness and the smallness of the units we are allowed or required to scan or interpret. And there is an association between our massified nature as a class and the bigness of the book and suprabook levels that may or may not be 'out there,' beyond the frame of the classroom, at what we suppose is the 'destination' of our learning to read. On the one hand, the tiny mind and the phoneme; on the other, history and the canon of literature. This is a model for living: a relatively hierarchized morality that learning reading in the classroom teaches – whatever else we may or may not learn, however good or bad we are at reading. In fact, we might learn the moral lesson better if we're poor readers.

There is also another set of analogic relations: between the space of the reading classroom and the space of the textual practices that occur there. And this analogic relation means we are always taught something more than reading when it is reading that we learn or fail to learn. Some examples follow.

The classroom has definite, familiar spatial arrangements. You can spot a classroom a mile away. It is designed to permit 'an internal, articulated and detailed control – to render visible those who are inside it. [That is] an architecture that would operate to transform individuals: to act on those it shelters, to provide a hold on their conduct, to carry the effects of power right to them, to make it possible to know them, to alter them.'[24] This architecture, in the broadest sense, produces and contains specific kinds of subjects, specific social identities. Student as against teacher is the primary one, but there are others too. The spaces one finds in the basal reader, to take only one example, also make up an 'architecture' with equally well sectioned boundaries and characteristic identities: the domestic space as against the public street; the city street as against the trip to the country and the obligatory farmyard; Dad versus Mom; the pet versus the little sister. If these boundaries were not clear (let alone if they were inverted), nothing would be possible at all – in the classroom or in the text. This is a quite definite (if not absolute) morality; it marks off the bounds of moral play. We are to strive for equality here – equality presumably with the teacher, the model. Yet we must never reach it, for if we were equal with the teacher this could not be a classroom – a classroom in which we are to strive for equality, and so forth. The same is evident in the represented spaces within the basal readers. Mom is utterly *not* to be Dad. The domestic space exists only because it is *not* the public street. Babies are *not* pets.

In the space of the text and the space of the classroom, one is never alone but is defined by a position in a grid of relations. The story of 'being lost' is so popular here, perhaps, because there is always a resolution, a return to the familiar hierarchy. Outside the text, outside the classroom, outside the family: these are all spaces from which one must eventually return. To be in neither place is to be nowhere. Aloneness and other spaces always dissolve back to 'here,' to 'now,' to a dependable and familiar presence. This same presence was demanded, to mention only one case, by the charity schools in the 1870s: that the child be present at school or within the family. Hence Barnardo's photographs by means of which 'children absconding from our Homes are often recovered and brought back . . . [or] . . . have been recognized by parents or friends and finally restored to their care.'[25] Under a similar kind of injunction, basal reader characters exist in certain proper places but do not think – at least they do not think very much. They say, mostly, and they act a little. But they are always 'in play,' being watched.

In the class and in the early reading book there is routinely, in any given case, an authority to be appealed to or to intervene: there is no possible relativistic space of play or debate over relations of authority. They are always merely given. Over each text and each classroom hang the twin lights of truth and falsehood; on and off, binary, digital. Nothing goes unresolved. Nothing is left indefinite. Neither space allows 'maybe' to hang around for long. In the class and in the text, the middles tend to be excluded. Representation merely happens: the question of representation itself is unasked, the problem unmentioned.

Class and text: each marks clear space and time zones. There is the school timetable, but also the cycle of the family day, week, year. That institution, the family, constitutes a main site, while its 'cycle' constitutes a main technique, for the regulation of the child. As Donzelot writes, a number of mechanisms of policing have been designed since the nineteenth century to 'shepherd . . . the child back to spaces where he could be more closely watched: the school or the family dwelling.'[26] And each of these sites and techniques is part of a more general armature of regulation, representing historically 'a decisive shift from the total power of the monarch to the infinitely small exercise of power necessary to the discipline and productive exploitation of bodies accumulated in large numbers.'[27] The early reading book is clearly a case in point.[28] It tells us about where we are all supposed to be when we're, precisely, not in school space. It is rarely self-reflexive; it rarely opens a possible space for reflection on (let alone critique of) the school or the family. School and family practices are 'natural' – always were, always have been. The family home is ever present and thoroughly normal. Not so the classroom. When it does figure in the reading book, it is treated very carefully. In comic books, in trash: these are the proper moments and spaces for the classroom to be subjected to humor and criticism. On another tack, one rarely finds the reader *in* the reading of early school readers, for that could open up a potentially plurivocal space, a difference. Again the reading is paced, cycled, calendared – series 1, book 1, and so on. These are no more and no less than filing systems, forms of objective and external benchmarking. One is, unarguably, 'up to' a certain point in the story, the book, the series. It is simply not open to question, reflection, difference, undecidability. The basal reader and the reading classroom exist in an utterly archaic New-tonian space. They exude more certainty than the monastery.

At school we read a very particular kind of book from the vast range of kinds of books that there are. It is a schoolbook. As much a school as a book, then. We know, all along, that no one but schoolkids reads them and that they read them *in* school – just like us. The books and the readings are almost unimaginable outside. They are like the materials of labor specific to a highly partic-ularized, if widespread, kind of factory. The schoolbook is as spe-cific to its site as the precision gasket punch is to the car factory; as the heavy-duty industrial buttonholer is to the sweatshop. We use different machines, for example, at home, or in other readings, in other sites whether for fun or for a different kind of necessity. The schoolbook tries to limit its possible uses to *one* and only one. It al-ways tries to write of similitude and against difference: it is the most successful attempt at writing-against-difference we can imagine in a posttheological world. If it had only one use, then it would have only one meaning, and only one truth. It has, it strives for, one reading. It begs to be taken as the paragon of the limitation of reading to a particular essence – which, as we have seen, is a mark of the pyschologistic theories of reading that produced it. The school reader tries to be the very model of this technology: one is supposed to read it only one way. In fact, the triplet of teaching, textbook, and authority asks to be read one way. That way is sometimes called 'literally.' And it is no coincidence that at the same time that it limits reading to singularity, to the definite space of the classroom that is other than home, the basal reader also al-ways speaks of 'home' or some relation to home. Why is this? Is it to taunt, to mock, or to frustrate? Is it as if the factory machines did not roar and scream but said, quite gently, 'freedom, freedom, freedom'?

For many – perhaps all – of us, these 'homes' that the basal reader shows are always imaginary. They speak to us as if they were actual homes, but they are always overneat, overly well lit, well laid out figures of the imaginary. They are just like advertisements in this respect, and they retain something of the politics and ethics of advertising. What they advertise is a model of the modern home. They show that a certain architecture (the children's and the parents' bedrooms being separate, for example) is good; that a certain set of domestic relations is good; that it is normal and expectable for there to be television, good sewers, hot and cold running water, visits by doctors, good and beneficial relations with older generations, plenty of nourishment, no scarcity of basic essentials, gas and electric power, heating and warmth, a roof that doesn't leak. The basal reader advertises precisely what contemporary advertising cannot: what is taken for granted, unglamorous, and yet, as we shall see, part of a very specific technology of, as Ian Hunter puts it, 'morally managed "experience,"' 'regulated freedom,' and 'supervision through self-expression.'[29]

Psychologistic readings of reading focus on the reader in the classroom as a relatively pure consciousness and on the text as an effect of a relatively pure grammar. For them reading is the meeting of grammar and consciousness. In order for it to be so firmly in place (in psychoeducational studies of reading and in professional pedagogy alike), this quite specific version of the subject-object double requires a pair of assumptions that are also problematic (for those studies and that pedagogy) when clearly spelled out. The first assumption is that reading is always reading *as*. It has to be so in order to be, for just one example, reading-as-consciousness. The second assumption is that interpreting a text always changes not only the text but the reader – it changes what counts as the reader. These are insights derived very loosely from Heidegger, and they have a number of consequences, as follows.

To say reading is always reading as: this is to say that it has an 'as-structure.' The as-structure of reading shows a multiplicity of possible extensions of the 'as.' Grammar and consciousness are only a couple, and they are limited. What we read the school text as (qua readers) is not grammar. We do not read it as grammatical rule so much as grammatological ceremony. We read it, for example, as a *world*, as a moral sample or example, and so forth. Both in and after the moment of merely scanning the text – in and after the moment of consciousness of the text, which is to say in and after the moment psychoeducationalism calls 'reading' – what we read the text *as* has its effects on what we become. For what we become is, among other things (often things in concert with this training in reading), effects of just these sorts of texts. The as-structure of the reading and its subject-effects are not separable and discrete moments in the way models of 'reading and context' would prefer. What then would be the as-structure of reading for someone beginning to read in the classroom?

To read in the classroom is to read inside a particular kind of mechanism that was produced in the nineteenth century in Europe – for most of us this machine is a variation on the English model. But the machine of the classroom is not just a *producing* machine; it too is produced. It is both a product and a producer. What it is a product of and what it produces (as effects) is a set of specific techniques related to a kind of contradictory ethics. That is, the nineteenth century's twin goods were culture and utilitarianism.[30] The popular schools were designed to provide both the romantic goal of self-enlightenment and the cultural and spiritual development of the full personal being of the child as well as the citizen-worker, the useful tool of the state.[31] In Donald's words, they were both 'intimate' and 'secure.'

To read a text here, and to read it as a moral world – here – is to read oneself as the ethical-moral effect of these twin, oppositional requirements. One is invited to become a kind of double being: the model of full selfhood and the model of selfless citizenry. What does this dual being look like?[32] On the one hand, it is in training. It is supposed to be traveling *towards* fullness of being, along the course that is often mapped into 'stages' by psychoeducationalist pedagogy. And so it continually hears of its own incompleteness. The welfare techniques that constitute the space of the popular school classroom require that the reading subject aim to achieve 'equality.' But equality with what? With what model or exemplar? The only concrete exemplars in the class are the teacher and the text. And so we read the cozy scenes of the 'normal' family within the text as identical with the fantasy homelife of the teacher. The teacher is 'Mother' (less often 'Father'), and the reader is her 'son' or 'daughter' – and I refer, of course, to the names of characters in books. The popular schools, as they were founded at the beginnings of mass education in the nineteenth century, were projected specifically at the literacy of the working class: at almost nothing other than their literacy. And so it is little wonder that the basal readers eventually came to contain fantasies of middle-class life. This – formed around the exemplary text-teacher-authority triplet – is precisely what one must imagine oneself as 'equal' to in the act of reading. The text is read as exemplar in a very literal sense.

The liberal reformist education manuals of the nineteenth century continually represent the school as a machine – but a machine that is humane, that is anything but mechanical; one that reaches the heart and soul of the child. It is built in such a way as to normalize collectivities and to individualize persons at the same time: in fact, to do each through the other. Each acts as a means to the other's end. 'Utility' and 'culture' – to return to the shorthand – are not opposites so much as a single technical strategy. Now the 'soul' will be bared and attended to; now the skills will be taught. These are double moments of a *single* and, only apparently, contradictory ethical armature.[33] They make classroom knowledge possible. So to read the texts specifically designed for this space, *in* this space, is to construct oneself and be constructed as the bearer of this knowledge. One is an incomplete soul moving, if successful, to 'full being' and 'full consciousness' – the very consciousness, be it noted, the psychoeducationalist model of reading assumes to be *already in place* so that reading can take place. But one not only is incomplete in this 'internal' respect, one is also an as yet useless, incomplete member of a utilitarian citizenry. So the story goes: one *will* be a full member, one day, if one reads properly, but one is not that yet. The school is always a hypothetical space in the utilitarian state, a section where 'training for' is separated out, taken out of the mainstream citizenry, a space of preparation. The classroom reader, in this preparatory space, reads himself or herself as someone who is 'not ready yet,' 'not fit yet.' When he or she reads or writes in school, this action is called 'work.' But it is also called 'schoolwork,' and it is made very clear to the schoolchild that this does not mean real work. The school is a space of the imaginary presocial – of social inauthenticity, as well as the space of personal-developmental incompleteness. The real thing is always elsewhere and elsewhen. The loci of that elsewhere and that elsewhen are fictional spaces within fictional spaces. For example, it is what the character called 'Daddy' does when he goes off, out of the narrative, 'to work'; and it is specifically not what the character called 'Mommy' does in the domestic space. It is alluded to by the arrivals of such emissaries as mail carriers and furniture movers, by interesting scenes in the street such as excavations; very occasionally it will be shown in the form of farmers (within the sub-genre called 'The Trip'), though these are more often character types than working farmers.

At the same time, the reading is supposed to be a means of repairing these disequalities and incompletenesses of the reader: a means of making a 'whole person,' a unified, noncontradictory, neurosis-free, autonomous subject. In short, a fiction. The example is not confined to the primary or elementary school but migrates through the education system as far as the university. Think, for example, of how the university English department checks and balances its student readings: the poem is scanned and one offers one's reading. The reading may be, say, too personal or else too didactic. It may be too romantic or too formalist. Eventually a reading is arrived at within the correct range of judgment and discernment, with the correct balance between personal response and scientistic overaccuracy. Then it is graded. Its producer-recipient is congratulated, or else not, and so on. But this technique, as Hunter shows, emerges out of specific social programs, first assembled in the nineteenth century and specifically within the space of state-administered urban welfare directed at the working class.[34] This was and is an ethical practice, one of the armatures of which is the specific ethical practice of the classroom – the balanced, healthy reading. It goes along with the other aspects of urban welfare reformism: diet, health, medicine, policing, housing, domestic architecture, sanitation, and so on. The techniques of reading we have, then, have much more to do with threatened and actual outbreaks of cholera in nineteenth-century British cities than with natural developmental proclivities or with romantic 'civilizing' designs. Healthy readings are only a single manifestation of a widespread and general movement for popular education against infestation. To read a beginning reading book is to have, for example, bodily, spatial, psychological, and sexual impurities written off one's life agenda. Working-class children specifically do not read the details of their own working-class daily lives: no dirt, no drunkenness, no overflowing sexuality, no deviance or sedition of any kind, no masturbation, no incest, no sickness, no lonely old age, no death. Readers read themselves a very specific – yet also uniform and widespread – personal ethics, a corrective to their own possible or actual moral defects. The classroom is where one both finds oneself and finds oneself wanting.[35]

At the same time, the degree to which readers have learned this lesson, the degree to which they have moved somewhere along the staged and plotted road to correct morality, is measured. And it has tended to be measured by quite technicist and utilitarian matters such as the 'speed of response' readers are able to show to a new text, to an 'unseen,' or by cloze tests, by the ability to translate print into correct phonemes and vice versa. In short, there is a whole array of psychobehavioral – mostly blatantly physiological – observations, checks, and corrections. A major site of decision making as to the effectivity of the quite ethical techniques of training can be the reader's body, for it is the body that is a major target and recipient of welfare ethics overall. Yet there is also the culturalist-romantic form of response, the form in which the reader is (one hardly dares to say) 'tested' by the aesthetic techniques of the composition and the comprehension test. In the way that the first popular schools had playgrounds built into their designs so that teachers could see their charges at play – a slice of the 'real life' of the streets – in order to know their 'true' and fundamental selves; so the composition or the guided writing of the comprehension exercise led out the 'inner thoughts,' the supposedly true psychic life of the pupils. They were asked to give their intimate preferences, their tastes, their most inner and private images at the behest of a rhetoric of self-fulfillment whose goal was to 'really know' the child.

The adjacent measures to uniform basal readers in the emerging cities of the twentieth century were such urban revolutions as providing multibedroom houses, which prevented fathers from polluting daughters; connecting these houses to adequate sewers so that massed bodies lured from country to city could be protected from their own wastes; making minimum standards of health care available on a scale unknown in any other time and place, thereby protecting children not only from death and disease but also from the constant visibility of death and disease as natural sights. And one should remember here that the popular school itself was (and often still is) a crucial and focal instrument in the provision of health and health training. In this period there also emerged the cop on the beat, providing both supervision and superintendence of a new street-centered population: a secure and visible adult in the street as well as the school. The teaching and policing professions have very parallel histories in this respect. All of these, and other, measures were measur*able* in their effects on the body of the child, who was sick less often, lived longer, did not get molested so frequently, did not masturbate so regularly, and so on. These frequencies could be measured: the techniques had their exact quantities of success and failure. The techniques the frequencies meted out, techniques for preventing the physical and moral degeneration of the working class, included the extension of basic literacy. Reading – of a quite specific kind – was healthy and could consequently be relied on to have its measures of success, its assessments, in a way analogous to the other healths. These came to be measures of bodily duration, type, psychophysiological behavior, and so on.

Overall, because reading emerges as a site of correction, its aesthetic demand is virtually identical with its ethical-corrective demand. One reads *as*, and one reads oneself *into* a particular kind of being. But the correction ethic means that I read the schoolbook to find what is lacking in me, and so to develop the techniques of finding self-lack more generally. There is a particular demand that I have a visibly personal relation with the text – visible, that is, to the teacher – and that it be assessable for its lacks against some norm or grid of the standard reading subject. More often than not this is a statistical norm, a bodily frequency and regularity. The regime of the classroom and the regime of reading are practically identical: they are regimes of regulated freedom, to reinvoke Hunter.[36] Children are invited and expected to be no more and no less than themselves – for now – right in front of the teacher; to make an utterly free, unconstrained, and personal response to the text in the best child-centered tradition. And this is exactly so the teacher can see how the children actually *are* – how they are in what *counts as* their essentially expressed being. The children are not coercively controlled in the act of reading – not forced to scan and derive like a slave or a computer's disk-reading head – for that would only repress and constrain and so would not do what is, above all, necessary, which is to *display*. What is displayed is how well children's 'inner being' measures up against a well-calculated benchmark. Left to themselves, free to express whatever it may be exactly as they wish, in this process emerge themselves – their mental contents, their wishes and desires. They come out, into the play of scrutiny. The philosophies of 'child centeredness' and 'normative skill-based constructs' look like formidable opposites, motives for grand-scale debates. But while the debates go on around these apparent antinomies, what is hardly seen is that they are poles of a single educative strategy. They are 'reciprocating tactics' within that single normalizing-individualizing strategy.[37]

From this investigation, we can begin to see that effective semiotic investigations of specific social-semiosic practices (in this case reading-in-a-classroom) are parergonal; they need to be situated *on the frames* of the practices they investigate, in the spaces between 'inside' and 'outside' the text, where broad historical and local community relevances meet and have their effects. They cannot be performed either purely conceptually (in terms of a general history) or purely empirically (in terms of the ostensible surfaces of signs). Although they have to attend to the local density of here-and-now matters of how signs are actually made to mean, they also have to acknowledge that this almost always sits in a broader social, political, and historical space occupied by a community of sign-users. The not-signs that, among other matters, are used to give signs their meanings are not fixed and (still less) universal for any given sign (or even type of sign). Rather, they are locally and historically malleable: and their mobility stems from the fact that they arise not from general theories of semiosis but rather from actual communities of users.

The locally specific (working from ostensible signs alone) and the historically relative and relevant (working from the conditions that make signs possible): two forms of discourse analysis (each using the term 'discourse' in a quite different way) have recently begun to move into these two analytic spaces. The first is ethnomethodology, the study of the routine grounds of everyday social practice. The second is Foucauldian genealogy, the study of the kinds of human subject it is possible to be today in terms of the historical conditions and knowledges (discourses) that ground those possibilities. Each is, so far, distinct and confined to its (nevertheless broad) specialism. What the idea of an effective semiotics opens up is that these two positions not only can but must be combined – even at the risk of jeopardizing the purity of each, even at the risk of developing a form of semiotic analysis that neither would recognize as its own. The point would be to arrive at a kind of analysis that was both answerable to specific 'naturally occurring' materials (which ethnomethodology is but genealogy is not) and responsive to broad sociohistorical changes in the fields of knowledge, power, and subject production (which genealogy is but ethnomethodology is not). If we have to work from the available analytic traditions, then effective semiotics might be thought of as a Foucauldian ethnomethodology, or else as an ethnomethodological genealogy. The terms matter less than the idea of a direction for semiotics as it is (necessarily) situated in its own moment of analytic history.

In the first two chapters of part 2, I shall speculate on the generic contours of such an endeavor by wondering whether it might not be possible after all to set up some formal (indeed formalistic) ways of conceiving of an effective semiotics along these lines. For surely the idea of the frame and framing – with its double fixity/mobility of the sign and its double locality/historicality – must have at least some general terms, levels, and prototechnical vocabulary. Although we have seen (indeed, began with) the problems of abstract semiotic formalism, without any formal vocabulary at all we may risk moving semiotics into a space of quite radical indeterminacy, a space where anything goes by the name of 'analysis.' Yet to succeed, this protoformalism would have to be responsive to the *possibility* of semiotic indeterminacy (as well as its opposite, and as well as the spaces *between* indeterminacy and its opposite) insofar as this may arise as one of the (presumably innumerable) devices and techniques actually used *in practice* by communities of sign-users – and this as opposed to a general (or *in principle*) axiomatics of signs. So our question becomes: Is there a possible formalism for effective semiotics that avoids the problems of falling into fixity and thereby overdetermining sign-uses before any empirical encounter with them? This is the topic of chapter 6, which attempts to answer this question by mobilizing the ethnomethodological concept of reflexivity. Then, in chapter 7, I go on to take up my earlier question: How can ethnomethodological and genealogical modes of analysis be combined? In that chapter (as in this one), I investigate how children and young persons are actually trained in practices of sign-use: how they become subjects of, and in, semiosis.

PART 2   From Formalism and Ethnomethodology to Ethics

6. Reflexivity, Problems, and Solutions

I shall begin part 2 in a way that at first seems almost a contradiction of the way I began part 1. There I argued against semiotic formalism on the grounds that it de-effectivizes semiosis, removes it from what Wittgenstein called 'the stream of life' and attempts instead to totalize the diverse processes of semiosis by finding a general rubric for their operation – on the model, to some extent, of the ways linguistics attempts to find a general grammar behind the extremely diverse uses of language.[1] Now I want to ask whether it is possible, after all this, to construct a formalism for effective semiotics itself, one that will account for the diversities and differences of principles upon which actual sign-using communities practice semiosis in all its variety. But this formalism is not for its own sake. On the contrary, it acts as a summary of what we have found so far. It is nothing but an assembled reminder of a set of positions already adopted. And in addition, this formalism is designed to account for and introduce a further analytic concept, Garfinkel's concept of reflexivity, upon which the arguments and analyses of part 2 partly depend. Why reflexivity? What is its position in developing an effective semiotics?

In his *Studies in Ethnomethodology*, Garfinkel rarely refers to social practices in terms of signs, and he never considers questions of semiosis. Still less does he see ethnomethodology as in any way related to semiotics. However, in one crucial passage he does refer to the stultifying effects of thinking about communication (or 'usage') in terms of signs and referents:

> Although it may at first appear strange to do so, suppose we drop the assumption that in order to describe usage as a feature of a community of understandings we must at the outset know what the substantive common understandings consist of. With it, drop the assumption's accompanying theory of signs, according to which a 'sign' and a 'referent' are respectively properties of something said and something talked about, and which in this

fashion proposes sign and referent to be related as corresponding contents. By dropping such a theory of signs we drop as well,
thereby, the possibility that an invoked shared agreement on
substantive matters explains a usage.[2]

Instead of such a semiotic position, Garfinkel proposes that what
he calls 'usage' can in fact be explained in terms of community
members' knowledge(s) of *how* signs are used. They do not share
agreements 'on substantive matters' but rather agree on 'methodological' ones: hence the term 'ethnomethodology.' Communities,
on this account, are assemblages of common ways of getting
things done or (to use a terminology from chapter 3) of making
things happen. Garfinkel's crucial theoretical insight involves,
then, that we substitute analyzing *how* something means for the
(more traditional) notion of analyzing *what* it means.

Perhaps the most central of Garfinkel's concepts for describing
this essential effectivity of semiosis (to use a term that continues to
distort his own position) is reflexivity. According to this principle,
how a sign (or for Garfinkel, 'usage') means is always reflexively
related to the type of situation it is used in. The sign and the situation type mutually elaborate each other. For example, if I say
'Open your books to page 60,' this may make sense because it is
said in (and very important, as part of) a classroom lesson and the
one saying it is audibly the teacher. In its turn, that *this is* a classroom lesson is (in part) a sensible and mandatory understanding of
the situation for all concerned by virtue of the fact that someone
(audible as a teacher) can say, in it, such things as 'Open your
books to page 60.' Lessons are made out of such utterances – that
is what they are. And that they are lessons provides the grounds of
understanding for the utterances in them. Upon such mutually reflexive (or 'incarnate') practices does the very possibility of society
depend, in Garfinkel's social theory. Society is irremediably practical; it is constructed from (and as) practical activity, and practical
activity is irremediably reflexive. In acting in particular ways, that
is, members not only rely on their community's methods for doing
so, they also display that it is these methods (and not others) that
they are acting upon. Social practices are meaningful not because
of their 'contents' but because they display the grounds of their
methodic production and understanding. To 'understand' a sign,

then, is to be able to see in it (as an activity) what its productional methods must be.

We can begin the elaboration of our effective-semiotic formalism, then, by abstracting from Garfinkel's position and adapting it for our own ends: every sign, S, is part of an activity, a. But after Garfinkel, it is more than just 'part of' an activity. Anything that might be construed as part of a sign and that is not relevant to its deployment in an activity (though it is hard to imagine what this might actually be) is trivial. Or at least it is irrelevant to effective semiotics. Hence the term 'sign' can almost be *replaced* by the term 'activity.' 'Almost,' but not quite, because of the following caveat: Since a community's activities are methodic – that is, since they are not just any activities ('behaviors') but must *display* their intelligibility as part of a specific form of life – we can say that a sign is a *methodic* activity. Its internal relations are relations between activities and the methods, m, communities use to produce them – to get them done and hence to understand them.

Activities are local (here-and-now, synchronic) accomplishments, even though the methods used to produce them may be deployable from locality to locality within a community (and perhaps even between some communities). Therefore they have a historical (there-and-then, diachronic) trajectory.

In being a methodic activity, ma, every sign is not 'aimless'; it is a solution, s, to a socio-logical problem that a community has, albeit a routine problem, faced continually, day in, day out. A sign's external relations, R_2, are the ways it acts as such a solution.[3] Hence we can derive the following formulas:

(1) $S = \text{def } ma$ 'A sign is a methodic activity'

(2) $m \, R_1 \, a$ 'Methods bear a relation to activities,' *or:*

(2.1) $R_1 = m/a$ 'A sign's internal relations are the relations between its constitutive methods and activities'

(3) $ma \, R_2 \, s$ 'Methodic activities bear a relation to solutions to socio-logical problems,' *or:*

(3.1) $R_2 = ma/s$ 'A sign's external relations are the relations between its methodic activities and the ways its acts as a solution to socio-logical problems,' *or* since (1):

(3.2) $S\,R_2\,s$ 'A sign bears a relation to the ways its acts as a solution to socio-logical problems,' *or*:

(3.3) $R_2 = S/s$ 'A sign's external relations are the relations between the sign and the ways it acts as a solution to socio-logical problems'

(4) $R_3 = R_1/R_2$ 'There is a relation between the internal and external relations of a sign'

(5) $R_3 = fS$ 'The relation between the internal and external relations of a sign is the meaning of the sign, fS'[4]

Nick Hartland has argued that R_1 and R_2 are 'reflexive' in the sense elaborated by Garfinkel and Sacks.[5] This is important for the field of ethnomethodology, since it solves a long-standing problem in that domain of inquiry – a problem with some bearing on our current investigation. Traditionally, and as we have seen, ethno-methodologists (for example, Wieder) argued that there is a reflexive relation between *utterances* and the types of social *events* they form a part of.[6] By 'reflexive' they meant (to repeat) that each is used to elaborate the other. So in Wieder's example, when a convict answers a guard's question by saying, 'You know I won't snitch,' the utterance derives its sense by being part of a convict-guard interaction in a halfway house (a type of detention center for drug offenders). That is, it relates to an elaborate 'code' of conduct that convicts assume to be in place when guards are addressing them such that, in this case, it can be assumed that the guard's query is not 'casual' or an inquiry into the well-being of the convict, for the convict's sake. Rather, the question is taken – retrospectively, after its production by the guard – to be a request or demand that the convict give the guard some information that may be detrimental to the convict or his fellow inmates. Hence what the utterance means, here and now, depends on the situational specifics of its being uttered. But the reverse is also true, according to Wieder's use of reflexivity. The sense of the convict-guard interaction is given by its being done precisely in these terms, with these words and others like them. It would not be a 'convict-guard interaction' if it did not include such responses to inquiries – it would be another order of affairs entirely. Hence the type of event lets you know what the utterance means or does; and the type of utterance lets you know what the event is. The two are reflexive, precisely in Garfinkel's sense. And it is because of this that we can say everyday activities provide for and display their own 'intelligibility.'

This type of *general reflexivity* (which ethnomethodologists take to be an omnipresent feature of everyday activities) is an important discovery about everyday life in general. It shows that the meaning of everyday utterances is not guaranteed by general structural principles outside and beyond the events they compose and that mutually compose them. But once discovered, it leads to very little else than its multiple and chronic rediscovery in exactly the same form everywhere.[7] It becomes more like *a principle of ethnomethodological inquiry* than something that can generate analytic findings about the specificity of everyday utterances. In short, it can turn into the very thing it sought to avoid: a general principle for guaranteeing meaning, albeit at the level of *how* meaning is achieved rather than of *what* signs mean. And for this reason empirical studies of reflexivity have been very low on the ethnomethodological agenda.[8] Indeed, we must now suspect that the problem with Garfinkel's original conception of reflexivity is not that it relates utterances to activities but that it relates *specific* utterances to *types* of activities such that the idea of a 'type' carries the same implications as grammatical or formal semiotic typologies.[9]

Hartland's refinement and reconstruction of the concept of reflexivity restores the possibility of its being used to find specifics (as well as 'types' or general methods). First, he returns to a basic ethnomethodological premise (and one entailed by the principle of reflexivity): that the activities persons can be observed to engage in in everyday life are methodic; they are 'produced' by methods (including typifications but not reducible to them alone) specific to the occasions of the production and understanding of those activities. The problem with this version of things, however, is that – on the face of it – it makes the notion of 'social order' seem redundant. For if methods were utterly unique to occasions, then the social order would have to be made up all over, time and time again, from occasion to occasion. Each event would be singular, constituted by a radical difference from all other events. In early ethnomethodology, the Schutzian concept of typification solved this problem to some extent. But as a better attempt at a solution, stemming from about 1970, Garfinkel and Sacks began to promote the idea of 'transferability.' According to this principle, the transfer of methods from occasion to occasion is itself every social member's *occasioned* accomplishment.[10] Hence this (as it were) metaaccomplishment guarantees social order. But this requires a further reliance on the famous Sacksian assertion (or perhaps 'paradox'): that members' methods are both *context-sensitive* and *context-independent*. Hartland solves this problem by saying, simply and brilliantly, that R1 itself is reflexive. That is, *methods* are relatively stable from occasion to occasion. They constitute a kind of bedrock of social and local-historical order. But the *activities* they generate are occasion-specific.

As he shows in his study of magistrates' courts, there are generally available methods for giving descriptions of persons (here magistrates giving descriptions of accused persons), but the actual descriptions they produce are unique to these specific describers, described persons, and circumstances of description.[11] But the methods reflexively depend in a crucial sense on the descriptions they generate, and vice versa. In practice they are always methods for doing specifically this (and not some other) kind of description when viewed synchronically, but they have the diachronic property of being able to be used elsewhere and at other times.

We can illustrate this by looking at two of Hartland's examples. In both cases the magistrates find there is a degree of *control* their respective defendants should have had with respect to driving along the highway. There is a methodic principle (as Hartland shows) that magistrates *should* find the areas and fields over which defendants ought properly to have control but over which, in the case of the 'crime' in question, they did not happen to exercise control. This lack, effectively, *is the crime*, even when the particular lack in question does not involve a breach of some specific legal code (though it can involve such a breach in some cases). In Hartland's first example, however, it is *the driver's lack of control of his own emotional relations* to other drivers that is in question – he has run into the back of another vehicle because of his frustration at its slow speed. In the second example it is *the driver's lack of control of his own vehicle* that is in question: he has not allowed for poor road conditions and has 'accidentally' run into another car. The words uttered by the magistrates in each case are almost identical: they amount to the fact that the driver should have, and could have, exercised more 'control.' They depend on exactly the same methods for giving descriptions of felonious drivers. But each description fits the situational specifics of the case in its own unique way – there is a crucial *difference* between the two types of control as (described) social objects. Hence broadly based *methods* are reflexively bound to unique *activities* (in this case descriptions).

This is Hartland's account of R1 as a reflexive relation. But he then goes on to argue that there is another type of reflexivity: that between methodic activities (in this case the produced descriptions) and 'socio-logical problems.' Socio-logical problems are not to be thought of as troubles, or as the sorts of things that perplex people and create anxiety. Instead they are the most ordinary things in the world and stem from Sacks's *methodological* heuristic. Sacks argued that it can be sociologically productive to view social practices as solutions to problems.[12] In several of Hartland's analyzed cases – and again I truncate his detailed analyses – there appear to be no good reasons why magistrates should not make prison sentences part of all their dispositions. They have to *find* reasons for not doing so; that is, for giving fines, suspending drivers' licenses, and so on *rather than* handing out prison sentences once someone is found guilty (that is, preponderantly, lacking in control). And as Hartland shows in an overwhelming number of cases, the magistrates find that prison is 'relevant' to defendants (where finding prison relevant is itself a case-specific methodic accomplishment). And the key to this resides in a locally relevant assessment of the degree and type of 'control' the defendant is deemed to have had (but did not exercise). Hence the methods and activities of magistrates (for example, methods of describing and actual descriptions) furnish solutions to this specific socio-logical problem: Why *not* order a prison sentence? And that they act as solutions furnishes the sense of their descriptions. The two are reflexively related (R2).

Another example of a socio-logical problem and its solution (analyzed empirically in the next investigation) is, How is it that people can become sexually competent in societies where that competence is expectably practiced in private and to the exclusion of noncompetent observers? In chapter 7 I suggest that there are secondary systems of elaboration that accomplish this: from voyeurism to dirty jokes, a whole range of ways of finding that events can be 'sexualized' so precompetent sexual practitioners can 'check' their knowledge as a community, one against the other.

Taking just one instance, a piece of sexual graffiti can be understood insofar as it can act as a solution to this routine problem; and the problem is constituted *as* a problem (at least in part) because the graffito (an activity for which specific methods of accomplishment provide for its intelligibility as a 'competent' instance of sexual graffiti) exists as a solution to it. Each provides for the sense of the other. Otherwise we would be hard pressed to understand the function of, say, genitalia drawn on a toilet wall, and if we were unable to find such things (in fact, quite a large range of things), we might assume there were no such problems with sexual competence. This is not to deny that drawings of genitalia cannot be used in other ways, even when inscribed on toilet walls; and in turn, it is not to deny that they are the only solutions to the problem. But they *can* be used in such a way; that is, when they *are* so used. And this last phrase does not involve a tautology: that they are (sometimes) so used is documentable with respect to their users' own formulations of them as specifically those kinds of objects.

One interesting feature of Hartland's second level of reflexivity, then, is that it begins to approach the phenomena encountered in more 'macroscopic' social and political investigations than is usually the case in ethnomethodology. The term 'macroscopic' should be shown here under erasure, for it can easily buy us into an argument whose very terms may – as a consequence of work in critical ethnomethodology – be spurious. That is, it is routine in non-ethnomethodological sociology to assume a rough division between micro and macro social orders and events.[13] According to this division, the 'micro' social domain consists of such things as language, face-to-face interaction, intersubjective meanings, social-psychological phenomena (such as intentions and motives), and so on. By contrast, the 'macro' domain supposedly consists of such entities as patriarchy, class, the state, the economy, power, and so forth. I do not want to present arguments against this model of affairs, for there may be no arguments for or against it. Rather, it appears to be a basic assumption of certain kinds of sociological theorizing – 'naturally' basic to both 'macro' and 'micro' schools, whether in the name of asserting distinctiveness or assuring synthesis.

What I ask instead is whether it may be possible for an effective semiotics to avoid making this assumption in the first place, dissolving the problem rather than first inaugurating it and only then solving it. What Hartland's reconstruction of reflexivity accomplishes appears to be precisely this type of dissolution.

First, it prompts us to examine everyday semioses as both produc*ing* and produc*ed*: producing the sense of socio-logical problems and produced as solutions to them; such that anything that might count as a social object is not taken as fixed and simply waiting (like a 'natural' object) to have its properties examined by a neutral observer. Rather, any social object is a problem-solution doublet, unfixed, in process, and always available to new and different creative treatments (lay *and* professional).

Second, it suggests that 'micro' phenomena are not merely sociological flotsam and jetsam (or technically, 'epiphenomena') whose apparent patterns are the 'observable' effects of 'deeper' social currents that in themselves remain mysteriously unavailable to the untrained eye. This mistake stems fundamentally from the micro/macro division itself, and against it we are prompted to consider everyday activities as material practices that (as methods) constitute and (as activities) are constituted by the very stuff and doing of social order, disorder, structure, anarchy, or whatever it is that is being accomplished in and as a form of life.

Third, it gives no special privilege to what are traditionally conceived of as 'micro' phenomena; that is, it avoids having to make an argument – common in phenomenological sociology – about the 'production' of 'actual' social objects in 'consciousness.' Instead, it is able to consider (if it must) the domain of consciousness as a material one, not specially privileged, and existing as a relation between methods and activities.

Fourth, it refuses to reify occasion-independent methods and occasion-specific activities into overall general social categories, pervading all of society (or all of *a* society). Insofar as it might wish to address questions of the state, of ideology, of power in general, of capitalism, and so forth, it must do so tentatively, with the terms under erasure, as standing for massive blocs of socio-logical problems and solutions whose connections and relations are yet to be demonstrated. These 'objects' of 'scientific' sociology can be seen, that is, as solutions for problems posed within, and specifically within, the form of life of 'scientific' sociology. They need to be treated as such in the first place, rather than as definite and fixed objects that must inform social theory from the outset.

In the next investigation, I shall introduce a social-theoretical base for effective semiotics, and as part of this I want to investigate the domain of socio-logical problems and solutions. That base preserves the time-honored tripartite sociological distinction between theory, methodology, and research. The *theoretical* part of the investigation offers some remarks on two quite theoretically distinct sociologies, those of Foucault and of Garfinkel. By displaying some family resemblances between them, it aims to generate basic study policies for exploring everyday forms of semiosis. The *methodological* part works from those basic policies and deals with the specific socio-logical problem mentioned above: it asks what can be done when competent sexual conduct is formally required but when 'training' is made available only indirectly, if at all. The *analytic* part of the investigation examines an empirical case of a possible solution to that problem. It deals with a case of lecturing in which notions of moral and immoral sexual comportment and talk are, respectively, recommended and discouraged 'by the way,' 'secondarily,' or 'as an aside' to the main business of the lecture.

7. Ethnogenealogy: Public Methods for Private Practices

As foreshadowed in the previous chapter, I now pay some attention to the possibility that ethnomethodological social theory can be used, at least in part, as a basis for effective semiotic investigations. To achieve this I shall compare and contrast it with the archaeological/genealogical approach of Foucault. The impetus for this comparison and contrast is that these two approaches – ethnomethodological and Foucauldian – represent the two extremes of social theory that, I have argued, an effective semiotics must be able to encompass. To put the matter bluntly: ethnomethodology is the social theory par excellence that has been able to generate detailed findings about concrete social situations and the forms of semiosis that produce them (and that, reflexively, they produce). On the other hand, Foucauldian discourse analysis has been superbly capable of situating discourse in terms of its general effectivity as means of producing (and being produced by) forms of knowledge, power, and subjectivity in their broadest sociohistorical senses. In the previous chapter we saw that an effective semiotics should be able to range from the most basic of semiosic practices (the sheer intelligibility of signs or methodic activities), via the level of socio-logical problems and solutions, to the historical embededness (and suprasituational availability) of semiosic techniques within communities. To use a shorthand, this range might be thought of as reaching from the 'situational,' via the 'social,' to the 'historical': from ethnomethodological to Foucauldian relevances via a possible common ground.[1] But are these traditions of social theory and analysis not incommensurate? As we will see, the answer is both yes and no. There are very definite differences between the two traditions, but there are also crucial points of 'touchstone' where they meet – points that may be central for the development of effective semiotic analyses. Naturally enough, this meeting ground can be seen to have its basic formations in the 'social' sphere I have just mentioned, the sphere that effective semiotics projects in terms of socio-logical problems and solutions.

To make another contrast, albeit briefly, such highly distinct social-theoretical traditions as ethnomethodology and Marxism have both proposed that social practices be taken as solutions to problems or contradictions that arise for community members. Marx makes this recommendation in the eighth of the *Theses on Feuerbach* when he asks us (in an almost Wittgensteinian way) to treat social life as essentially practical: 'All mysteries which mislead theory to mysticism find their rational solution in practice and in the comprehension of this practice.'[2] A vaguely similar theory exists in the works of Harvey Sacks, where he treats socio-discursive phenomena such as speaker-sequencing as problems to be faced by community members (or 'practical actors') and for which *collectively* available solutions can be invoked – in this case the turn-taking organization for conversation. In both cases this is a social-theoretical heuristic. Community members may be completely unaware that their forms of life are fraught with 'problems' of basic conduct for which 'solutions' can be found, as opposed to, say, highly overt problems like how to get the car fixed. Thinking of everyday practical events as problem-solutions is an *analyst's* invention, a heuristic. But, I argue, it can be analytically rewarding.

In both ethnomethodology and Marxism, there is a notion of 'logical' conditions underpinning the very possibility of social life. To be sure, this can sometimes be more overtly structural, even reified, in Marxist analysis (cf. 'the real foundations'). The ethnomethodological tradition, by contrast, prefers to make reference to a formation of perceivedly normal *appearances* to which community members can and must orient themselves in the course of their sense-making practices. And for ethnomethodology this formation is by no means fixed or objectively given. Rather, it is continually remade 'for another first time' on every interactional occasion.[3] Nevertheless, both traditions posit a relatively stable source of 'problems' (a 'problematic,' perhaps) to which semiosic practice is a 'solution.' In what follows, I shall preserve this general outline as a heuristic for analytically understanding how signs (methodic activities) work in social life.

Moving now to Foucault, here the problem-solution metaphor

or heuristic is not so clear. This may be because his concerns are effectively outside those of mainstream sociology, in spite of his incorporation into sociology and social theory.[4] Foucault's focus of attention, especially in his earlier work on discourse,[5] is turned fairly exclusively on the conditions of possibility of discursive orders as such. Yet it can also be said that Foucault does not always separate these discursive orders or regimes (which constitute the social fabric) from the particular circumstances or practices in which they are 'played out.' Indeed, in the work of his 'middle period,' and especially in the case studies *Pierre Rivière* and *Herculine Barbin*, Foucault comes to concentrate almost exclusively on particular instances or conjunctures within the webs of competing and contradictory discourses and on the kinds of *social subject* they produce – social subjects who must find equally discursive 'solutions' to their problematic situations in the form of available techniques such as the confession, the diary, and the erotic journal. Two matters are worth noting here. First, these 'early' and 'middle' preoccupations might give us some grounds for distinguishing between discourses (problem conditions) and discourse or discursive actions (techniques or solutions), such that it is largely the former (for example, 'conditions of possibility') that have survived in recent Anglo-American readings of Foucault, at the expense of the latter. Foucault, for some, has become a general theorist, despite his insistence that theorization and particularism ('eventalization') are not incommensurable. Second, the work of Foucault's middle-period texts can be seen to directly parallel ethnomethodological work on competing readings of social events; for example, Pollner's seminal analyses of 'reality disjunctures.'[6]

In both Foucault and ethnomethodology, it is possible to locate an abiding common concern with the local production of institutional orders, even if ethnomethodology is more consciously 'analytic,' preferring to 'say' how socio-logical problems and their practical solutions work rather than to 'show' how they *might*, as possibilities. In this respect Foucault refers to 'eventalization' (as opposed to generalization), whereas Garfinkel prefers to think of 'invariance' (Discourse) as a function or effect of contingency (discourse).[7] Both, however, reject the idea that social practice is merely an effect of structurally given forms or ideal-rational rules behind the surface of visible action. Thus Foucault writes with respect to rationality:

> My basic preoccupation isn't rationality considered as an anthropological invariant. I don't believe one can speak of an intrinsic notion of 'rationalisation' without on the one hand positing an absolute value inherent in reason, and on the other taking the risk of applying the term empirically in a completely arbitrary way. I think one must restrict one's use of this word to an instrumental and relative meaning.[8]

And Garfinkel:

> It is not satisfactory to describe how actual investigative procedures, as constituent features of members' ordinary and organized affairs, are accomplished by members as recognizedly rational actions *in actual occasions* of organizational circumstances by saying that members invoke some rule with which to define the coherent or consistent or planful, i.e. rational, character of their actual activities. Nor is it satisfactory to propose that the rational properties of members' inquiries are produced by members' compliance to rules of inquiry.[9]

In this respect, in Foucault as well as Garfinkel there is a common method, and this means not 'accepting' social facts that must be explained *after* the fact; rather it means, in Garfinkel's phrase, catching 'the work of fact *production* in flight,' which I see as essential to any effective semiotics. The analyst does not 'deny' social facts: this is not what a 'constructionist' or 'effectivist' position means, for it could only lead to a kind of social solipsism. Instead, social facts become problems whose solutions must be practically constructed by community members. Passages from Garfinkel's *Studies* on the accomplishment of social facts appear uncannily parallel to Foucault's treatment of the construction of truth(s) and especially to some of his later thoughts on the question.[10] Both writers find their topics in the relation between work (activities) and conditions of possibility (available methods) that, in quite local circumstances, lead to certain accounts being heard and accepted as 'true' or as 'the facts,' where this analytic method contrasts with those that try to adjudicate between different accounts' veridicality (for example, theories of 'ideology'). If, however, Foucault wants to construct a genealogy of such discursive problems and solutions in terms of technologies of power and subjectivity, Garfinkel's attention is much more clearly turned towards their contemporary (synchronic) architecture – that is, to the specifics of their local material construction as against their 'historicity.' But as we have seen, for all this there is no in-principle reason why the synchronic (architectural) and the diachronic (genealogical) perspectives (to use a crude approximation) should not complement one another, especially if there is a more fundamental agreement vis-à-vis method: namely, localization-eventalization, albeit at different levels of empiricity.

Both Foucault and Garfinkel have been associated with a 'textualist' or even skepticist position on questions of truth; yet nothing could be further from the case. If an investigation attends to how an expression (for example, a 'statement' in Foucault or a 'usage' in Garfinkel) comes to be *counted* as true, historically or situationally, this does not mean the investigator is skeptical of that expression's status as true once it has been so counted. If, to use a shorthand, 'convention' guarantees truth, this does not make it the poor relation of other candidates for truth conditions or grounds (such as correspondence with reality or rational cohesion with other expressions in a theory). If truth is relative to, and dependent on, the very social methods and activities that secure it, this means, if nothing else, that it most certainly exists. The absence of some form of absolute truth (for example, literal descriptions that are independent of the methods and activities that render them sensible, or in different language, independent of 'interpretations') does not mean truth is absent. Indeed, as Heritage argues, the essential indexicality of everyday expressions (their lack of semantic fixity) does not, for Garfinkel, separate language from truth; rather, it is the very mooring of language to truth.[11]

A further difficulty in locating overlaps and resemblances between Foucault and Garfinkel is their quite different uses of terms such as 'accounts' and 'discourse.' No doubt Garfinkel's terminology is more clearly related to Anglo-American empiricist ideas about speech (*paroles*), whereas Foucault's stems (albeit critically) from Continental concerns with language in general (*langue*). But this is a very broad generalization, especially since both theorists are concerned to revise our routine thinking about these concepts.

Nevertheless, a reading of Foucault's position on 'statements' and their differences from 'speech acts,' 'sentences,' and 'propositions' clearly shows his reluctance to think of discourse in terms of a pregiven language system or grammar and his preference for considering local and situational specifics first.[12] And this is quite parallel with Garfinkel's initial remarks in *Studies in Ethnomethodology*.[13] Both theorists have a preference for treating language in ways other than that of any formalist linguistics. To this extent Foucault's conception of discourses (or discursive formations), perhaps via their proximity to concepts such as 'bodies of knowledge' or even 'paradigms,' is not incapable of at least a rough equation with Garfinkel's idea of perceivedly normal patterns of accounting and institutional frameworks of accounting. In both cases it is not merely an already given 'normal subject' who knows how to wield such 'equipment'; rather, subjects *become* normalized (they become community members) in and as the very course of the repetition of certain discursive formations as opposed to others. There is also a sense in which Sacks holds conversationalists to be constituted in and by the very conversational forms that speak them: for example, the teller and hearers of his 'dirty joke' are at least as much the products of *it* as it is of *them*.[14]

Continuing this line of reasoning, Garfinkel's rejection of sociology's 'ironic stance' towards ordinary life and his idea that it can therefore avoid 'constitutive analytic theorizing' have distinct parallels with the work of Foucault's 'middle' period, in which he refuses to offer simply another 'scientific' account of positions adopted by marginalized persons such as criminals and perverts. Neither theorist, that is, would argue that 'scientific' accounts (including their own) can assume privilege over 'lay' accounts. Instead, either of these might become topics for analysis. Foucault, for example, will work from the specific confessions of a multiple murderer or from the evolution of economic discourses in general.[15] Garfinkel too will work on a case of a transsexual 'passing as a woman' or on a night's work in an astronomy laboratory.[16] In fact, ethnomethodology can by no means be defined by a sphere of proper objects; it works with anything 'from divination to theoretical physics.'[17] Moreover, in both Foucault and Garfinkel there is at least an implicit criticism of the forms of privileged knowledge the social sciences often assume in relation to their analyzed objects.

Nevertheless, Garfinkel's policy of positive *indifference* towards questions of value is much more explicit than anything in Foucault.[18] Foucault (by contrast with say certain versions of Marxism) might share Garfinkel's *analytic* abstention from political-moral judgments about ordinary or popular practice (Pierre Rivière is presented as anything but a cultural dope). But his numerous interviews suggest that Foucault's overtly descriptivist – he sometimes calls them 'positivist' – histories are to be read as forms of social critique and even intervention: Foucault's remark that he is 'a good distance away from politics' is surely somewhat tongue in cheek.[19] Again, Heritage shows how Garfinkel's work is quite capable of examining the means by which, for example, 'research scientists both preserve an underlying commitment to the unitary character of objective scientific knowledge and exploit this commitment to advance their own theoretical positions' and by which other local-political effects are accomplished.[20] To this extent ethnomethodology's formal restraint in the domains of value, ethics, and politics is not necessary to its overall social theory: if literal description is ideally unavailable (and this is a central tenet of ethnomethodology), then a purely descriptive sociology of everyday life is as subject to this same condition as any other social formation – hence the question of the political-moral grounds and consequences of the analysis cannot be ruled out in principle. Theoretical action and debate cannot simply be severed from civil action and debate by a programmatic statement. Indeed, that very programmatic statement could not be other than a political position.[21]

Although it's true that I want to ground the social-theoretical component of an effective semiotics in *both* Foucault and ethnomethodology, it is obvious that these theoretical corpora are far from unified in themselves; and they are certainly in no position to be formed into some kind of grand synthesis. Hence my remarks must remain very general – working towards an analytic mentality rather than firm and eternal principles. Foucault's minute investigations in the counterhistory of ideas and Garfinkel's highly piecemeal analyses of everyday cognition and conduct have their bases in completely separate intellectual traditions. Their respective views of phenomenology, to take only one example, are almost but not quite antithetical. Foucault writes:

If there is one approach that I do reject, however, it is that (one might call it, broadly speaking, the phenomenological approach) which gives absolute priority to the observing subject, which attributes a constituent role to an act, which places its own point of view at the origin of all historicity – which, in short, leads to a transcendental consciousness. It seems to me that the historical analysis of scientific discourse should, in the last resort, be subject not to a theory of the knowing subject, but rather to a theory of discursive practice.[22]

To be sure, Garfinkel's use of phenomenology is critical – perhaps even 'materialist' or 'actional' – rather than transcendental. Most genres of ethnomethodology have now moved clear away from Schutz's phenomenological-anthropological constants (such as 'the reciprocity of perspectives'). One could imagine Garfinkel's broad agreement with Foucault on the importance of discursive practice being over and above consciousness.[23] He has nevertheless been willing to retain a certain phenomenological orientation and to contribute positively to the debate on phenomenological sociology.[24] But more conclusively than this, Garfinkel and Foucault can be seen to be in rough agreement on phenomenology's traditional adversary, structuralism, particularly in its highly mechanistic forms – and this despite the early Foucault's reliance on some versions of structuralism, particularly Georges Dumézil's.

What their respective analyses of 'discourses' and 'accounts' aim to do are quite distinct matters. Foucault's earlier work, for example, centered on the archaeology of official and scientific forms of knowledge (such as structuralism itself), while Garfinkel was still attempting, empirically, to show up the 'background expectancies' of everyday life (initially theorized by Schutz) and to argue that these expectancies are crucial grounds for any form of social action, including conflictual action. However, Garfinkel's concept of reflexivity has always ensured that acts or activities have more than a purely constitutive role: instead, they should be thought of as both *constituting* broader social 'objects' and *constituted by* generally available 'methods.'

Having mapped out some general ethnogenealogical principles, let us turn now to a particular set of practices: sexual learning. Foucault, in the first volume of *The History of Sexuality*, argues strongly against a Freudian version of sexual discourse as essentially 'repressed' discourse.[25] Instead he shows how modernity continually transforms sexual practice *into* discourse. The technology of the confessional is the major means by which this is achieved. At a crude level of approximation, just as the panopticon solves the problem of how to 'know' the exterior behavior of 'transgressive' or 'unruly' individuals (prisoners, mental patients, and so on), so the confessional solves the problem of how to know the interiors of all who might *potentially* transgress. Foucault, however, does not think of the confessional as a technology imposed from the top down; rather, he locates a 'will to confess' what are effectively 'private' practices and desires, such that the 'private' becomes an eminently social and institutional space guaranteed in part by the continual transformation of sex into discourse.

To this extent it would be a mistake to begin with the idea that learning sexual comportment is essentially repressive. Instead, the problems it poses lie in the relations that exist between official and local discursive activities; for example, between 'sex education' (morality, hygiene, and so on) and 'folk knowledge.' Although the problems are multifarious, they can be expressed in the form of a central contradiction. The public discourses on sexuality (manuals, for example) are specifically recipient designed for the already sexually competent (that is, they aim to improve performance or to overcome problems with existing performance capacities). At the same time, sexual practices are largely conducted in private, at least in Western societies (there are legal penalties for public sexual displays). Thus, although privacy allows a degree of freedom of conduct among the already initiated and for the novitiate alike ('openness' necessitates more facile surveillance and direct policing), the learner in such 'closed' regimes faces greater pedagogic difficulty than, say, the Samoan adolescent (if Margaret Mead is to be believed on that score). To be constrained by a 'will to confess' rather than a direct panoptic gaze means, in effect, to be debarred from 'observational learning': if the policing observer cannot observe, then neither can the policed-observed 'object.' In societies of this type, characteristic of modernity, how can sexual competence – one of the requirements of general social competence – be learned at all? The novice effectively faces the problem of being required to become competent and yet having no obvious or direct resources for acquiring that competence.

Learning sexual comportment is to some extent not unlike learning comportment in any other life sphere. According to at least one reading of Heidegger on the question of comportment (*Verhalten*), this is simply a term for how, in any familiar situation, we 'cope.' For Heidegger this does not necessarily involve the mediation of acts of consciousness; rather, it is a question of 'human activity in general,'[26] part of that being that is a conjoint self-and-world and that, therefore, needs no equivalent or intermediary concept of mental activity. Hence, when we act competently this is part of our *intentionality*, but that intentionality is no more than a matter of 'directing oneself toward' something rather than the intervention of a mental act between an 'action' (self) and a 'goal' (world). Hence it can be called 'purposive action without a purpose,' to use Dreyfus's term.[27] Dreyfus goes on to say that this

> occurs in all areas of skillful coping, including intellectual coping. Many instances of apparently complex problem-solving which seem to implement a long-range strategy, as, for example, a masterful move in chess [or sex?], may best be understood as direct responses to familiar perceptual gestalts. After years of seeing chess games unfold, a chess grandmaster can, simply by responding to the patterns on the chess board, play master-level chess while his deliberate, analytic mind is absorbed in something else. Such play, based as it is on previous attention to thousands of actual and book games, incorporates a tradition which determines the appropriate response to each situation and therefore makes possible long-range, strategic, purposive play without the player needing to have in mind any plan or purpose at all.[28]

This suggests, though, that in *learning* chess, outside and prior to the mode of familiar coping, the player must be purposive, must have a plan 'in mind,' must be attending to the technical specifics of the play. The problem for the one who would *learn* proper comportment, then, in chess, sex, or elsewhere, is quite different from simply enacting or embodying the already-learned proper orientation of the master. A specific attention, in this case, *does* seem to have to be paid. But does this simply return us to a pre-Heideg-

gerian phenomenology of intention? Dreyfus implies as much. But
could there be, instead, even in the sphere of *acquiring* the techniques of coping and comportment, quite material forms of problem-solutions? Could learning something, *itself*, be a particular
form of directing oneself toward: a socio-logical practice without
need of ghostly mental equivalents to guide it?

If so, the sexual learner is very much in the position of Garfinkel's jurors, who must display legal competence and respect correct rules of juridical procedure in their decision making without,
in any official way, knowing how such procedures routinely are, or
routinely should be, carried out.[29] Similarly – and not coinciden-
tally – they are in the same position as Agnes, the transsexual of
Garfinkel's study, of whom Heritage has written: 'Her task in
managing, constructing and reconstructing her social identity is
. . . perhaps well caught by the famous Neurath-Quine metaphor
of being compelled to build a boat while already being out on the
ocean. It was unavoidably a bootstrapping operation.'[30] Remember that Garfinkel uses the Agnes case to show that sociosexual
identity is, for 'normals' (as he calls them) too, a continual problem of conduct for which countless unseen solutions are in operation every day but to which neither the community member nor
the investigator has 'empirical' access – except perhaps in 'special'
cases *such as* that of Agnes. The Agnes case is, then, effectively a
'naturally occurring' breach experiment. What I would suggest is
that the one who faces the problem of becoming competent in sexual conduct faces exactly such an 'anomic' or breached situation,
an in-built socio-logical contradiction.

The contradiction in a nutshell is this: If private, how learned?
There is indeed a thesis that runs through many sexological studies
and argues that doing sex is natural and that one does not have to
learn it.[31] This thesis, dominant in psychology, common sense, and
(more pertinently) in many of the discourses on official sex education, works through concepts such as 'instinct' and 'natural pro-
pensity.' Although it partly solves the problem, it leaves open another problem as its legacy: it requires an ideal-typical notion of
'natural sex' and leaves a socially arbitrary residue of practices that
come under the classification of 'deviance,' 'unnaturalness,' 'un-
healthy practices,' and the rest. When engaged in – and many
learners, not being apprised of the very classifications they are

learning, *must* engage in them – these produce sanctions, guilt, and shame. Thereby one contradiction is displaced by another: if natural, sex must simply be done to be learned. But just which practices are natural is not available until one is a competent practitioner and therefore discriminator. Hence 'deviance' is built into a training that would ideally omit it. The route to the natural becomes 'structurally' paved with shame. So let us drop, for now, the 'natural sex' thesis as a resource (though it remains an interesting topic) and look to other possible solutions.

It could be objected at this point that of course modern sex education is 'up to the job.' As I write – though not when I first formulated these ideas – every society, almost without exception, has engaged in massive and expensive campaigns to attempt to halt the spread of the HIV virus and in doing so has been forced to become more explicit not only about sexual practices but also about intravenous drug use. Nevertheless, such campaigns routinely revolve around what *not* to do sexually, rather than what to do. Even when highly explicit, they assume that readers and viewers already know what certain sexual techniques are: they then become *explicit* precisely about the details of the curtailments, limitations, and caveats. One set of materials states:

> Making the first move might be scary, but more guys than you think have sex with other guys. It's natural, and if you're safe you'll have a great time. And what's safe? Kissing, cuddling, licking, stroking, wanking, oral sex (avoid cum in the mouth), vaginal and anal sex with condoms and water-based lube (such as KY-gel).[32]

All of this leaves open the questions of who is to have sex with whom, where, and when; what these various types of sex and sexual objects are; how they are to be performed; and perhaps most important for many sexual learners, how they are to be performed *well* – that is, what is to count as having had 'good sex' or at least having 'done it like everyone else (who is competent) does.' Again, to some extent the dominant sexological idea that these things come 'naturally' appears to prevail. There is still no single technology, social space, or institution where a sexual novice can learn the basic physiologies of sex; learn methods of 'hygiene' and safety (countering the acquisition of HIV, sexual diseases, unwanted pregnancy, and so forth); learn to enjoy and know his or her own competence in sex vis-à-vis others; come to understand and realize the more abstract notions of desire, love, and sexual relation*ships*; and appreciate the details of sexuality peculiar to the different available sexual 'permutations' – heterosexuality, homosexuality, bisexuality, and so on, let alone actually practice sex in such a way as to turn the information above into effective knowledge.

Imagine a society in which sexual practice is conducted 'in private,' for the most part by individuals alone or between couples (and more rarely, small groups), relatively stable membership of couples is expectable, and adults are expected to be sexually proficient. In such a society there are two distinct possible solutions to the problem of sexual learning. Sexuality can be learned either by experimentation or by 'secondary systems of elaboration' for sexuality and sexual discourse, where the relations between these two themselves raise further problems. The first solution has the built-in socio-logical trouble of directly threatening the requirement of relative stability among couples. Experimentation and learning relatively stable coupling are potentially contradictory and indeed have led those against sex education to associate official sexual training with promiscuity. The second solution has a slightly less troublesome upshot: it produces the sexual learner as 'voyeur' or 'exhibitionist,' for it requires access to 'official' competence through such unofficial discourses as pornography, graffiti, folk wisdom, dirty jokes, locker-room talk, and so on, through a whole range of activities and practices (signs) that can only be called 'furtive.' It requires listening and looking for the sexual in whatever discursive resources might be available, intentionally sexual or not.

One clear and almost literal instance of this problem-solution is the type of graffiti that requires the reader to fill in sexual words that have been replaced by nonsexual substitutes. Clues to the 'original' sexual words are given by their positions in the rhyme scheme. Two examples from toilets. First:

> There was a young lady from Bude
> Who went for a swim in the lake
> A man in a punt
> Stuck his pole in her ear
> And said you can't swim in here 'cos it's private

Second:

> Shakespeare was a man of wit
> On the tail of his coat he had some buttons
> One day whilst walking by St Pauls
> A woman grabbed him by the arm
> She said I see you are a man of pluck
> Come to my house and have a ham sandwich
> Some are a penny, some are a bob
> It all depends on the size of your ham sandwich

Note in these cases that the 'repaired' versions are not particularly interesting or funny – in fact they tell more of violence than sexuality (though the two are often connected in graffiti). Their 'point,' it seems is simply to act as a kind of furtive cloze test: Does the hearer know the sexual word replacements? If so, one has found that one knows what some other person knows. If not, one can ask, for example, 'What dirty word rhymes with "punt"?' and so on.

Turning to another example: as Sacks has shown, such matters as where and how one is expected to laugh during and following the telling of a dirty joke can be taken by youth cohorts as marking one's competence: not just one's conversational competence, but one's sexual competence.[33] Indeed, in terms of the activity of listening and responding to dirty jokes, the two competences cannot be clearly separated. Similarly, competence can be hidden from parents or other authorities, for example, by abstaining from laughter in cases where dirty jokes provide for appropriate laughter 'slots.' Learning when to laugh, learning to display that one has gotten the point – in this case, in a joke about fellatio, where that practice, as part and parcel of the joke, indeed as its 'point,' is left unmentioned but hearable for those who can recognize it ('I told you never to talk with your mouth full') – shows that one knows just which practice is being referred to in such elliptical ways. It shows that one is a member of a certain community of recently acquired sexual competence, that one can recognize a specific sexual practice from what nonmembers (precompetents) hear only as a blur of indexical particulars.

Community members, in this case, can narrow down the indexical potential of an utterance like 'I told you never to talk with your mouth full' so that very practice of narrowing – marked by laughing at a highly specific moment – is a community practice, a practice specific to a community. The activity [telling + laughing] is methodical; in fact, as Sacks shows, it is highly methodical, since it involves incredibly precise sequencing and timing: the telling has to be set up for the laughter to occur at a *very* specific instant, such that any laughter that is even a fifth of a second late can be heard as a response to the already 'existing' laughter rather than to the point of the joke.

In another sense, the method [sequencing + precision timing] reflexively produces an activity [telling + laughing] that is thereby intelligible as a *community* activity, and reflexively, the community in question is given its sense of itself (of 'what it is for us' or 'what we are') by being constructed as and through such activities as this [telling + laughing] along with numerous others. At a further level, the (reflexively combined) methodic activity comes to be used as a solution to the broader problem of sexual learning: as a kind of 'voyeurism' or, perhaps, 'écouteurism.' And this is how I would want to *use* a term such as 'voyeurism.' It is to be understood as naming a secondary elaboration of the sexual, or as a mode of transition between discursive competences – between the marginal (the furtive) and the official-sexual. Insofar as it at least attempts to conjoin such formations of competence, voyeurism can be thought of as sexual training by metaphor or, more generally, by figure of speech. Training can be tropic. So 'voyeurism' is a metaphorical term only, but one that glosses essentially metaphorical-tropic *practices*. If (and this is speculative) voyeurism or other strategies of secondary elaboration came to be embedded in a community as 'popular memory' – that is, as a means of solving socio-logical problems more generally – we would then be able to locate its historical meaning.

Yet if voyeurism is at least *one* way of solving the pragmatic problem of sexual training, if it is a way of overcoming the contradiction between requirements ('outcomes') and available resources, it has a further problem associated with it. For voyeurism is always folded back into the very domain of the sexual practices it would discover. Being, as Heritage notes, a 'bootstrapping' exercise, it is always an instance of the events it refers to. Garfinkel (in his sense of 'reflexivity') suggests, as we have seen, that accounts (utterances or 'usages') are always incarnate in the practices they account, and in this case we have seen that they are: voyeuristic utterances such as ['Don't talk with your mouth full' + laughter] are always already sexually imbued, for the community in question. They are not just isolated practices ('dead' linguistic signs); they are always already sexual practices. That is, for example, it's 'sexy' to speak this way – if furtively so. 'Talking dirty' is not just talking *about* sexual activity, it *is* an example of sexual activity, just as 'talking or thinking through possible crossword solutions' is part of solving crosswords. Here we might note that the (perhaps) dominant discourse on the 'naturalness' of sexuality and sexual learning actually categorizes voyeurism (or furtiveness) among its residue of *unnatural* sexual practices. Therefore it outlaws the very systems of secondary elaboration it seems to require. The problem of learning thus becomes one of seeing without being seen, leaving the sexual learner always potentially in a position akin to the impostor.

In this light, we can begin to see how an analysis of various sexual issues might be made. We can point to the conservative reaction against the continued existence of, or even the introduction of, sex education in schools (for example, the campaigns conducted over recent years by the fundamentalist Right); or to the parallel United Kingdom debate on the access of 'minors' to medical advice and prescription of sexually necessary items such as contraceptives that came to a head with the notorious *Gillick* court decision in favor of such interdictions.[34] To make sexual training 'official' (by medicalization or education) is unacceptable to those who argue that the sexual-moral is in fact 'natural' and therefore the province of (supposedly) equally 'natural' institutions such as the family – as opposed to 'social' institutions such as the surgery, the family-planning clinic, or the school. To make sex a matter of extrafamilial discourse, it is argued, is to make it subject to unnaturalness, to potential promiscuity, and so forth. That is to say, certain communities (which could be collected together by an analytic term such as 'the Right') have an interest in restricting the semiosic potential of sexual terminology so it is their own rather specific versions of these terms that have official currency. To 'let the terms go' into uncontrolled circulation is not, for these communities, merely a linguistic matter: it can, in and of itself, be considered promiscuous, proliferative, and unnatural.

The struggle, for these communities, is against the very contradictions outlined here. Those contradictions, for the 'Right,' ought not to exist. Yet what this leaves out of account is that the absence of official training means not only that secondary systems of elaboration must be constructed as a socio-logical requirement of competence for those whose families find the positive transformation of their own sexuality into discourse harder than the interdictory policing of their children's potential sexuality, but also that a chance to engage sexual learners in surveillance by using the sex lesson as confessional is forgone. Consequently, no matter which side of the debate one takes (for or against the proliferation of sexual information), the inherent contradictions of sexual learning in a sexually privatized society are not *solved*. They are simply displaced to a slightly different terrain.

The point of an effective semiotics of sexual learning, then, would not be to adjudicate such debates, but rather to examine everyday activities (signs) – including the activities of the debates themselves – whereby practitioners who are faced with the omnipresent problem of learning actually handle the central contradiction that is preserved despite any matters of policy.

Turning now towards 'exhibitionism,' another issue that could be handled using the theoretical apparatus outlined here would be that such aspects of social semiosis as displays of masculinity/femininity could be treated as surrogates, or metaphors, for sexuality after the manner of the dirty joke example above. Here we could hypothesize that, again, because sexual competence is privately practiced but must be publicly displayed (and given an embargo on its public display in any *direct* way), it will be displayed metaphorically in certain forms that are not 'intrinsically' sexual, such as physical toughness and swearing (in the case of masculinity) or modes of dress, deportment, and hairstyle (in the case of femininity). That is, if the membership category 'grown man' or 'grown woman' carries with it the category-bound activity (or predicate) 'sexually competent,' then displays of 'grown-upness,' whether sexual or not, can get that activity (or attribute) seen.[35] As Sykes puts it,

> The inmates of the New Jersey State Prison have changed the criteria by which an individual establishes his claim to the status of

male. Shut off from the world of women, the population of prisoners finds itself unable to employ that criterion of maleness which looms so importantly in society at large – namely the act of heterosexual intercourse itself. Proof of maleness, both for the self and others, has been shifted to other grounds and the display of 'toughness' in the form of masculine mannerisms and the demonstration of inward stamina, now becomes the major route to manhood. These are used by the society at large, it is true, but the prison, unlike the society at large, must rely on them exclusively.[36]

The adolescent, like the prisoner, is cut off from full participation in traditional adult forms of, for example, maleness, and it is no coincidence that ethnographic studies of male youth communities, such as that of Willis, show the same concerns with highly masculinist displays:

> The ambience of violence with its connotations of masculinity spread throughout the whole [youth] culture. The physicality of all interactions, the mock pushing and fighting, the showing off in front of girls, the demonstrations of superiority and put-downs of the conformists, all borrow from the grammar of real violence. The theme of fighting frequently surfaces in official school work – especially now in the era of progressivism and relevance.[37]

'Borrow[ing] from the grammar of real violence': The phrase aptly catches at the ways the voyeurism-exhibitionism 'solution' is essentially a metaphoric-tropic one and indicates a potentially fruitful domain for further inquiry.[38]

If, for learners, the 'sexual' has to be read for within semiosic displays that are not intrinsically and overtly sexual – that is, via secondary systems of elaboration – the range of displays and occasions that could therefore come to be read as 'sexual' is potentially vast. An event such as a sociology lecture could be a case in point. Below I present a fragment of such a lecture. It is interesting on two counts. First, it discusses sexuality 'as an aside' and to this extent is an instance of the secondary systems of elaboration that, I am suggesting, can become routinized ways by which precompetent persons can learn adult sexual competence. Second, it also *addresses* (makes a topic of) those secondary systems themselves – especially pornography, dirty jokes, and party talk. In a double way, then, it is an empirical case that both acknowledges and instances the problems and solutions I have referred to above in a very speculative way.

The fragment consists of a transcript of a sociology lecture to university students. It is, in ethnomethodological terms, a 'naturally occurring' instance of talk; that is, I came upon it for quite nonanalytic purposes and not in the form of a tape but as already transcribed. The transcript was made for professional and pedagogic purposes. I present it below with only the identifying details of participants changed, as the normal conventions demand.[39]

1 LECTURER: (.) so I think we'll simply call off our class for today (.)

2 Before you leave, Mr Howard (.) you need to go by the Sociology Office

3 Mr Howard here? Yes (.) I guess they have some papers for you to sign

4 Now, also, before you leave, I'd like to have some of this stuff passed out (.)

5 How many people are enrolled in the course?

6 Terry, would you give me a hand on some of this stuff?

7 Would you hold up your hands, so we can get it to the persons enrolled? (.)

8 Now I think there are (.) I have two extra copies (.) there are more copies

9 I don't think we've run off enough to get them distributed to all the members of the class (.) so you'll have to allow some time like the middle of the week before we can possibly run off more

10 And I think I'm certainly going to change my ways of (.) if I give it to any of you then I'm going to give it to all of you (.)

11 The [untranscribed] paper is rather heavily revised (.)

12 Now this is an old [untranscribed] paper, it's on [untranscribed] interpretation; it's possible that some of you already have seen it (.) if so then it won't be of interest

13 If you'll just raise your hand if you need it (.)

14 Well, there'll be more materials (.)

15   There are other copies of the [name of paper], so I'll be glad to give them to you after class

16   Now I have, also, the copies of the [sex change] paper are available, and for those of you who didn't get any, if you'll see me after the break, in my office, I'll be glad to furnish a copy

17   Now let me tell you what this is about

18   There are a set of about eight studies that make up a book that's been sent to the publisher (.) it goes under the title of [name of book] – you needn't pay any attention to that

19   The thing I want to call your attention to is that in that [sex change] paper (.) that's a lurid title (.) as you can imagine (.) and I must ask you, as adults, – it's not for party talk

20   I mean (.) sure it's for party talk (.) but it's not to pass around the way one would pass around Toots and Caspar

21   You know what I'm talking about

22   So it's not a little bit of pornography that's kinda gotten loose from [the university] (.)

23   Now I tell you that because the person is very much alive and in the area (.) and, also, I have a collaborator (.) we intend to pursue the work more deeply than has been done here (.)

24   If it's turned into a scandal, there's no possibility of doing anything more

25   I'm not even afraid of the suit (.)

26   I'm just afraid of the mortification, and it would just be so unprofessional for it to be turned into a mere matter of (.) what shall we say? (.) of a dirty story

27   There's plenty of room for ironic and, you know, pornographic comment; it's after all a gal who's made a sex change (.) or a guy who made a sex change

28   So I ask you, treat it as your own property (.) and where persons have good reasons to read it (.) let's say with educated interests (.) okay, fine (.)

29   Otherwise, I ask you to keep it to yourself

30   I'm talking about such things as parties and smokers (.) and all the various ways in which one can in any course in sociology, you know, acquire the stories that turn one into the party cheerleader

31 Now, I tell you that I can't take any [untranscribed]; there's nothing to be done (.)

32 If you do it, then you simply will have done it (.) and in that case, as I say, any excuse will do (.)

33 So I ask you to take particular care (.) and don't use it as an interesting sex story

34 [Omitted from this transcript]

35 And, now I give it to you to read in order that the course will be enlivened for you and, I hope, for me, if you read it

36 You can take it for granted that I'll be happy to hear any of your comments

37 That goes without saying. Okay.

This stretch of talk has some obvious features. It is monologic: one speaker addresses an assembly of listeners who do not speak in return. Also, it accomplishes a number of tasks such as 'educational housekeeping' (1–16); preparations for reading (17–37); and cautions on the uses of texts (19–33). We, and the participants, can see this from a number of features of the talk. Its monologism is evident not simply from the sheer absence of turn exchange. In addition to this, the auditors are directly characterized in a number of ways: as persons who should raise their hands rather than speak (7); as individuals such as 'Terry' and 'Mr Howard' who should respond by their actions rather than their talk; as students enrolled in the course; and by contrast, as people who happen to be present but are not enrolled, people who have presumably 'dropped in' to hear the lecture; as ones who listen and read and who are, potentially, 'enlivened' (35); and as 'adults' (19). That is, they are not characterized as speakers for the purposes of this occasion. Their talk is referred to, but it is deferred to occasions outside and after the lecture; they are thought of as talking, that is, in their capacities as party-goers (30), as people who attend 'smokers' (30), as possible distributors of comic books (20), as potential users of sociological texts as pornography (22), as tellers of dirty jokes (26), and as professionals (26) – or, since this seems to contrast with the other designations, as novitiate professionals who might be doing sociology.

The lecturer's version of things allows his students a number of possible subject positions, then, and each has its benefits and its drawbacks. For example, using the 'Sex Change' paper as a stimulus for titillation will have the benefit of turning them into 'party cheerleaders.' But this will do the profession (sociology) no good whatever: thus the students are to decide, based on what they do with the 'sex change' paper, whether to be professionals or to opt for the more immediate plaudits to be had from being the life and soul of the party.

However the choice is formulated (and there are several options here), the audience is not simply a collection of just any listeners and potential speakers, undifferentiated and uncategorized. They have – that is, they are produced in the talk as having – determinate features, typical activities, characteristics, and apparently well-known or obvious ways these fit together. Each 'type', however, is constrained to be silent for now but a speaking subject of a certain type later. Some of these subject positions require those who are currently listeners to make choices at a later point, in and during some typified future. So, according to this formulation of the audience, it's almost impossible to be constructed as both an adult (19) and someone who would 'pass around Toots and Caspar' (20). Categories of persons, courses of action, and typical narratives seem to fit each other in a fairly precise way. At the most elementary level, as 'students' they are constructed as people who 'read'; as 'party-goers' they are constructed as people who might wish to be 'cheerleaders,' and so forth, and each of these types and courses of action appears to be embedded within typical narratives. For example, this version of things assumes that student parties could not be places where people read or have 'professional' exchanges. That is, the lecture talk makes (and makes available) not just possible courses of action but typical sequential arrangements of events within them (narratives).

Consequently a number of activities hearable in the talk ('educational housekeeping' and the rest, listed above) are accounted so as to be designed for recipients; that is, they are accounted in terms of who is being addressed. In turn, this matter of 'who is addressed' is itself a construction of the talk; it is a construction of how, to take another example, 'cautions on the uses of texts' should operate for just this (projected) class of persons.

Let us note another fairly obvious feature of the lecture fragment: it is discursively constructed as an 'aside.' By this I mean that it occurs at the periphery of the main reason for the occasion – the work of lecturing. We, and the participants, can hear this in a number of ways. It occurs at the end of the lecturing work itself: 'We'll simply call off our class for today' (1). Here the cohortive plural 'we,' which is routine in classroom talk, is used for a while but soon gives way to the more directive 'you' in which the lecturer is differentiated from the class cohort.[40] Further, the talk in the fragment assumes that the listeners ('you') will shortly leave the setting (2). Also, the talk occurs in the discursive space that Schegloff and Sacks have called the opening up of a closing.[41] The formal business of the class has been closed in line 1, but using a routine method for reopening prefiguredly closed occasions, it is in fact reopened: 'Before you leave . . .' (2), 'also, before you leave . . .' (4). It is classically in such spaces, according to Schegloff and Sacks, that activities incidental to the main reason for the occasion are accomplished. The 'before you leave' device prefigures two such peripheral tasks: the 'housework' ('Before you leave . . . you need to go by the Sociology Office') and the work preparatory to reading ('before you leave, I'd like to have some of this stuff passed out'). With those activities duly framed – providing methodically for their intelligibility – and 'under the auspices of' the work preparatory to reading, a third activity can proceed – namely, the cautionary work.

This is announced by a preface that is not so routinely associated with reopenings as the 'by the way' and 'before you leave' types, and so it is perhaps to be heard as less incidental than the other activities, as more 'substantive': 'Now let me tell you what this is about . . .' (17), 'The thing I want to call your attention to is . . .' (19). Note here, however, that it is possible to hear (especially from line 19) that it is *not* the cautionary work itself that is being framed, in the initial instance at least, by the call to 'attention.' That is, the lecturer says, 'The thing I want to call your attention to is that in that [sex change] paper . . . ,' but the first 'that' is never grammatically completed. Instead the lecturer moves to a topic that is 'touched off' by the mention of the paper: he refers to the luridness of the title (as it were 'by the way'), and it is this new (and initially framed as incidental) topic that frames the cautionary work. Hence the cautionary work emerges as an aside (a touched-off topic) within a reopened substantive occasion (lecturing) within an aside ('Before you leave').

So while we, and the students, can hear that a closing has been reopened, and that 'sidework' or peripheral activity is expectable, we can also hear (within a nesting of activities) that the work of lecturing is somehow continuing with a (possibly final) substantive activity, namely, cautioning. This cautioning intersects with and builds in the divisions between types of subjects (potential readers) that we have already examined, especially the division between the 'professional' and the voyeur-exhibitionist ('a little bit of pornography,' being 'the party cheerleader,' and so on). Lines 19–33 of the fragment address *and* construct (a) categories of persons with respect to (b) their later reading and conversational activities concerning (c) how to handle sexual discourse. The split between the categories of 'professional' and, for example, 'dirty story tellers' is accomplished methodically by an interlocking of that category distinction on the two terrains (b) and (c). The categories 'professional' and 'voyeur,' from the device 'types of reader,' offer a polar contrast that is accomplished by the lecturer's invoking parallel contrasting category-bound activities for each: 'having educated interests' in sex and 'having good reasons for reading' sexual histories on the one hand, versus 'telling dirty stories,' 'reading sexual history as pornography,' and 'being the party cheerleader' on the other.

To refer to and construct the students as potential types of subjects (as opposed to others) means that the type ('Who I am') will emerge later *depending on* moral choices as to how they eventually read and talk about the 'sex change' paper. Reflexively, to instruct the students in *how to go about those readings and tellings* (as well as with whom and where they should do so) is to construct them in terms of the (above-mentioned) subject types; they can in the end be *only* professionals or pornographers; that is the total range of possibilities. It is not difficult to hear which of the reading types and (reflexively) subject types the lecturer prefers. The choices are not given as morally identical or equal: one is morally recommended and the other morally discouraged. Hence, and this may or may not be typical of morality work, the students are locked in not only to a reflexive set of subject and activity types but also to the respective moral valences of each.

Beyond this, there are further aspects of the typical courses of action the lecturer assumes for the students. The lecturer relies on the expectancy that initial courses of action (party talk and so on) will not simply 'stop at that'; rather, he assumes they will flow through into a broader community where such specific and highly local courses of action can build up into typical patterns and narratives. That is, he appears to be aware that texts and talk have potential in terms of historicity (popular memory). They are not merely occasional or occasioned events (though they are this too), but they have effects of a more lasting and effective kind. They can thereby generate further courses of action with their own (typical but not necessarily predictable) consequences. By moving from subject types to activity types, and from those to the domain of socio-historical consequences, the lecturer constructs a version of his community (his 'world') as one with a narrative structure where 'narrative is the presentation of *at least two* real or fictive events or situations in a time sequence, neither of which presupposes or entails the other.'[42]

Of the two possible narratives the students are given as choices, one goes as follows: The students read the 'sex change' text as publicly distributable dirty stories; the person who is described in the material somehow hears about this and thereby comes to be hurt; the lecturer who wrote the paper is either sued or mortified or both; the collaborative project is halted; scandal is brought upon the university. . . . Here the ellipses can represent hearable but unmentioned further consequences (the professional disrepute of the lecturer in national sociological forums and so on). In the second narrative the students treat the text as their 'own property' (28); they read it for the most part in a privatized fashion; they show it, if at all, only to persons with 'educated interests'; the scandalous consequences of the first narrative are avoided; the sociology course is 'enlivened'; the lecturer, perhaps, gets to hear the students' professional comments in the way usually associated with collegial feedback. Note also, the first narrative allows the 'sex change' paper's semiosic potential to proliferate. It gives it the status of a broadcast text, broadcast to who knows which specific communities with their own interpretive regimes. The second narrative ensures that the semiosic potential of the text remains fairly narrowly confined to a local subprofessional reading. The first narrative, in the strict sense, is after the manner of the typical cautionary tale or *conte morale*; the second is an adjunct of this, 'the happily ever after' story. The latter is clearly the morally recommended (perhaps even required) story, though not without some wistful modulation: 'If you do it [proliferate the text], then you simply will have done it' (32). No doubt the modulation could be read as a tautology.[43] But we can hear it otherwise: 'If you do it,' that is, proliferate the text, 'then you will have done it,' that is, brought the first (negatively valued) narrative into existence.

So what can be heard in this lecture is a variety of professional gatekeeping, relying on an attempted 'normalization' of a reading population. From a wide range of available uses or readings of texts (in principle), two narratives for their 'usage' are uniquely invoked, each with its own morally (and by implication legally) sanctioned consequences. (Though note also that the publication of a 'sociology' book containing exactly the same paper does *not* entail 'a little bit of pornography that's kinda gotten loose from [the university],' even though there is very little control the lecturer-author could have over that reading and its historical upshot.) A particular domain of sexual discourse and practice – transsexuality, though others would do – is thereby shown to have two dimensions: the professional-clinical and the dirty-voyeuristic. This is clearly in line with, and draws on, more generally available selection and inclusion criteria on sexual talk as a whole. That is, when it comes to naming sexual body parts and acts, two relatively exclusive discourses are available: the clinical ('penis,' 'vagina,' 'intercourse,' and the rest) and the dirty ('cock,' 'cunt,' 'fucking'). The clinical and the dirty are at least relatively exclusive in that sentences that contain mixtures of the terms can be heard as 'ungrammatical.' What is important, however, is that relatively direct transforms between the two can be made. They are easily co-translatable, and so one problem for the 'policing' of sexual talk is to ensure that instances of the clinical do not get readily translated into instances of the dirty and vice versa. Yet it is precisely the 'dirty' form in which the secondary systems of elaboration of sexual learning take place. Consequently sexual learners are, as we have suggested, caught in a double enfolding of the contradiction (double bind?) already surrounding their learning attempts. They are prohibited from direct instruction and similarly instructed to avoid adjacent circuits. Without the resources available to act as adults, it is nevertheless assumed that they can treat sexuality in an 'adult' way (19), with discretion, as 'property' (28), in a way that is responsive to ellipticals like 'You know what I'm talking about' (21), and so on.[44]

Returning to Foucault, it would be interesting to compare the version of the student and student life in the lecture fragment with his (Foucault's) analysis of the conditions of students in a more general social and political framework. He writes:

> The student is put outside of society, on a campus. Furthermore, he is excluded while being transmitted a knowledge traditional in nature, obsolete, 'academic' and not directly tied to the needs and problems of today. This exclusion is underscored by the organization, around the student, of social mechanisms which are fictitious, artificial and quasi-theatrical (hierarchic relationships, academic exercises, the 'court' of examination, evaluation). Finally, the student is given a gamelike way of life; he is offered a kind of distraction, amusement, freedom which, again, has nothing to do with real life; it is this kind of artificial, theatrical society, a society of cardboard, that is being built around him; and thanks to this, young people . . . are thus, as it were, neutralized by and for society, rendered safe, ineffective, socially and politically castrated.[45]

On the one hand, we can see that the work of lecturing we have just analyzed is geared towards this general picture of studenthood; it attempts to keep the politics of sexuality, in this case, 'on the campus,' in 'educated' and 'professional' hands. On the other hand, it appears to acknowledge that such policing (the restriction of the indexical potential of 'academic' texts) will not always work. The system can and will leak, texts will get out of control, students do have lives, issues, politics, and morality 'off campus.' The techniques of exclusion cannot be guaranteed, and this may be precisely why they have to be repeated and brought into focus 'for another first time,' time after time.

Foucault, especially in *Discipline and Punish*, has shown how, historically, official scientific discourses have constructed their own positions of dominance by effectively marginalizing competing ('popular' and no doubt much more semiotically proliferative) discourses and how, at the same time and by the same techniques, they have produced relatively normalized subjects through which general 'flows' of 'power' can move effectively, efficiently, and thus be reproduced. What this analysis of lecturing has shown, perhaps, is that professional scientific discourses achieve this in highly localized ways while still drawing on generally available (recursive) community resources: categories of subject, typical courses of action, narrative structure and predictability, and so on. One finding, then, is that scientific discourses on sexuality (here sociology) have built into them techniques of 'enfolding.' By this I mean that those discourses are not simply produced in a 'linguistic' dimension or field but are also produced and reproduced in a political-moral dimension or field of moral action. To speak 'sociologically' (within and as a scientific discourse) is also to recommend its forms of indexical 'closure' (to retain the shorthand expression) as a morally sanctionable way of speaking, writing, and acting – where 'sanction' can be heard either positively or negatively. To speak and write 'professionally' and 'technically' is never to speak in some kind of isolation from the broader civil domain within which professional and technical talk are done; at the very least, to speak this way is to speak *on behalf of* the professional and the technical as 'the good.' This enfolding is, I suggest, a major means by which nonprofessional, 'popular' discourses become marginalized historically. Techniques of what Foucault would call 'power' (surveillance, confession, normalization, and the rest) are constituted in and as that double grounding that (and this may be news) is itself worked up through commonly available discursive methods. This is true at least at the level of 'intelligibility' – the basic level of methods and activities – for the resources involved are such ordinary things as membership categorization devices.

Traditional ethnomethodology gives us techniques for analyzing and locating these discursive methods. It allows us to see how methods and local-social activities mutually produce one another and provide for each other's intelligibility. But it can go no further than this. It puts the second level of semiotic meaning (actionability – the level of socio-logical problems and solutions) on the agenda; but ethnomethodology largely eschews concepts that look as if they might have more than local relevance, that look as though they might be 'imposed' by theoreticist rather than local interests, that look (to use Garfinkel's favored term) as if they are part and parcel of 'constitutive theorizing.' For me this limits, before any actual investigation, what is going to count as 'locally relevant.' As we have seen in the analysis of the lecturing transcript, what is locally relevant to the lecturer goes well outside the domain and confines of the lecture theater. Members' local relevances, therefore, do seem to be more than just restricted to local settings.

I want, from here on, to explore some of these possibilities (under the names 'actionability' and 'historicity'), assuming, for now at least, that the discipline of ethnomethodology can be left to the task of investigating the question of sheer intelligibility (the reflexive relation of methods and their accomplishments). Hence, in the next chapter I take up these themes in a relatively abstract (even formalist) way, returning to the levels and forms of semiosis as *relations* (R_1, R_2, and R_3) encountered earlier in chapter 4. By now it should be clear that R_1 is the level of 'intelligibility' (signs as methodic practices); that R_2 is the level of the 'actionability' of signs (their use as socio-logical problems and solutions); and that R_3 is the level of 'historicity' (the embedding of actionable formations in community histories such that semioses can be rendered available – in various ways – outside single localities of use).

8. Intelligibility, Actionability, and Historicity

It seems to me that Hartland's conjecture we investigated earlier (that R1 and R2 are reflexive) is unassailable. By a very rough method of reductio ad absurdum, if R1 were not reflexive, members would be unable to rely on methods from occasion to occasion. They would effectively have to create the entire social world anew for every situation, and as a consequence, situations would be totally independent of one another, or discrete. If discrete in this way, then situations could not leak into one another but would instead be finite and specifiable quanta – 'packets' of social action. But then members would have to at least carry some notion of 'packet' from packet to packet in order to be able to see that each situation was in fact a new one. If this could happen, then at least one method (the method of discerning packets, whatever that would look like!) would be occasion-independent, leaving us with a contradiction. Hence R1 is a reflexive relation.

A similar argument could be made from the second consequence of R1's being reflexive: that activities can be utterly unique, creative, and context-dependent without therefore being unintelligible. If R1 were not reflexive, all context-dependent activities would be unintelligible. If there is at least a context-dependent social activity that is intelligible (which we must assume, since semiotics is the investigation of precisely that), then R1 is reflexive.

The argument for R2's being reflexive is not so clear-cut, for as we shall see, it depends on the assumption that social practice is absolutely 'secular'; that is, completely severed from the action of metaphysical forces. If methodic activities could not *possibly* be reflexively related (as solutions) to socio-logical problems, then those methodic activities, though intelligible (R1 being reflexive), would be conducted entirely for their own sake. They would have no purpose other than to display their own intelligibility. If we assume that some methodic activities are of this kind (and I think it is reasonable to conclude this, both from Hartland's investigations and from the self-evidently reasonable assumption that not every social activity will have a purpose outside itself where *some* cases of mathematical calculation, sociological investigation, chess playing, and so on could conceivably be cases in point), it still does not mean all methodic activities can be of this kind. There must be at least some methodic activities that solve socio-logical problems: otherwise there would be no quotidian way of solving such problems. Magistrates, to return to Hartland's example, would always order prison sentences; precompetent sexualities would remain that forever – excluding acts of God. (No doubt there *are* those who would thank God for not being sent down; and those who would thank Nature for making them sexually competent.) Barring those acts, insofar as there are socio-logical problems, methodic activities must be what exist as solutions to them.

The only other possibility is to hypothesize a 'controlling hand' in social life that 'magically' solved socio-logical problems on our behalf. This would have to be something like a transcendental structure or principle of history, for the 'medium' in which socio-logical problems exist is history, just as the 'medium' in which methodic activities exist is everyday life. This would mean imagining an underlying mechanism that guided historical change such that, when socio-logical problems were solved we would say that the principle was acting on our behalf, and vice versa when they were not. Then we would have to imagine a metaprinciple that would be the principle by which the first historical principle 'decided' whether the problem would be solved (whether history would be beneficent or not). And I'm not sure that the iteration of metaprinciples would stop here, so that we might have to hypothesize a final and absolute principle of history that stipulated where it *did* stop. That is, we would need to have a decidedly anthropomorphic conception of history that was at the same time divine and totally outside collective human agency. In effect this would amount to saying that there are methodic activities (such as making decisions, stipulations, and so on) that go on without an agent (or have a very ghostly agent). And here we reach a fundamental limit – an ethical limit. One either imagines ghostly agents (who happen to act just like human beings, as it turns out, only on a 'bigger' scale such that R2 is no more and no less than God's version of R1), or one does not. Since the social world would look identical under both hypotheses and – perhaps more important – since there seems to be some empirical evidence that everyday methodic activities can, for some classes of occasions, solve socio-logical problems, it appears fairly clear that the 'secular' version is going to be more productive. Without it, for example, there would be no possibility that any variety of semiotics could have strategic value for social intervention. Indeed, the very notion of social intervention would disappear.

Hence I believe there are conclusive grounds for taking R_1 as reflexive. And since R_2 does not *exist* for methodic activities that do nothing other than display their own intelligibility, there are at least compelling grounds for assuming that, when R_2 exists, it is a reflexive relation. Henceforth I will assume both of these are the case. But this leaves us with the question of R_3 (the relation between R_1 and R_2).

There is a straightforward answer to this question: Since R_1 and R_2 are both reflexive, R_3 would be the very reflexivity that binds them. The answer may be correct, but if so, it is trivially so. Perhaps the argument could be left at that; but the consequences would be devastating for our investigations, since, as we have seen, R_3 is held to be *the* meaning of a sign (but see below for a refinement of this view). If R_3 were no more than a statement of the ubiquity of reflexivity in general, then all we could say about the meaning of a given sign was that it displayed reflexivity in general: this would be all it would 'do,' its only and ultimate use. This has to some extent been the kind of conclusion drawn by some ethnomethodologists – that reflexivity is only a general principle and not open to investigations that will deliver 'news' as their findings.[1] What this suggests to me is as follows: If the Hartland conjecture is correct, as I assume it is, then 'reflexivity' is in fact two things (R_1 and R_2). This is precisely what makes it empirically investigable. However, R_3 is neither a third type of reflexivity nor reflexivity in general. Instead, I offer the following conjecture: R_3 is recursive.

A recursive operation is 'a process that operates on the product of its own operation.'[2] This broader notion of recursivity dominates popular accounts of chaos theory – the analysis of complex, nonlinear systems.[3] In the stricter mathematical sense, 'recursivity' is the near synonym of 'computability,' 'algorithmicity,' and 'effectivity.' A set of natural numbers (for example, the set of even numbers) that can be generated by an algorithm is called 'recursively enumerable': a given algorithm works on a first number (the smallest natural number of the set) in order to generate, as its product, the next number of the set. It then works, recursively, on *this* product of its own prior operation to generate the next number of the set, and so on. In the case of the set of even numbers, we can see that the algorithm in question would involve adding 2 $(x'=x+2)$. If such an algorithm can be found for a given set, then the set can be computed; it is 'effective.'[4]

I shall not argue that signs are effective in exactly this way, though of course a limited number of them will be within the restricted domain of mathematics (or even within some of its even more restricted subdomains). However, I do want to argue that R3 is a *process*. R3 is a historical process in the sense used above. More specifically, it is the process that relates historical to quotidian processes. And this historicity is made possible by the fact that methods (as opposed to the specific activities they produce) are context-independent and therefore, to whatever limited a degree, diachronic and by the fact that such methods can be deployed *from one occasion to another* as solutions to socio-logical problems. Accordingly, a sign has meaning insofar as it is a reflexive *methodic* activity that is reflexively connected (as a solution) to a socio-logical problem of a general, communitywide, or historical kind. R3, if recursive, would then be equivalent to the way a community 'learns,' to its 'popular memory' (the 'folk wisdom' of teenagers, for example, or the 'unspoken know-how' of magistrates). Or in other words, insofar as a methodic activity can be used to generate a product (in the form of a problem-solution), it can also be used again to *operate on that product*, and so on recursively. It therefore becomes a generally available methodic activity for its community – available for use in the solution of problems, as yet unknown, that will be generated out of social practice (where 'social practice' means the use of methodic activities, either simply for the sake of displaying their own intelligibility or to solve socio-logical problems). Accordingly, it is quite possible that some problem-solutions will be used discretely and uniquely, as 'once-offs': in which case they will have no relation, R3. Or to put it another way, R3 will be null. In cases where a problem-solution is *effective* on more than a single problem, however, R3 will be recursive, assuming that the problems it is effective on will be generated out of the very methodic activities that provide for R3. Hence we can see that:

R1 is reflexive and necessary – all social activities are methodic; all methods generate activities;

R2 is reflexive and contingent – it will not exist in cases of *merely* autointelligible methodic activities but will in cases that provide problem-solutions;

R3 is recursive and contingent – it will not exist in cases where problem-solutions constitute singularities but will in cases where they are 'stored' or reusable on community-generated problems.

Examples of R3 would occur, then, wherever a community treated a socio-logical problem as one of a genre of problems, such that genres of solutions to it would be known to be available. R3 is the domain of sociohistorical knowledge within a community or, to use a shorthand, 'popular memory.' Clearly, analytic work in this domain will involve more than any semiotic formalism or systemics can guarantee. Such matters will not be easily read from the surface of social texts. Instead they will require more painstaking inquiries and involve what might even be called a 'historical sensibility.' In many cases they will no doubt demand that the investigator be absorbed in community practices for some considerable period. Accordingly, distinctions between 'investigator' and 'community' might become, productively, blurred.

An example of R3 in operation concerns the availability of 'secondary systems of elaboration,' as I have called them in reference to the sexual competence problem. That is, the graffiti, dirty jokes, locker-room talk, voyeuristic practices, pornographic circulations, and so on constitute a *collection* of solution-types. They are collected by virtue of their quasi-unofficial status such that they can elaborate the primary (or official) modes of elaboration open to sexually competent community members. Hence members can know 'in future' that 'naturally unknowable' (but essential) aspects of community membership may be accessed by secondary systems of elaboration, remembering that this term is no more than an analytic collecting device for numerous varieties of quite specific and precise methods.

A consequence of what we have ascertained so far would be that many signs are meaningless! In fact, only signs that display R_3 would be meaningful in the strict sense. And to an extent I want to preserve this formulation – so that the term 'semiotics' is strictly used only for the analysis of sign-uses as solution-types in a particular community's *history*. This would be the strict definition of a sign's meaning. However, since R_3 is a function of the relation between R_1 and R_2, it is also possible to think of all three relations (R_1, R_2, and R_3) as forms or types of meaning, or as 'contributing' to a sign's meaning. In one sense it is also true to say that the three 'values' of R are separated only by a kind of temporality, one that is coextensive with social time. Accordingly, R_1 is intralocally temporal; R_2 is interlocally temporal; and R_3 is supralocally (or historically) temporal. Note that all signs that display R_3 *must* also display R_2 and R_1; that all signs that display R_2 *must* also display R_1; and that all signs *must* display at least R_1. That is, all signs are intelligible; some of these act as solutions to socio-logical problems; and some of these solutions become part of 'popular memory.'

If we allow all three forms of R to constitute a sign's meaning, then the types will be distinguished as follows. R_1 is meaning (as use) as intelligibility (the mutual intelligibility of methods and activities); R_2 is meaning (as use) as a problem-solution in social-actional practice; R_3 is meaning (as use) as a community-historical possibility. In what follows, however, unless it is clear that some other theory of meaning is being discussed, I will reserve the term 'meaning' (or, to distinguish it, 'historical meaning' or 'historicity') for R_3 and refer to the other two domains, R_2 and R_1, as 'actionability' and 'intelligibility' respectively.[5] These 'levels' are the topic of the next chapter, where they are further unpacked in relation to the ethnomethodological concept of indexicality.

9. Indexicality's Horizon of Possibility

In this investigation I shall begin with our first semiotic level, intelligibility (R1). In the ethnomethodological literature I have been drawing on as a basic social theory for semiotics, the meaning of a sign (or more strictly a 'usage,' 'utterance,' or 'expression') is frequently confined to this level of intelligibility. This is achieved by a central ethnomethodological concept that is somewhat broader than the concept of reflexivity and also less easily definable or directly usable in semiotics: indexicality. Indexicality is usually referred to as the context-dependence or context-sensitivity of any utterance.[1] The thesis is that the 'meaning' (that is, the intelligibility) of an utterance is dependent on, or sensitive to, its context, where 'context' is to be heard as the highly local or in situ embedding of a stretch of language. Here the notion of context is such that it is immediate and audiovisually available, on the scene of the utterance itself.[2] It is whatever is pertinently on hand for the interpretation of the utterance right here and now – for any particular 'right here and now.'[3] In this restricted sense the concept of indexicality would not be very important for our investigations, since it appears to be confined to the specifics of everyday scenes and, as a concept within a theory of meaning, it appears to take 'meaning' to mean 'intelligibility' *only*.

But perhaps in another sense the concept of indexicality could be useful to effective semiotics. That is, all three of the 'levels' of sign-use we have so far identified appear to have context-sensitive aspects. At the level of R1, 'context-sensitivity' appears to mean exactly what ethnomethodologists have meant by 'indexicality'; at the level of R2, 'context-sensitivity' would mean the sensitivity of particular solutions to their particular community's socio-logical problems; at the level of R3, 'context-sensitivity' would mean 'community-specificity.' Given the choices above, it is the last of these that would be most pertinent to our inquiries here. And so I now offer a semiotic reconceptualization of indexicality; for if 'indexicality' could mean 'community-specificity,' then it might (at the least) give us a key into this crucial semiotic concept. It might mean that we could begin to think of communities as collections of 'what happens' (to return again to Nancy's definition) in the *handling of indexicality*.

In order to rethink indexicality in this way, it is clear that it has to be taken from being merely (and perhaps trivially) bound up in (and as) an essential constituent of empirically available social encounters and must instead be thought of as a *critical* rather than just a *descriptive* concept. Hence I propose a very slight shift in the ethnomethodological concept of indexicality, taking it towards 'critique' – that is, towards actionability (R2) and historical meaning (R3). This appears to be necessary if the concept is to have any value for effective semiotics.

By 'critique' I mean *something like* the premise of the irreducible *différance* of any sign as it (the premise, that is) is currently used in what might be called 'critical theory' (CT).[4] 'Critique' would then mean any form of analysis that worked from this premise – one that can be alternatively expressed as a reaction against axiomatic or algorithmic theories of meaning (such as that of Wittgenstein's *Tractatus*) and that insists, against such theories, that any intelligible communication is achieved not by virtue of the intrinsic properties of signs (such that, for example, they map directly onto the world), but only by virtue of an essential semiosic instability of any sign *in principle*. I take this critical potential to be implicit in the concept of indexicality – even though, as I argue, the full potential of the concept has not yet been exploited in ethnomethodology (EM) itself.

I want to argue for a partial rethinking of the concept of indexicality from 'within' EM and 'between' EM and CT. It could be argued that the abiding effect of Garfinkel's *Studies in Ethnomethodology* has been, despite the insistence of some practitioners, its impact on social *theory*. That is, Garfinkel's theoretical solution to the problem of social order is utterly unique – to the point where there are probably now only two forms of social theory – social theory and EM. Garfinkel's radical hypothesis is twofold: that the social order is underwritten discursively, and that discursive stability ('meaning' or 'understanding' or both) is achieved via practical actions upon expressions that are in principle indeterminate or indexical (rather than stable). Putting these two hypotheses together, EM is founded upon the radical insight that social homogeneity (in practice) is predicated upon discursive heterogeneity (in principle). Every sign's intelligibility is always the effect of muddling through, making do, with unstable sociodiscursive conditions. In this sense Garfinkel's insight partly overlaps (and predates) the founding premise of CT, whose locus classicus is Derrida's *Of Grammatology*.

The premise of the in-principle instability or indexicality of intelligibility, shared by EM and CT, is nevertheless 'taken up' in distinct ways within each domain in terms of its conception of social-textual practice. CT takes instability (*différance*) to be either inherently discoverable in otherwise seemingly definite and closed texts (such those of Saussure or Rousseau) or celebrated in the case of 'naturally' indeterminate texts (such as the postmodern novel). In certain cases the boundaries between CT and its 'object' texts become blurred, so that CT enters self-consciously into social-textual practice.[5] One of its principal aims is to explore and exploit any possible relation between civil debate and action, on the one hand, and theoretical debate and action on the other.[6] This may mean that in the literary domain, for example, the distinction between a fictional work and a critical work becomes – is made – deliberately unclear.

EM, on the other hand, has attempted to show how discursive indeterminacy is *worked*, in practical actions, by members, so that it may be 'overcome' if not 'repaired' in any ultimate sense, so that its 'repair' is only ever 'for the moment,' 'for all practical purposes' – thereby generating intelligible communications or 'practical understandings.' Although no EMist has ever argued that EM itself is 'outside' or beyond such fundamental methods of social accomplishment (hence leaving a constantly possible, if rarely actualized, relation between civil debate and theoretic debate),[7] there has nevertheless been, in EM, an 'analytic' tradition (as against an interventional tradition) such that EM's aim is to *describe* social accomplishments in terms of members' methods for handling the open texture (indexicality) of linguistic expressions.

Hence there are two distinct directions one can proceed based on the premise of indexicality/*différance*. The *single* thing I shall argue for at present is that these two 'directions' are not incommensurate either in principle or in practice, since, among other things, they both reject objectivist and formalist versions of how signs can 'mean.'

One upshot for EM would be that we could not decide a priori whether an indexical expression (or sign) is going to be, in practice, worked *towards* definiteness and stability or, on the other hand, is going to be, equally in practice, worked *towards* amplifying its essential (its always already given) polyvalency. Indeed, it might be possible to see that this distinction between semiosic identity (discursive stability) and semiosic difference (discursive indeterminacy) does not constitute an 'either/or' possibility for any given sign.

Instead, it might be discovered that there is an array of possibilities, across this continuum, with any actual expression's actional 'uptake' in respect of the array being highly dependent on contextual particulars. John Heritage puts EM's position on members' actional uptakes of indexicality succinctly in terms of 'making definite sense with indefinite resources.'[8] This formulation, which is widespread but by no means universal in EM, makes the a priori assumption that 'definite sense' is always what is made, empirically, in actual situations of social-moral choice. Instead, we should leave that question open before inspecting particular details of those arrangements. It is not impossible to conceive of (or indeed to discover) practical situations where quite *in*definite senses are permissible or even required. Cases in point would be some (but not all) instances involving:

- poetry
- madness
- bold hypothesizing (à la Popper)
- expressionist art
- certain popular texts (*Total Recall* and *Twin Peaks*, to cite two examples)
- postmodern fiction (Calvino, DeLillo, Pynchon, Joyce, and others)
- quantum mechanical indeterminacies
- psychoanalytic interpretation of certain kinds (such as free association)
- surrealist 'automatic writing'

— various types of religious action and debate (where
   meanings are expected to remain specifically unclear)
— children's games and fantasy play
— musical improvisation
— dreaming
— playing 'Chinese whispers'
— punning
— irony
— making double-entendres
— playing with visual illusions (for fun or else seriously,
   as in the drawings of Maurits Escher)

To this we could add, no doubt, a much larger range of quotidian
events. As Wittgenstein puts it: 'Is it . . . always an advantage to replace an indistinct picture by a sharp one? Isn't the indistinct one
often exactly what we need?'[9] Or in EM terms, some forms of life
(law or classical mechanics, for example) may treat 'reality disjunctures' as 'puzzling events' requiring 'solutions' whereas others
may take them as unremarkable, as part of the routine business of
life as usual.[10]

Another way of conceptualizing indexicality has been in terms
of a gap or lacuna, a space to be filled in by specific methods.
(Mehan and Wood wrote of members' impulses to 'fill in the
rules.')[11] My premise is no more and no less than this: There are
more things to do 'with' a gap than simply to fill it, and there are
manifold practical situations of action where something other
than a 'filling' takes place. Rather than filling a gap, for example,
one may attempt to widen it, alter its shape, leave it in place exactly as it is, create another gap of a different sort in its place or beside it, ignore it, take it for granted, and so forth – a potentially
endless variety of 'types' of practice.

EM's initial theorization of indexicality envisaged a range of
possible ways of 'filling' gaps and went looking for them in practical, empirical instances. The limitations of this, to me, seem ho-
mologous with the limitations of logical and axiomatic theories of
meaning. The later Wittgenstein showed these to be unduly restricted by arguing that there is not just *one* language game but
many. He had in mind the propositional attitude that had served as
a model for *all* expressions within the traditions of formal logic. I

have in mind the gap-filling attitude (where expressions 'make definite sense') that has served as a model for *all* practical actions within many – but not all – traditions of EM. No doubt gaps do get filled, fairly definite senses do get made for all practical purposes; but there seems to be no reason why this specific variety should be generalized to cover all cases of 'gap work' or 'sense making.' This is especially so since the metaphor of a gap implies that some sort of firm ground lies to either side – so that community methods need only be designed in order to move from one firm terrain to another via gaps. What such firm terrain could be remains untheorized and unexemplified empirically.

Instead of conceptualizing indexicality as a gap, one could, for example, conceptualize it as a point – a *hypothetical*, unrealizable (or ideal type) zero degree at which an expression is not yet 'put into' social practice (pN). At this point, what we can call its 'indexical potential' would be indefinite.

Along one path emerging from pN (where the path represented the putting of the expression into social practice – putting the expression back into the 'stream of life,' as Wittgenstein has it), the expression would move towards another *hypothetical* point (po),[12] a point of ultimate closure, where its indexical potential would be so narrowed and honed that a single and final meaning would henceforth be forever invoked along with (or as) that expression.[13] Informationally, this point, po, would represent the lowest possible 'entropy' a sign could have. The path of the sign could be thought of as *converging* towards po, representing zero entropy. But the point could never be reached in practice simply by virtue of this paradox: that singular and final meanings would have zero information! Or more conventionally, no meaning without *some* divergence (difference).

This is how, for example, Husserl imagined the Pythagorean theorem, which 'exists only once, no matter how often or even in what language it might be expressed. It is identically the same in the "original language" of Euclid and in all "translations." '[14] By achieving this hypothetical point, Husserl argues, an expression 'keeps its ideal identity throughout all cultural development. It is a condition that allows communication among the generations of investigators no matter how distant and assures the exactitude of translation and the purity of tradition.'[15]

A second path – perhaps in the opposite direction – would carry the expression away from semiotic unity and towards another hypothetical point (p1),[16] a place of ultimate dispersal, where its indexical potential would be increased to an ideally infinite degree. Informationally, this point, p1, would represent the highest possible 'entropy' a sign could have (the semiosic equivalent of thermal equilibrium). The path of the sign could be thought of as *diverging* towards p1, representing maximum entropy. But this point, again, could never be reached in practice because of another paradox: that infinitely differentiated meanings would have infinite information – they would be able to say absolutely everything at once. Or more conventionally, no meaning without *some* convergence (identity).

So at point p0, the expression could mean only one thing; and at p1, it could mean anything at all. Neither of these points can, then, ever be reached empirically – the points represent 'tendencies,' 'impulses,' or 'habits' towards unattainable extremes. Before an expression reaches either point, it comes up against *practical* limits. (Moreover, the expression's starting point (pN) is itself an unattainable 'limit,' for no expression is ever *not* situated, always already, in the 'stream of life.') However, I *do* want to argue for the 'lines' or 'paths' in this model (one linear and semiosically convergent, the other nonlinear and semiosically divergent), which I will call *the paths of an expression's indexical potential*.

It should already be clear, then, that I am not proposing just another binary: say, between a totally unlimited and a fully limited semiosis.[17] In fact my second 'path' of indexical potential is not a single line at all. Rather, it is an array of lines, representing multiple pathways.[18] It is an impulse associated with trying to multiply and proliferate an expression's indexical potential. So, in one direction lies an impulse towards linearity and singularity; in the other lies no single 'direction' at all, but rather an impulse towards 'chaos' (in the sense of antilinearity) and multiplicity.

The ultimate limits-in-principle (p0, p1) of these directions (or one direction and one multiple direction) cannot be practically achieved – perhaps they cannot even be imagined. The two tendencies towards them have limits in practice so that all intelligible signs will have a p-value between 0 and 1. And because they are limits in practice, they will vary with the in situ specifics of any em-

pirical case. The abiding fruitfulness of EM has been its ability –
with some exceptions – to locate, with analytic precision, only one
(set of) these limits: the set produced by linear-singular methods,
those *designed* to make definite sense. My question (which I am
calling 'critical,' since it insists on the possibility of routine differences and contestivities in the domain of community-historical
meanings) is, What does an investigation look like if it accepts the
task of delineating *both* sets of limits instead of just one? That is, to
extend the metaphor, unlike the physical universe, which most
physicists hold always tends in one direction (towards maximum
entropy), the semiotic universe has no one tendency. There is no
equivalent of the second law of thermodynamics in the semiotic
universe.

A criticism of EM would be that it, for the most part anyway,
conceives of the semiotic universe (society) as always tending towards low indexical potential despite its practical unachievabil-
ity;[19] and a critique of CT would be that it works the other way,
imagining that most signs tend towards dispersion despite the attempts of, for example, philosophers and logicians to contain
them.[20] Hence, for all the insistence on difference in CT (in fact, because of it), it is just as singularizing as EM. On the physical metaphor, CT holds to a kind of semiotic equivalent of the second law
(all signs can mean by virtue of their tendency to high entropy).
The effective semiotics I am proposing would hold that move-
ments *towards* the equivalent of the second law *and* towards its
opposite are empirical community matters and cannot be deemed
in advance theoretically or as 'natural tendencies.' This is another
way of putting Schutz's dictum: that the 'data' of the social sciences are always of the second order for, unlike the data of the natural sciences, they are always already 'interpreted' in advance by
the communities under investigation.[21]

Even within particular communities (or subregions of the semiotic universe), there will be occasions when high-entropic sign-
paths will occur and others when low-entropic sign-paths occur,
even though there may be community 'tendencies' – such that, for
example, we would expect a community of Platonists, by and
large, to favor low-entropic paths (minimizing difference and
maximizing identity) and a community of relativists to favor high-
entropic paths (maximizing difference and minimizing identity).[22]

In this case EM and CT would themselves be respective examples of such communities.

Practical limits along the linear-singular axis (towards po) will take the form of such things as, 'enough is enough for all practical purposes.' The question here for members, as it were, is how to keep the path relatively singular and linear; how to prevent it, at any point, from breaking up into an array of multiple meanings; and how far the path should be extended in the direction it is traveling (in the extreme case, 'as far as possible' or 'until we get to the truth'). Practical limits in the other direction (towards pι) will take the form of 'how to say more and different.' The parallel question here, again for community members, is how to proliferate lines of the path, how to invent new ones, and how to extend currently existing ones as far as possible (again in the extreme case, 'as far as possible' or 'until truth cannot possibly be an issue for us'). Although these can be called different *forms* of socio-logics, they could also be referred to, in their specificity, as textual technologies or reading-writing technologies. But it is clear that the indexical potential of signs (in principle) can, if we allow it to have (roughly) 'closing' or 'opening' directionalities,[23] lead to a whole array of socio-logical problems and their solutions (in practice). It is in this sense that the concept of indexicality may be of use to effective semiotics. For if we assume that indexical potential can 'go either way,' we may be able to identify methodic actions of (again, roughly) 'opening' and 'closing' that potential. One classic study here is that of Latour.[24] As he has shown in the case of scientific communities, some 'closing' methods can solve, or at least (since extremes are unattainable) guard against, the problem of having a particular sign 'misused' or 'misinterpreted' by another community (perhaps a rival) or by 'revisionists' within one's own.[25]

If in everyday practice a sign's (in-principle) indexicality can be made practically 'definite' (EM) or practically 'indeterminate' (CT) – to invoke a cumbersome shorthand – then an analysis that empirically investigated this *overall horizon* of possibility would, in the sense intended here, be critical. It would be a critical semiotics, perhaps, for it would leave open the possibility that not all social-discursive practice actually *achieves* social order (let alone 'consensus'), but that some instances have such things as disorder, conflict, contradiction, struggle, and antagonism not merely as actional achievements but *as part of their taken-for-granted background and foundation*; that is, in terms of the reading-writing technologies (language games) they routinely occur in and as.

How is would relate to questions of 'politics' in the broader sense is an as yet open research question and one not easily answered at present. But I shall speculate that one could arrive at a critical definition of 'the political' where that term meant no more and no less than the traditions that come, historically, to inhabit a form of life or community, as that community's routine ways of dealing with the practical limits of signs' indexical potentials.[26] In this sense the question of where and how to limit a sign's potential might be a socio-logical problem – moving the analyst already to the level of actionability (R2). Such limits (the limits of commentary) may even be in contention from community to community, and the resultant 'border disputes' appear to be marked by the principle Lyotard calls the *différend* – a principle to be discussed in chapter 13. For now we could speculate that the expression 'ethnopolitics' might be appropriate to such cases, since it acts as a kind of mnemonic, continually referring the analyst to the location of politics in (and as) *situated practices*.

So, in terms of a practical ethnopolitical analysis, we might begin to ask how it is that communities of sign-users could actually 'work' a text's indexical particulars *towards* point p1; that is, expand its potential towards semiosic indefiniteness. Are there communities – pace ethnomethodology – that actually do this, that *require* the signs they find in their everyday lives to be 'opened up' to multiple meanings or uses? I shall pursue this in the next chapter, where I look at a cinephilic reading of a song-and-dance sequence from a well-known musical film, *Singin' in the Rain*.

10. Signing in the Rain

As an example of an actual site where indexical expressions are left open and indeterminate as part of a specific textual design, and as part of the practical accomplishment of a community's basic understanding of its representational materials, let's look at how a particular community, musical comedy fans, 'reads' popular Hollywood films.[1] I will focus on one such fan's detailed reading: Alain Masson's account of the 1951 film *Singin' in the Rain*.[2]

Masson deals with the song-and-dance routine around 'Good Mornin',' which is set in the Hollywood villa of Don Lockwood (Gene Kelly). He shows how the villa is filmed in such a way as to turn it into a completely impossible and unrealizable architectural space. At the same time, this utter indeterminacy *of space* is not a problem for him or for any musical comedy enthusiast, because 'fan' readings expect and require that in such films precedence will be given to dancing and human movement generally, so that logical spatial relations take a backseat. The set, in such cases, should become an *ideal* dance floor, even to the point of overlooking and subverting the everyday, commonsense assumption that actual interior spaces should be both spatially consistent and stable in design. The filmic dance floor both multiplies the theatrical space (by adding levels) and transgresses it by adding and subtracting 'logical' spaces in the service of an almost complete freedom of movement. If a wall or an alcove that is clearly shown in one shot happens to get in the way of the choreographic requirements of the next shot, it is simply removed, or else turned into a doorway leading to another, previously nonexistent room. In this way a continuous viewing of the film will not allow the viewer to 'reconstruct' the exact dimensions and design of the building in which it takes place. More than this, though, it will not allow the reconstruction of any physically possible space whatever. For example:

The camera enters the villa through a window, thus proclaiming the wall's penetrability. But why enter this way? In fact, where is the door? Apparently, nothing could be simpler: for at the end of the hallway, behind Kathy Selden (Debbie Reynolds), one can make out a double door. The only problem is that when the actors cross the few stairs between the dining room and this room, we certainly recognise the hallway but, where the door previously was, there is now a lot of room to dance, between these stairs and the magnificent chest, which was barely visible behind Kathy. The double door is nowhere in sight. Where we expected a way out, there is now the outline of a kind of alcove. But it hardly seems to matter. The three accomplices go down a few steps and we see them in the lower entrance hall. There's no door here either. Where there should be one, to the left of the bar, in front of the staircase, there is now a further extension: the small lounge room.[3]

In this sense, architectural spaces can open and close 'at will' – that is, according to the logic of choreography rather than geometry – to allow the passage of the dance and the dancers.

Here are some further examples. At one point the characters go into the kitchen, and the camera follows them until they end up next to a window recess. Then the camera moves to a point inside the kitchen to 'receive' them: but now they are shown in a different position, next to the refrigerator. At another point, the dancers ought to pass through a space that has previously been established as a doorway, but in order for the camera to follow them, its platform must take the place of the doorjamb so that the 'logical' set is cut through by the camera itself. Later the camera moves continuously and unhindered through the hallway, showing it as a completely open and uncluttered space. But a few seconds afterwards this same space is occupied by a hat stand that Masson describes as resembling a candelabra. Its sudden and unexpected appearance on the scene is far from being an error in continuity. In fact the characters themselves seem bewildered by it – they seem drawn to it and point it out explicitly. Masson is led to the conclusion that 'the space is transparent, the filmic area unlimited.'[4]

If we add to this that from time to time it is necessary for the film to switch around the spatial relations between objects (for example, exchanging a parallel arrangement for a perpendicular one or else making space for a stool to be used in a dance routine where no such space, let alone the stool, previously existed), and if we also consider that the shapes of major internal items (particularly stairways) can change according to the number of musical beats or choreographed steps required – and more remarkably, that solid walls from where the camera-viewer ostensibly films or watches can simply give way into an extra proscenium, effectively breaking the boundaries of the screen itself – then it's clear that no routine application of the documentary method of interpretation and no prospective-retrospective sense-making procedure is going to work here, even for such simple and factual matters as getting a sense of the layout of the building.[5] 'The rooms' distribution lacks logic and makes it difficult to conceive of any relationship with the outside world. From room to room, the house seems to be forever growing.'[6] What is important about this example is, I think, the following.

Indexical particulars (shots) can clearly be exploited as much 'for' their indeterminacy as 'against' it. Indeterminacy of this kind is not a problem for members of certain communities (in this case musical comedy enthusiasts). Though it may defeat commonsense background assumptions just as much as any ethnomethodological 'breach study,' it needs no 'repair' and leads to *anything but* disjunctive or anomic relations between the text and its viewers. This is *clearly* a question of the form of life or community in which the text routinely occurs, and not a property of anything that could be called 'the text itself.' In a courtroom, for example, and by way of contrast, such 'reality disjunctures' would have to be re-solved or reduced to questions of determinate versions of time and place with logically possible and empirically specific coordinates.[7] On the contrary, the spatial and architectural indeterminacy in *Singin' in the Rain* (for song-and-dance fans) is an *expectable* part of the *mise-en-scène* in musical comedies. Its *absence* would cause problems, not of logic but more of magic and, at least, of taste. That is, for Masson-as-fan, physically possible and logically con-sistent (let alone actual or 'naturalistic') interior structures would only lead to highly uninteresting (unviewable) dance routines and to a 'feeling' of being inside 'a stable with its row of stalls.'[8]

Without the opening up of the indexical potential of the camera shot, the genre of the musical comedy would be without what is for its fans an essential ingredient: what Masson calls the 'intimist' dance routine.[9] The term is significant, for the idea of intimism is borrowed from painting, where it refers to works that are carried out *devant l'objet* (in the actual presence of the object) and impart a 'mundane,' 'intimate' and 'immediate' or even 'life as usual' character to their object. In this sense ordinary members of particular communities can be said to have routine expectations of quite massive indeterminacies when it comes to particular *forms* of 'life as usual.'

Accordingly we have – via Masson's exceptionally detailed insights into how enthusiasts like him view musical comedies – not been able to investigate a series of signs (camera shots) at anything other than the level of their intelligibility (R1). The level of *sociological* problems (R2) has not been broached. As I have said, these transgressions of logic are specifically *not* a problem for this particular community. A musical comedy *without* such devices might, by contrast, throw up certain problems for the community – though this would always be speculation in the absence of a complex empirical inspection. In this sense, investigations of indexicality will not *necessarily* provide us with semiotic insights at the levels of actionability (R2) and community-historical meaning (R3). But it is clear by now that different communities act in distinct ways, even with regard to the basic intelligibility (R1) of signs. (For example, we could imagine topographers or topologists treating the spaces used in *Singin' in the Rain* in a very different way.)

The importance of these considerations – ethnomethodological theory notwithstanding – is that they lead us towards a discursive characterization of the concept of a community we have previously characterized only in terms of 'locale.' In fact, it could be said that a community is (at least among other things) an ensemble of methods where at least one possible way of characterizing those methods would be to ask how they act with regard to 'opening' or 'closing' the indexical potential of the signs they work on *and as* (for methods are a productional constituent of signs rather than separate from them). The signs, one wants to say, are what they *are* – for a community – by virtue of, among other things, how it produces them as indexical 'openings' and 'closings.' More important still, perhaps, we have seen that these specific kinds of method are tightly imbricated with a community's identity. Thus, for example, to read a scenic 'impossibility' in *Singin' in the Rain* as a 'continuity error' would be to mark oneself as clearly being an outsider. 'We,' in any given case, might be directly understood as, for example, 'those who read so as to proliferate and appreciate the indeterminacy of architectural spaces in musical comedies,' 'those who require a specific set of mathematical symbols to have a definite and restricted domain of applicability' (see chapter 12), and so on.

But does what we might call the 'polyvalency' of signs – their 'working' or 'effecting' towards multiple meanings – always remain at such extremes? The cases of communities that work the opposite way, towards delimiting semiosic 'uptakes' of the signs in their domain, are legion, particularly in religious and scientific circles. (Think here of the precise value of certain physical constants, or the charges of blasphemy to be brought against those, like Salman Rushdie, who 'invade' the sacredness of religious signs.) But along this imaginable array that extends from 'open' to 'closed' forms of intelligibility (R1), are there any 'medial' cases? Such cases would be communities that would go 'so far and no further' in opening up their semiosic activities to polyvalency. If these communities exist, an effective semiotics would want to know the methods by which they achieve such practical limits between open-endedness and semiosic closure. It would want to know, in terms of actionability (R2), the details of the socio-logical problems involved in finding such points of closure and solutions used to effect them. One possible community of this kind is a group of fans of the comic (or comic book) *Batman*. In the next chapter I shall look at how these fans *limit* the semiosic potential of the words and graphics they read.

I now want to examine a case of another community – readers of *Batman* comics – who, like musical comedy fans, frequently look for and expect semiotic multiplicities in comics texts. However, in this case my question will be, Where, in a practical sense, does this polyvalency come to an end? For after a historical investigation of how these multiple possibilities have emerged, we will see that there are limits to the 'openness' of such readings; there are points where *Batman* followers can go so far (in terms of semiosic indeterminacy) and no further. This does not mean they could not (physically, cognitively, and so on) read 'beyond' such points, only that were they to do so, their community membership would shift. The point here is to see that what a community *is* is highly imbricated in the methods it has available for making texts intelligible.

Turning to a slightly different comic genre, William Gibson writes in the introduction to the 'graphic novel' version of his cyberpunk novel *Neuromancer*:

> Translation is a peculiar business, particularly for monoglot novelists who find themselves in print in languages they know they'll never learn to read. . . . The edition in front of you is something else: it's been translated into a language I can read, one I've known for a long time. Walt Kelly taught me to read. I was having trouble, in school, with reading; my mother, for some reason, decided the thing to do was to read to me from *I Go Pogo*. It worked. Soon I was reading myself to sleep with Albert and Pogo, unaware that I was simultaneously absorbing mega-doses of Mr Kelly's gently savage political satire. It probably had something to do with the pictures.[1]

Gibson's idea of the comic as a 'translation' is a very interesting metaphor, since it assumes there is a (visual-verbal) *language* of comics into which, for example, a text originally composed in another language can be shifted. It suggests a specific community that writes and reads this language – yet one for whom any description of that community would be relatively 'transparent' to it.[2] That is, the very general community of comics readers is open to anyone with eyesight, a dollar, and a local newsagent (or various substitutes for these). Unlike some other communities (football players, for example) it does not make interactive contact with other members obligatory – though it does *provide* for interaction via readers' pages, comics conventions, fanzine exchanges, and so forth. The comics-reading community is, for itself and to itself, nontopographic and noncoeval, to repeat Fabian's terms.[3] To this extent, in certain circumstances, it could allow any member a relatively unconstrained range of possible readings – readings that need not be 'checked' against any community consensus. However, when readers *do* engage in exchanges of this kind, more concrete community competences may form in order to check, extend, or even constrain the range of possible readings. Such membership-repair and gatekeeping functions make reading technologies a matter of public record.[4] So although not just any reading of a particular comic will count as competent within a community of comics readers, the range of methodic activities for the production and consumption of readable text within that community can be massively 'open' or indeterminate.

It is possible to identify, in certain New Wave comics, a definite recipient design towards this indeterminacy – starting with the 'underground' comics of the 1970s – many of which have now been bought by the big comics stables, particularly Marvel.[5] A case in point is *Groo: The Wanderer*, where narratorial voices and narrator-characters (as well as the writers in 'Groo-grams,' the almost obligatory letters page) practically compete to be more *un*certain than each other as to what may or may not be happening within the nonstandardly arranged frames, and also within the community of readers itself. Thus, from 'Groo-grams':

> A few months ago I was captured by a small group of Iranian terrorists, and forced to write a letter to Groo (God bless him). In it I praised Groo (may he rest in Peace), saying really odd things like 'Make me Groo.' I actually think it was a quite humorous letter. This is why I knew it would not see print. I don't believe a funny letter has ever appeared in Groo (as a matter of fact, nothing funny has). Now that I have been released, I can write of my

own free will, and correct the wrongs of the Iranians. (Make me Groo.) Groo is not funny, he is stupid. He doesn't wear pants. Do you find a cat on Groo's head, on the cover of issue #20 funny? I don't. Mulch is stupid too. Note I asked my brother to write this for me (that's me), so he'll probably stick parentheses all over the place, in places they should not be (make me Groo). So until my brother actually writes a real letter to Groo (may he rest in peace), instead of putting little messages all through this Groo letter (make me Groo). Hasta Luego.

Joel Pierce

N.K., Rhode Island

P.S. Please print this letter twice[6]

The letter *is* printed twice. The limits, in *Groo*, are paradoxically thus: for readers, everything is allowed except a literal reading.[7]

Clearly, then, some comics forms can involve a textual and disseminatory economy that at one extreme can be highly *laissez-faire*. Subversive readings abound, are encouraged, are even required. Thus for cultural theorist Tony Bennett, 'Batman 1989 was, above all, a self-consciously double-leveled Batman calling for a similarly double-leveled reading response.'[8] But this polymorphous hermeneutic can, if extended into a general principle, be quite problematic. A case in point would be the developments in the *Batman* texts of the late 1980s and early 1990s, developments that are perhaps more subtle and convoluted than Bennett's term 'double-leveled' can adequately capture.

Batman changed a good deal during the 1980s – some readers even date the point of change to the early 1970s.[9] It barely resembles the simplistic mock warfare between the outrageously wooden Batman-and-Robin (on the side of good) and a variety of comic crims (Catwoman, Riddler, Joker, and so on) that was so successfully satirized in the 1966 *Batman* television series (with Adam West and Burt Ward), complete with 'Holy this' and 'Holy that' from Robin and plenty of ZAPs and POWs. In a move that influenced, and was later influenced *by*, the 1989 *Batman* movie,[10] the Batman character ceased to be the Caped Crusader and became the Dark Knight. Eventually this diversified into a number of forms. Among these are the three perennials: the traditional *Detective Comics* series (but now allowing a slightly weirder set of possibilities to prevail); a highly adult spooker called *Legends of the Dark Knight*; and the 'standard format' *Batman* comics themselves.[11]

There exist massive intrageneric differences between these various formats – itself an instance of semiosic dispersal. This difference and dispersal suggests distinct readership trajectories, both within (some) formats and between them. Here it should be remembered that comic books can be historically traced to the daily newspaper comic strips; that they were initially aimed at adult audiences; that the heyday of comics was during and after the Second World War, with comics designed for the 'sex and heroics' market of troops on active service, who took easily to the portable, disposal, and quickly consumed comics art form; that it was only in the 1950s that comics came to be thought of as a kids' product (largely under the direct influence and intervention of social psychology and its interest in 'juvenile delinquency'), so that, since the seventies, it has been an uphill battle for comics writers and publishers to reestablish the 'original' adult market. In this sense the use of the epithet 'kidult' is appropriate to comics only as one (perhaps minor) possibility among many.

DC Comics, for example, used to include (inside the front covers) a catalog titled 'DC List This Week,' with each publication followed by a code showing its 'quality' and its 'audience.' The legend to the list included the following types: 'Standard Format,' 'New Format,' 'Deluxe Format,' 'Available at Select Outlets,' 'Prestige Format,' 'Graphic Novel,' 'Collected Edition,' and 'Suggested for Mature Readers.'[12]

In the process of this shift in markets and genre alteration, Batman worked alone, without Robin, for quite a few issues – Dick Grayson having graduated to superhero status in his own right as Nightwing and Jason Todd having been savagely murdered by the Joker – though throughout 1990 each issue worked through a long process of grooming an indecisive Tim Drake for Robinhood.[13] This move towards the lone individual brought with it a new brooding and existentially self-doubting Batman: a 'new man' unsure of his position in the world, reflecting on his own possible cowardice in hiding behind a mask, considering his closeness to the underworld, even coming to think from time to time that he is responsible for the very existence of certain criminals by being the paradigmatic agent of law enforcement and thus constituting a space of opposition, a challenge to the one who would be the equal and opposite ultimate criminal. Accordingly, the graphics have changed from the earlier schematic comic book heroics and towards a graphically 'realist' representation of 'unreal' gothic horror. The paradigm is less the detective and more the Dostoyevskian existential protagonist, contemplating good and evil as abstract concepts.[14] At the same time, the official cultural 'level' of the stories has been upgraded from a situation in which practically no intertextual references were required to one practically teeming with external points of contact – literary, cultural, and political.[15]

But for all this latitude, there's a bottom line, a point where the reinterpretation closes off, a limit beyond which any reader who is to remain competent is effectively reduced to a single line of interpretive choice. We can see a critical example of this by looking at the interpretability of the relations between the figure of Batman and his adversaries. Here it's important to remember that there's always a set of possible confusions and reidentifications: *Batman* today rarely involves a mapping of hero and villain onto a black-and-white morality. From the start *Batman's* originator, Bob Kane, deliberately cast his hero in the *form* of a villain (from the 1926 movie *The Bat*). But how far can this go? Is there a point at which Batman simply does have to be read as 'the good' in the face of an utterly unequivocal villain?

Almost all the new Batman adversaries are seen to have morally positive characteristics, and this is also true of the revamps. The Riddler is now highly intelligent, if psychopathic; the Joker is subtly witty, even though his jokes bear a strong relation to his bizarre unconscious, and so on. To this extent they exist as colorful (if repulsive) constituents of an imaginary American society. But the rarely seen adversaries of America *itself* have no positive features. In this sense, the bottom line in interpreting *Batman* comes when its version of American self-identity is threatened. The reader, whoever he or she may be in any other sense, is always and without fail 'interpellated' as an imaginary American – if only for the duration of the reading.[16] But in an important sense, that *américainité* – since it is supposed to be distributed across the whole social body of at least one nation – can get its self-understanding only from the outside, from another imaginary that is specifically *not* American.

Hence a totally deheroicized other has to emerge, diegetically, from time to time, one with all the marks of the alien, the outside. Perhaps since Gorbachev, America (and even more so *Batman's* America) has had a cultural crisis in this respect: no clear, legitimate, and strongly marked other *from* which American self-identity can emerge. In its place are only a string of smaller others, a loose thread for that identity to hang on to: South Africa for a while (*Lethal Weapon II*), Japanese trading markets (*Punisher* comic), Saddam Hussein for another few months (*Fires of Kuwait*), and so on.

A three-part serial in March, April, and May 1990 (*Batman* nos. 445–47), 'When the Earth Dies,' took the unusual (but precedented) step of removing Batman from Gotham City and from America altogether.[17] This is unusual in the sense that Batman lore in the early 1990s attempted to establish the hero as an extension of the city.[18] In the 'Dark Knight/Dark City' sequence (nos. 451–54) particularly, Batman's brooding and doubtful interior was directly and explicitly mapped onto Gotham's own deep and murky history. Indeed, and perhaps to mark the continuity of theme, 'When the Earth Dies' opens with Batman – back in Gotham – fighting the Slasher, a serial killer who uses power tools to carve up his victims:[19]

> [Batman] *knows* this city. He knows every street, every intersection, every back alley, every sewer, every tunnel. *All* of Gotham is his city. Not just the Upper East Side Park Row brownstones, or the midtown business district, or the downtown financial areas. The Black and Spanish ghettos, the parks filled with transients, the Bowery with its addicts, they are part of his city too. And they are also his to protect. (no. 445, 1)

Hence the scene is set for connections and relations between Batman – hence Gotham, hence America – and its other, so that there's a complex set of associations, allowing multiplicities and diversities and the overlaying of 'personal' characteristics onto 'local urban' and 'national' characteristics, and vice versa. As wealthy capitalist Bruce Wayne, Batman flies to the USSR, ostensibly to aid the ailing economy by starting a branch of Wayne Enterprises there. His real but secret mission, however, is as Batman. The conceit is that any enemy of glasnost is an enemy not just of the then USSR ('Russia' throughout this pre-Yeltsin comic) but of Bush's new world order.

The enemy, in this case, has a previous connection with Batman. In an earlier sequence, 'Ten Nights of the Beast,' America had been threatened by a secret agent – the KGBeast – trying to assassinate the United States president. Naturally Batman gets to sort him out. Early on in 'When the Earth Dies,' a Soviet official explains to Commissioner Gordon that the Beast was (or has perhaps now been officially reinterpreted as) a 'renegade' (no. 445, 5). It turns out that the Beast had a protégé, the NKVDemon, whose mission is to kill the top ten men in the Gorbachev regime because of their pro-Western crimes against true Marxism (sometimes called 'Stalinism' in the comic, though the Demon mostly seems to idolize Lenin).

Again, the Demon has none of the positive characteristics of Batman's American adversaries. He's a monster of huge proportions, complete with a whole armory in his hammer-and-sickle utility belt, a red devil's mask with horns, oversized incisors, and a wicked line in overdone boy-meets-tractor Marxism. At first meeting, as they fight, he continues to talk, drooling all the while: 'The Beast trained me, American. He fed me special *steroids*, making me stronger than any man. . . . My skin was hardened, my nerves partially deadened so I cannot feel pain. I am virtually impervious to harm' (no. 445, 18). This old USSR, incarnate in one who is barely a man, because it is much *more* than a man, fights dirty. It takes steroids to give it unfair advantage in competition; it has no real human sensations; its end is to destroy America (Batman), and that end will justify any means.[20] At the same time, the Demon is shown to take a perverse pleasure in being and doing all this: '[Batman (to the Demon)]: I don't fight for the thrill of battle. And I don't fight unless there's no recourse' (no. 445, 19). However, the Demon gets away when Batman calls in Soviet police reinforcements. He gets away because, in a repetition of the issue's opening words, now applied to villain rather than hero, and to Moscow rather than Gotham, 'He *knows* this city. He knows every street, every intersection, every back alley, every . . .' In this sense the repetition puts the Demon, more squarely than any other previous adversary, in direct opposition to Batman in 'content' while sharing his structural position within an inverted America. It is to this extent that (at this point) a very narrow range of readings – perhaps even a single reading – is available. To read any aspect of the Demon positively, against the comic's recipient design, against the Batmanian semiotic, is to move beyond the community's threshold of readability. At this point the methods of reading would become excessive to the kinds of activities that are 'proper' to the community in question. Hence, according to our first level of meaning (given in chapter 6 as $S =$ def *ma*), the text would become unintelligible. The Demon marks a clear limit, not to be transgressed by any Batfan or any 'American.' It tells, by negation, clearly where and who one must be. The only alternative is not to read or – which is the same thing – to read from within another community.[21] This is not to make a schoolmasterly stipulation but to offer an empirical observation about a specific community's limits of intelligibility.

It is possible for *someone* to read the Demon's prayer before his portrait of Lenin (no. 447, 7–8) ironically, subversively, and so forth, against the comic's clear designation of it as within the genres of madness:

> Vladimir Ilyich Lenin, you shaped our world which that . . . that *man* [Gorbachev] seeks to ruin. You pointed out the *truth* which he corrupts into *lies*. You showed us the way which he seeks to *change*. I look at our world and ask if we are better today than we were, and my answer is *no*. Once we were a *happy* people, now we are depressed. Once we firmly held an *empire* in our mighty hands. Now we permit that empire to *flee* us and rush toward the decadent *West*. Now this, Vladimir, this is the new world they want to begin on your *birthday* – this world which will merge East and West. Which will force us to forsake our proud heritage. All the glory you sought for us, Vladimir, all the greatness you aspired to – all that makes us *unique* and *strong*, that *pretender* to your greatness seeks to *destroy*. I strike on *your* day, Vladimir Ilyich Lenin, I strike in your *name*. And in your name *we shall triumph*.

To read it with irony is *possible* in principle, simply because of the truism that any text can be so read, because of the underlying (in-principle) indexicality of every expression or text, and perhaps because one must, according to one's ethical position. But it is inconceivable to read it this way and keep reading or following as a bona fide *Batman* aficionado. One position likely to produce a subversive reading would be that of an 'outsider,' an expert in cultural studies, perhaps, who would then have to give up all pretensions to inside knowledge and to an emic approach to social practice (both of which are mainstays of contemporary cultural studies).[22] It could be, for example, that there is evidence outside the comics text to the effect that, in 1990, a sizable section of the then Soviet population wanted something other than traditional Marxism, Gorbachev, *or* American capitalism. But there is no space for any such alternative in any competent reading of *Batman*.

That is, the text cannot tolerate any statement beyond a certain point in the chain of 'reasonable' doubts, the chain of semiosic inference that is also the social-political range of the *Batman* language game. The game's whole understanding of the world, its taken-for-granted foundations, cannot be taken beyond this point of not-doubting.[23] It is not a paradox, in terms of this text, for Bruce Wayne to speak *literally* of 'an ordinary citizen with incredible wealth' and thus to have it assumed that, postglasnost, with successful Americanization, any Soviet citizen could be one, and (presumably, human nature being what it is) 'they'd get used to it' (no. 447, 9–10).

That this supposedly implicit limit – the point at which any intelligible reading of *Batman* must approach zero degree – was actually displayed on the surface of an issue of the comic was an important problem for a number of *Batman* readers. Making the limit so clear, not defining it by negation, not leaving its exact coordinates in suspension, marking it with such an inelastic and 'cheesy' villain; speaking and graphically displaying, perhaps, what all *Batman* fans knew but never needed to say – appears to have removed a degree of subtlety from a readership that has increasingly come to accept some indeterminacy as a principle of reading – in fact as a principle of textual *realism*:[24]

> I've just read BATMAN #446. I've always enjoyed Marv's stories [Marv Wolfman, writer], but I have a quibble. The NKVD doesn't exist anymore; it was a forerunner of the KGB (others included the Cheka, the GPU, the MVD, and the MGB) that existed as such from 1943 to 1946. I never got to read 'Ten Nights of the

Beast,' so maybe I'm missing something important about the origin of the Beast and the Demon. Still, it seems like you've fallen victim to Cheesy Villain Name Syndrome (along with Horns on the Villain's Head Syndrome). . . . Of course, mine aren't the only tastes you're catering to, but I wish you'd avoid the temptation to have these ridiculous costumed super-villains. I prefer BATMAN to DETECTIVE partly for its greater realism, and the generally close correspondence between Bruce Wayne's world and ours. . . .

Michael Boydston
Austin, TX.
(no 451, 24)

Interestingly enough, the producers of *Batman* are being taken to task here for allowing the principles of (or the limits of) intelligibility to be made explicit. Boydston situates his complaint in terms of a community history as it relates to 'actual' history. He expects there to be a nexus between the two (even if he has missed one of these crucial links). But not only have the 'events' of both histories been transgressed, so has the history of expectable forms of reading within the community. To show the limits graphically is to transgress a tenet of realism: it turns the characters (or at least the villain) into stereotypes. It makes them wooden and uncomplicated, against the assumption that 'Bruce Wayne's world and ours' should be related, practically the same, complex: worlds in which, precisely, one does not so much *encounter* the limits as live and read by them. The solution to the problem of explicitness is an insistence, finally, on 'realism': this is where interpretations come to an end for Boydston and many other letter writers. And 'realism,' by this definition, is something that is to be shown but not said, something on which representations should be built but that should never be explicited as such. Its explicitation is its transgression. The producers have, then, produced a text that is a problem for its readers, and its solution is an insistence on the tried-and-trusted historical forms of sense making 'proper' to *Batman* writers and readers.

'Realism' for the Batfan means the representation of everyday relativities, complexities, and paradoxes. In this way we can begin to see that neither 'realist' nor 'relativist' theories of meaning could hold universally, for all cases. In fact the terms 'realism' and 'relativism' are overgeneralized and theoreticist glosses for specific community methods and activities. In some communities we can discern tendencies towards semiosic relativism in the form of established community methods for *maximizing* the indexical potential of its 'proper' texts. In others we can discern realist tendencies in the form of equally established methods for *minimizing* that potential. But it is also possible, as we have just seen, that even relativist methods have 'realist' limit points – points where the continued expansion of intelligibility must come to a close. Too much explicitation of the principles of intelligibility generates obviousness, to which a return to 'realism' becomes a solution.

In the next investigation, I will examine a highly 'realist' community: mathematical physics. What is important in this case is that we can see how 'realism' – as, ultimately, in the case of Batfans – is less a basis for a general semantics than a particular community's defense strategy; how it is a set of means by which the community guards against its 'proper' signs being reinterpreted either from within or from elsewhere. Science and mathematics (along with a range of other communities) have a problem that arises from a paradox: they are expected to be 'open,' to be 'publicly accountable.' Their findings, according to many versions of what constitutes scientific method, have to be published in order to 'count' as genuine findings. This is one 'test' of their durability. At the same time, *public*ation offers a space of semiosic vulnerability. It makes science's proper signs available to whomever might wish to read them. One solution to this problem is 'rigorous definition': ensuring that scientific constants and values will be either quantitatively (empirically) or logically (theoretically) fixed in a variety of ways. So while, for example, humanities disciplines may 'borrow' terms such as 'entropy,' 'chaos,' 'equilibrium,' and 'force,' in doing so they can be shown to have transgressed the 'proper' scientific meanings of these terms by analogically shifting them out of their quantitative definitions or their logical positionings within a range of other scientific concepts. Realism, therefore, can constitute a bulwark against these types of invasion; it can become a kind of theft detector by marking the sign with a *further* sign of propriety. How does this work in practice?

12. Gatekeeping Logic

In his important ethnographic study of science in action, Bruno Latour has shown that scientists often have an interest in severely narrowing the indexical potential of signs within their own (scientific) domains.[1] That is, they can be seen to act in ways that prevent 'aberrant' uses of key pieces of terminology, formulas, constants, technical devices, forms of argument, and so on. If Latour is right, we could expect such 'gatekeeping' tactics to be at their most vigilant at those points where scientific communities come into contact with other communities. A particularly 'high risk' area would be popular science texts, where writers cannot control who it might be that comes to read, interpret, and, potentially, appropriate scientific signs. In this investigation I shall look at one such strategy of control as it operates in a popular account of mathematics and physics.

The mathematical physicist Roger Penrose has had great success with his popular work *The Emperor's New Mind*. There he makes strong claims against the idea that machines can be intelligent in the sense that humans are. By way of argument, he presents a very wide ranging discussion of events and discoveries in contemporary mathematics and physics and goes on to show that mind-machine analogies arise out of mistakes within and abuses of scientific ideas. It's quite clear from his writing that physics (and in particular the manipulation of mathematical-physical symbols) is not for just anyone. But this provides him with a problem on the other side: for he is precisely, in (and as) the very book that sustains his argument for scientific exclusivity, trying to make technical and professional details accessible to any reader. How can he be sure that bizarre varieties of physics will not ensue? How can he be sure that his part simplifications won't lead to 'ethnophysicses' springing up among the 'laity'?

One way he does this is to invoke a variety of logicomathematical realism: he argues that physical-mathematical utterances are not valid unless the one who utters them can show that they somehow map onto really existing equivalents in nature. Expressions that fall short of this criterion (which is presumably what non-professional instances would do) ought to be rejected. But there is no precise way this argument can be sustained without a certain kind of tautology arising. How could one *show* that there exists a 'real' pi to which a very, very long and complicated number corresponds? Somehow the number itself (or the best approximation of it yet calculated) has always to be, itself, the proxy for this real pi. Somehow it is the number's elegance that guarantees its attachment to what is *presumed* to be 'real.' But at the same time, only 'insiders' (mathematicians) can make judgments about what is elegant.

Hence, what starts off as a heuristic for getting mathematics done (a heuristic of the form 'let's imagine that mathematical expressions map directly onto nature') is transferred into an object of an entirely different epistemic status. It becomes a philosophical principle. And in fact, when it comes – textually – to arguing for mathematical Platonism, all Penrose can do is to make a stipulation (where in an ideal world he would be able to offer a proof). For example, writing about the real number system, Penrose asks:

> Why is there so much confidence in these numbers for the accurate description of physics, when our initial experience of the relevance of such numbers lies in a comparatively limited range? This confidence – perhaps misplaced – must rest (although this fact is not often recognized) on the logical elegance, consistency, and mathematical power of the real number system, together with a belief in the profound mathematical harmony of Nature.[2]

Having raised the possibility of an empiricist approach to number systems (that they should go as far and only as far as our experience, so that numbers like 10^{100} would be 'too big' to use), Penrose dumps it straightaway as a principle of faith. Naturally, if you believe that 'nature' has a 'profound mathematical harmony' (a phrase that is merely added to the idea of 'logical elegance' but is made, linguistically, to look as though it were entailed by it), then there is nothing else for it. There is no other argument to be entertained.

This is precisely the battle of faith that Penrose raises with Brouwer and other mathematical 'intuitionists' who believe that mathematics is no more than a social practice involving community-based rules for the manipulation of symbols. But note that he achieves this through stipulation rather than argument: 'Can [mathematical *objects*] be other than mere arbitrary constructions of the human mind? At the same time *there often appears to be* some profound reality about these mathematical *concepts*, going quite beyond the mental deliberations of any *particular* mathematician.'[3] Note the slippage between concepts and objects, as though statements about the one could be identical with those about the other – thus accomplishing their identity by attributing identical predicates to each. Note too that the main weight of Penrose's claim is taken by the phrase 'there often appears to be,' for he is in the predicament of not being able to prove that 'there is.' Note further that the naturalness of mathematical objects is contrasted *not* with their particularity to a community (which is Brouwer's actual argument), but with their situation in a particular person's mind.[4] This last slippage is between a semiosociological and a psychological account of mathematics as synthetic. Quite simply, one cannot simply substitute for the other; and a rejection of one is not a rejection of the other, if only because a semiosociological version of intuitionism would not need to consider 'the mental deliberations of any particular mathematician.' Penrose persists in this form of 'disproof':

> The very system of complex numbers has a profound and time-less reality which goes quite beyond the mental construction of any *particular* mathematician. . . . Later we find many other *magical* properties that these complex numbers possess, properties that we had no inkling about at first. These properties are just *there*. They were not put there by Cardano, nor by Bombelli, nor Wallis, nor Coates, nor Euler, nor Wessel, nor Gauss . . . such *magic* was inherent in the very structure that they gradually uncovered.[5]

Strangely (or aptly) enough, the Platonic properties of numbers are referred to here as their 'magic.' Mathematical symbols map onto mathematical objects by magic! And this is crucial to Penrose's argument throughout the book. For his view of specifically *human* intelligence is that it is able to intuit this magic, to see its beauty, to be driven by it, since it preexists all human action and thought. Human intelligence, to take this somewhat further, is aesthetic:

> The true mathematical discoveries *would*, in a general way, be regarded as greater achievements or aspirations than would the 'mere' inventions. Such categorizations are not entirely dissimilar from those that one *might* use in the arts. . . . Great works of art *are* indeed 'closer to God' than are lesser ones. It is a feeling not uncommon among artists, that in their greatest works they are revealing *eternal truths* which have a kind of prior *etherial existence*, while their lesser works *might* be more arbitrary, of the nature of mere mortal constructions.[6]

And this is precisely why machines cannot model human intelligence. Machines can only perform functions that are calculable (in Turing's very specific sense of this term): they cannot feel the sublimity of what they produce by such calculations. Human beings can do this, Penrose argues, through the 'anthropic principle': the belief (be it noted, belief) that 'nature' itself is specially constructed so as to provide for beings like ourselves, the proper interpreters of natural (hence mathematical) principles.

Penrose goes on to argue that the main bastions of insight into the mapping of mathematical expressions onto (hypothetical) natural objects are the two principles of logic: the law of the excluded middle and the law of contradiction. What he omits is an equally important *methodological* principle of logic: that nothing should be defined in terms of itself. In fact he has completely ignored this principle in his argument for (or statement of faith in) Platonism. If we now take this principle (call it the principle of external definability), we can see that it throws a spanner into the works of Penrose's argument.

The proposition Penrose wants to show to be true – let us call it proposition Q – is that mathematical truth is absolute. More formally, proposition Q would state: 'For all mathematically true statements, we have absolutely true statements.' As I mentioned above, he cites two axioms that support this proposition – the law of the excluded middle and the law of contradiction. Let us call these E and C. E states that 'a proposition is *either* true or false,' while C states that 'a proposition cannot be *both* true and false.' So it is now propositional *truth* that will go proxy for 'naturalness' or 'reality.' By satisfying E and C, that is, a consequently true mathematical statement will be considered Platonically real.

So, to put Penrose's position simply, Q (the absoluteness of mathematical truth) depends on E and C. If they are true, then Q is true. But there is a circularity to this, since mathematical truth is itself defined by this very same argument. Or to put this another way, mathematical truth exists only in a world where E and C hold, and where they entail Q (the absoluteness of mathematical truth). So we can see that this definition of mathematical truth *contains itself*: it contravenes the principle of external definability ('anything to be defined, say *x*, must be defined by a proposition which does not contain it, *x*').

Hence the absoluteness of mathematical truth can be stated only tautologically. If we believe it, it must be true: if we don't, it can't be. A further complication is this: as a logical argument, Penrose's position on mathematical truth seems to *require* the principle of external definability, yet it also seems to contradict it.[7] That principle seems to be *both* true and false at the same time. And if we remember back to the very beginning of Penrose's argument, we will see that this contradicts his own absolutely crucial axiom, C: 'A proposition cannot be *both* true and false.' And if that proposition doesn't hold, then the whole house of cards called 'absolute mathematical truth' looks very shaky indeed. It's clear then: either you believe Platonism or you don't; but you can't ground it on the standard logical canons. The social rather than logical paradox is that it's perfectly all right for *anti*-Platonists to live with contradictions of this kind, but not for Platonists of Penrose's ilk.

These peculiar grounds are those on which Penrose tries to deny a Brouwerian version of mathematics (the view that mathematics is cultural invention). But why does he *want* to deny it? Perhaps because that view would mean that whoever wanted mathematics, for whatever purpose, could have it and use it freely without the restrictions of professional control. The control comes precisely from the enlistment of Aristotelian principles for symbolic manipulation by a Platonic faith in absolutes. A curious philosophical mix. And these principles are in essence ones that guarantee a closely binaristic version of the world. In this version of logic, propositions are either true or false: there is no available space between the binary alternatives, and there is no possibility of combining truth and falsity in the same proposition. Commonsense logics of various kinds cannot operate: for example, the commonly held view that statements may contain 'a grain of truth' or that views and opinions can be true on some occasions but not on others. Mathematics is not allowed to slip into any domain of this kind. It is at once a strict binaristic formalism *and* a key to the 'magic' of 'nature's' own structure. The world is Platonically real for Penrose, and the essence of its reality is a binary logic. We are invited to share this – and thus to do mathematics on what appear to be narrowly professional terms – or to relinquish any desire to manipulate mathematical symbols. The signs are kept highly narrow and strictly within a specific community.

As with mathematics so with formal semantics, where a similar problem exists. Formal semantics treats natural language as though it were a calculus – a set of symbols to be manipulated according to a fixed set of rules. But at the same time it *believes* those rules are the key to the truth-functionality of sentences or propositions. Sheer calculability (a formal procedure) and truth (an onto-epistemological judgment) are conflated. Formal semantics makes the mistake of looking for the truth of descriptions as a formal property of their relation to the world.

If the argument from calculability to truth can be sustained in mathematics only by statements of faith, then this must be the case a fortiori in natural language studies. Accordingly, effective semiotics would want to take a more Brouwerian approach. This would mean that instead of analyzing descriptions in terms of their (natural) truthfulness, effective semiotics would be more interested in their (social, historical) plausibility. Let us take an example – another instance of graffiti:

The Beatles were: a great man, his side-kick and two props!

The truth of this description is eternally contestable: no amount of formal analysis (logical or semantic) will take us to a point where the linguistic matter maps onto a true (or indeed false) state of affairs. But at the same time, for any community with even the most meager knowledge of the Beatles, the description is a plausible one.

How do we know this? In terms of the semiotic model developed so far, we can say that the description sets up a problem: Which

Beatle is which? And anyone who knows the Beatles can see quite simply, at a glance, which is which. They find the solution right away, *even if they disagree with the truth of what it asserts.* The most ardent fan of Paul McCartney will still know that it is not he who is intended by the description 'a great man.'

Finding a puzzle solution in this way can establish the plausibility of an utterance for its reader. As with the sexual graffiti analyzed in chapter 7, displaying the solution displays one's competence. That is, it's just as *competent* to respond with 'That's a bit unfair to Paul' as it is to say 'Yeah, John was always the real leader.' The first response takes the initial utterance to be plausible but false; the second takes it to be both plausible and true. In this way the T/F criteria can be inverted whereas the plausibility criteria must remain constant – at least for any competent reading.

In everyday life, it's not agreement but understanding that is most basic to communication (that is, to community membership). If you don't understand, you don't get past first base and into the further space of agreement or disagreement. But this is not to say – on the contrary – that understanding, plausibility, and competence are always and necessarily part of any communicative situation. Sometimes 'first base' itself is *not* reached and – as I hope to show in the next investigation – this does not mean we have a case of 'failure to communicate,' 'distorted communication,' and so on. In fact, such situations may make it much more clear and obvious to all concerned just what it is to be social: to be a specific community member, a specific kind of social subject.

13. Converse Communities

For Penrose, numbers have meaning by virtue of their truth-functionality; his position on meaning is a Platonic realist one. Effective semiotics is able to *describe* how that theory of meaning works inside the community of mathematics in order for them to perform a kind of gatekeeping operation. But it would not be able to take on board a truth-functional theory of meaning as its 'own' theory, if only because Platonic realism is unable to provide descriptions of other communities' ethnosemiotic positionings. For example, it can find *fault* with mathematical intuitionism, but it cannot describe it in its own terms. Could effective semiotics, then, use an intuitionist position on meaning as the basis of its description of community relevances? Just now we have seen that the social-historical phenomena of plausibility, understanding, and competence may be more deeply ingrained (for any study of communication) than questions of truth and falsehood, and so intuitionism might fit well with this position. Let's explore it a bit further.

Outside mathematics, intuitionism is usually known as social constructionism. It holds that meanings arise because of various forms of community agreements or contracts. One subdivision of this position, *psychological* constructionism, would obviously be of little relevance to effective semiotics itself, precisely because it forms its idea of community out of a consensus of like minds. This is not a sufficiently materialist version of community, since it ignores the social-historical dimension of plausibility, understanding, and community competence. On the other hand, a fully social constructionism might bring us closer to a workable and pluralist position that could describe whatever community relevances we might locate empirically in texts, transcripts, photographs, and so on. But there is a further problem with such a hermeneutic theory of meaning: that it locates meaning as arising from community *consensus*. Why is this a problem? Can communication ever occur in situations that work without deep-seated forms of consensus?

Put more simply, if signs cannot be said to 'mean' by virtue of their attachment to fixed realities, if questions of absolute truth are no longer available, do we then have to be satisfied with the idea that some kind of social consensus or contract must be the 'key' to communication? Can't we go any further than this?

The traditional formulation of the hermeneutic view – that communication is always and irrevocably underpinned by consensus – is to be found in Gadamer. For Gadamer, consensus cannot be overthrown. Even when 'surface' misunderstandings occur, they are 'based' on a deeper, underlying ground of understanding. For example, if a misunderstanding is even to be recognized as such, then the participants must have at least the same recognition procedures in common. In Gadamer's own words, 'Is it not, in fact, the case that every misunderstanding presupposes a "deep common accord" [*tiefes Einverständnis*]?'[1]

In a later formulation of the problem (set up as a critique of Gadamer) Habermas argues that consensus can and often does lead to 'distortions' of communication. Yet though he is skeptical of ever being able to give precise details of the 'deep common accord,' Habermas nevertheless shares Gadamer's idea that it must exist (perhaps in some imponderable form):

> Is it not . . . the case that something like a 'supporting consensus' precedes all misunderstanding? We can agree on the answer, which is to be given in the affirmative, but not on how to define this preceding consensus.[2]

His in-principle agreement with Gadamer emerges even more strongly in the paper 'What Is Universal Pragmatics?':

> In other contexts one . . . speaks of 'general presuppositions of communication,' but I prefer to speak of general presuppositions of communicative action because I take the type of action aimed at reaching understanding to be fundamental. Thus I start from the assumption (without undertaking to demonstrate it here) that other forms of social action – for example, conflict, competition, strategic action in general – are derivative of action oriented to reaching understanding [*verständigungsorientiert*].[3]

Note that, for both Gadamer and Habermas, the assumption of foundational understandings is just that: an assumption – or rather, a stipulation of faith or (perhaps) of methodology. To this extent it is not unlike Penrose's faith in mathematical realism that I discussed in chapter 12. One simply begins this way out of a kind of conviction that this is how the world must be: that even the horrible must depend on the happy, the actual on the ideal.

In some Wittgensteinian and ethnomethodological traditions, this ideal of a deep consensus or 'common accord' is taken up in the form of an appeal to the deep-seated 'logical grammar' of everyday language. This must be shared by all participants if communications – even 'surface' conflictual communications – are to take place at all.[4] But (and this is my central argument) when communications take place between parties who are acting in those communications specifically *as* members of different and distinct communities, is it not possible that what will be contested will be *precisely* the respective 'consensuses' or grounds of each community?

In our earlier discussion of indexicality (chapter 9), we saw that the in-principle open-endedness of utterances could in practice come to be closed or at least narrowed by the communicative work of a specific community – or indeed, that some communities can work towards an opening and dispersal of indexical particulars such that ambiguity, inconclusiveness, and so on would be required and expected outcomes of 'competent' communication. In that chapter I wrote that a critical semiotics 'would leave open the possibility that not all social-discursive practice actually *achieves* social order (let alone 'consensus'), but that some instances have such things as disorder, conflict, contradiction, struggle, and antagonism not merely as actional achievements but *as part of their taken-for-granted background and foundation.*' Presumably this is going to be even more acutely the case when different community relevances are at stake. Let us look at some examples.

The following account is purely illustrative – and fictional. But I think it represents something that can happen in conversation:

> The dinner conversation quickly became a free-for-all, with everyone talking at once. At any given moment, four or five separate dialogues were going on across the table, but because people weren't necessarily talking to the person next to them, these dialogues kept intersecting with one another, causing abrupt

shifts in the pairings of the speakers, so that everyone seemed to be taking part in all the conversations at the same time, simultaneously chattering away about his or her own life and eavesdropping on everyone else as well. Add to this the frequent interruptions from the children, the comings and going of the different courses, the pouring of wine, the dropped plates, overturned glasses, and spilled condiments, the dinner began to resemble an elaborate, hastily improvised vaudeville routine.[5]

Somehow we just *know* that there are 'conversations' like this: forms of ordinary talk that don't easily square with the transcriptions to be found in conversation analysis; types of talk that work outside those subdisciplines of (linguistic) discourse analysis that insist on finding routines and methods 'behind' the apparent chaos of everyday conversation. Perhaps we should make it easy for such kinds of analysis and simply say that these are just not conversations, yet that would only make the analyst's position look completely self-definitional. But I want to try to begin to think otherwise. This *is* conversation: locally organized, situationally specific, and so on but so as to *be* disorderly, polyvocal, carnivalesque, converse, perhaps even chaotic. It may not have easily visible rules. In fact it may mean that there are parties in conflict who are out to defeat whatever rules they can find, local or general. But above all, it does have (in fact it almost radiates) pleasure.

Let's leave this, though, as pure speculation and turn to some nonfictional cases. As an initial attempt to show how membership, competence, understanding, or plausibility can be contested, let us briefly inspect some conversational materials my students and I collected, then move on to a fuller discussion of a fragment from the ethnomethodological literature.[6] The first instance is a telephone call:

1 Caller: ((Dials phone))
2 Answerer: Can I have your name please
3 Caller: Er, Jones
4 Answerer: And your telephone number
5 Caller: 335 3966
6 Answerer: 335 3566
7 Caller: No 335 3966 ((Caller can hear another phone ringing at Answerer's end))

    8 Answerer: 335 3966 I'll get right back to you to
                   confirm your order of a tape
    9 Caller: Oh, er, all right
   10 Answerer: ((Hangs up))

The caller in this case was also the student who transcribed and analyzed the tape. In her initial analysis, she speculated on the possibility that the answerer had received another incoming call at line
7 and, *for this reason*, had hung up in order to call her back later.
The student described the conversation as a peculiar one, as if the
answerer was playing some kind of weird game with her. But this is
clearly an instance of another type of event altogether. That type of
event might be called the 'dial-back precall.' It's a strategy used by
businesses that sell by phone – businesses that invite prospective
buyers to call them. Typical cases are fast-food outlets (where
meals can be ordered by phone for later delivery) and television
sales ads (for furniture, gadgets, and so on – in this instance a vid-
eotape). In such cases an initial contact phone number is given in
the advertisement. Interested parties are expected to call this number and to give their own names and a number in a brief exchange.
After this the business then calls back to ensure that the order is
genuine and not fraudulent or a hoax. Hence the dial-back precall
itself has minimal turns: ideally it simply involves the exchange of
a name and a number so that the sale itself can be transacted in an
immediately following call initiated by the business rather than the
purchaser. In fact it is so minimal that it can be (and occasionally
is) handled by a machine.

In this case it's quite clear that the caller is unaware of this genre
of call. She is expecting the sale to be transacted there and then.
She assumes that this is going to *be* the sales call. With this baseline
assumption about the event in place, the call's sequencing does indeed appear bizarre. It's almost as if the sale were being refused or
deferred in favor of another (represented by the ringing phone). It
seems to be a very peculiar way of doing business or making any
kind of money-for-goods transaction at all. However, when it is
read and understood as a dial-back precall (which is what it is for
the answerer), it makes perfectly good sense.

This is a fairly trivial example, but it does show that forms of
communication can take place (and successfully) *without* a 'deep

common accord' or agreement. In fact, in this case the deepest possible matter is in doubt: what kind of an event this *is*, 'what we are
doing here,' 'what's going on,' 'what it is am I supposed to do,' and
so on through a massive list of supposedly routine and baseline assumptions. This is a case where we have differential uptakes of indexical particulars: difference and, to some extent, conflict, but
not (yet) contestation.

In the next example, I show how a conversational participant,
far from displaying agreement where agreement is *expected*, refuses that particular uptake in order to display her sense of herself
as distinct from her interlocutor in terms of community membership.

> 1 K: *You don't have ta be – a top – brain –* as long as you've got
>   – um (.) a lo:*ve* for Christ an' you can *put* it over to the
>   kids an' they kno:*w* tha– you know that (.) .hhh *you* have
>   *got* (.) um a special love then you c'n (.) .hhh you c'n *do*
>   a:nything? (.) You know what I mean? – um (.) .hhh if you
>   lo:*ve* what you're *doing* – then you will *do* it well.
> 2 L: oh that's true – yeah

My interest in this fragment is what happens just after Karen says,
'You know what I mean?' It seems to be a 'transition relevance
place,' yet no turn exchange occurs there. According to Sacks,
Schegloff, and Jefferson, one mode of turn-transition in conversations is called the 'current-selects-next technique.'[7] At a 'transition
relevance place' (here, 'You know what I mean?'), the current
speaker selects the next by directly addressing him or her and requiring a response. Questioning (or interrogative) formats are typical ways of doing this, and current-selects-nexts may have the
name of the recipient (next speaker) tagged to them – though this
is not a feature of the present instance.

What I find interesting about this case is that the choice for
Linda (as potential next speaker) is not merely a surface-technical
one but also a deep moral one. To be heard to do an agreement
with Karen in this specific slot (and given a dispreference in conversation for disagreements) would be to align herself with a specific community membership, Christians – a community to which
Karen belongs but Linda does not. Technically she should speak at
this point, but morally she cannot, unless it is to do a disagree-

ment.[8] The moral choice, as it were, overrules the technical requirement. She waits until Karen offers a downgraded (not specifically Christian, not specifically religious) version of her proposition ('If you love what you're doing, then you will do it well') and
only then offers her acceptance or agreement.

Here we can begin to see conflicts of community relevances entering into a stretch of talk such that those different and distinct
relevances can be seen to have priority over what many analysts
have assumed to be deep-seated and relatively fixed conversational rules. A very basic assumption about the sequence-grammar
of conversation (namely, after a current-selects-next technique,
the selected person should speak) is in this case put aside lest
clearly distinct community grounds become confused.

We can see a similar phenomenon occurring in the following
transcript. Here an academic expert in popular culture ('Tony') is
being interviewed by phone, live on radio. Regular listeners to the
program know that the expert and his skeptical, more conservative interviewer ('Kenny') often engage in verbal sparring. As the
interview begins, again regular listeners will know that Kenny
ended the previous session by doubting the authenticity of Tony's
pro-feminist politics. That session ended (right on the regular
time, after several signals from Kenny that it was *time* to end) with
Tony making the sound 'Hm::::?,' marked by a clear upwardly ris-
ing contour. This in place of the usual closing procedures.[9] So as
the current session starts, we can hear this topic being taken up
again – a nice instance of a turn-pause lasting a whole week.

1 K: at twelve tuh *six* .hhh now to our *sen*sitive cultural com-
       missar who joins us each Tuesday ev'ning on Dri::ve,
       Tony, Mai?ller .hh putting at least er seven intriguing
       levels 'v meaning tuh th' mos' commonplace of or'nary
       be*hav*iour in our pop culture *slot* .hh like >f'r example<
       getting z:*apped* .hh or z:*app*ing as it is sometimes caused
       er called uh a >ref'rence o' course< to er *arcane video*
       be*hav*iour Tone >is 'at right?<
              (.)
2 T: .hh it may well be Kenny but as usual you've caught me
       totally off guard with your – *char*ming description of me,
       sensitive, when did I suddenly get this appellation

3 K: Well it w's – after you::r grov'ling 'nd er before the altar
       of post *fem*inist *fem*inism:: las' week er where you w'r
       reproving me fer not being politic'ly correct Tone s'I
       thought .hhhh obviously th– here's a man who's er .h
       chasing after >shall we say< er .hh sensitive new age
       s::*kirt.*
                (2.6)
4 T: I'd like tuh say th't Telecom's cut in here and there's some
       kinda communic( )ns breakdown=
                            [   ]
5 K: .hhh
6 K: =hahk y'k hah
            [   ]
7 T: (   ) -ing like tha' 'n we all know I'm thee –
       authentic f:eminized male 'v thee: –
       early *nine*ties
       [   ]
8 K: (hhh)   hah hah hah
                [   ]
9 T: Let's get *ser*ious

The interesting phenomenon here is the gap between turns 3 and 4.
By any standards it's a very long conversational gap, and – since it
occurs at a transition relevance place – it is clearly Tony's gap and
not Kenny's. Tony is expected to speak here: to do something in response to Kenny's strong taunt to the effect that Tony's pro-femi-
nism is actually a sexual ploy. Although at line 4 Tony jokingly offers a technical hitch as the reason for his silence, this is clearly not
what has happened. When I talked to him afterwards (more as a
fan than a colleague), he made it clear to me that he was simply fu-
rious and outraged at this insinuation. He was in fact in danger of
replying in terms that are unacceptable on radio. So being himself
a trained broadcaster, he held his tongue. This gave him time to
collect his response – and it also gave Kenny's show a dose of what
all professional broadcasters fear: dead air. It worked as a kind of
reprisal. Once the gap was over, Tony was able to use the 'Telecom'
explanation as a polite excuse (with his word 'communications'
conveniently blipped across by a tiny patch of broadcast silence),
and get on with his riposte.

As with the previous case, we can see that a technical requirement (minimization of gap – one of the major design specifications of the turn-taking system) has been passed over in favor of a moral requirement. In this case the moral requirement is for Tony to express his deep-seated community membership allegiances and his differences in this respect from Kenny's. For Tony, Kenny is overdoing traditional masculinism to the point of misogyny and inviting him (Tony) into an admission of his comembership in that community ('here's a man who's chasing after . . . sensitive new age skirt'). Off-air, verbal abuse might be the most effective reply, followed by a termination of the talk. Suitable on-air language would sound like a compromise – and the station's contract with Tony requires him to continue the talk somehow. Temporary but extended silence has the artful design consequence that it both generates dead air (as a direct and immediate reprisal) *and* allows the formulation of an overemphatic and ironic riposte that reminds Kenny – who, after all, is the host, the 'professional,' and ought to be going about his professional business of interviewing – of the purpose of the program ('we all know I'm the authentic feminized male of the early nineties . . . let's get serious'). As with Tony's earlier 'Hm::::?' sign-off, it allows (despite, and perhaps because of, its breaching of interview conventions) a deep-seated community-membership difference to be marked.

In the next instance, I look at an exchange between two senior high-school students, John and Rachel. They are taking part in a class discussion on 'Resources, Population, and Pollution.'[10]

1 J: You have to say what a resource *is*. You have to say it's useful; it's a natural product
2 R: What's natural?
3 J: That comes from the earth
4 R: But you have to tie everything together. To see how each one relates to the other, how they affect the product and um, the uses that we get from this product

The ethnographic work on geography classrooms from which this fragment arises[11] shows that Rachel has a very different basic and underlying notion of what geography is and ought to be than do most of the boys in her class (and to some extent the teacher). Crudley put, Rachel sees geography in terms of the environment and its proper ecological management; the boys treat it as a technical subject without any necessary moral component.

My interest in this fragment is the way these two community memberships work in it. At line 2, given the rest of Rachel's written and spoken contributions to the class, she is clearly questioning John himself about his use of the term 'natural.' She finds he's used it in a way that greatly conflicts with her idea of how the term should be used. John initially uses 'natural' to refer to artificial *products* – commodities that nevertheless have a basis in some natural substance (plants, animals, ores, and so on). For Rachel this use of the term is problematic. To her John seems to be confusing the natural and the artificial. She perhaps wants to engage him in debate about what is to be counted as natural and what not. Elsewhere in the same discussion, for example, Rachel tries on several occasions to get the rest of the class and the teacher to acknowledge a sharp separation between 'the natural' and 'the useful.' For her they are morally distinct: the natural *can* be useful, but it is not necessarily so; to think of it only in terms of its use is to degrade it. There is also a sense in which it is important in its own right regardless of utility. Yet her adversaries (the technical geographers) continue to conflate the two terms, even when 'picking up' and evidently 'expanding' on Rachel's own use of them.

In the fragment, then, John does not take Rachel's question to be criticizing *him* on this account. Instead, he takes it as a request for a definition – for information Rachel does not possess.

Elsewhere I have tried to analyze conversational questions into two broad types, Q- and N-types.[12] Roughly, Q-types question the material substance of the topic at hand; they are informational inquiries. N-types question the utterer; they are critical inquiries. 'Did you feed the cat this morning?' as a Q-type, simply asks whether the cat was fed. As an N-type it could be an accusation or a reprimand ('I know you didn't but you should have'). One interesting feature of the distinction between Q- types and N-types is that it can be decided *after* the fact of any question's having been uttered. That is, those who reply to questions can 'choose' to hear them as a Q-type or else as an N-type and to respond appropriately. Hence there are no guarantees for interrogators.

What seems to be at stake in our classroom fragment is this: By issuing her question as an N-type (which our other evidence suggests she is doing), Rachel is setting up the possibility of a conflict or controversy between community relevances (environmentalists vs. technical geographers). By taking the question up as a (less conflictful, less threatening) Q-type, John not only asserts his own community membership but asserts it as the only possible one: for by this same move he incorporates Rachel herself into a form of communication – that is, a community – based on information exchange (technical geography) rather than moral debate (environmentalism).

As a final example, here is a transcribed conversation from Jeff Coulter's *The Social Construction of Mind*:[13]

1 MWO: Dr . . . Dr K. asked us to call . . . to take you to hospital.
2 PP: Err . . . I'm alright as I am.
3 MWO: You know Dr K. and Dr S. that saw you last night –
4 PW: – Yes –
5 MWO: – they want you to go up this afternoon, and they've asked us to call . . . we've got the car with us, you know –
6 PP: – Aah, I, I'll make it in my own time// if you don't mind.
7 PW: //ya can't make it in yer own time.
8 PP: Course I can. (Pause of 1.5 secs.)
9 MWO: Err, well, you know, I mean Dr K.'s quite busy and he's made an appointment for you this afternoon at the hospital///( )
10 PW: //no harm to go and see him is there?//( )
11 PP: //no, I–I'd rather go on me own I . . . I
12 MWO: Won't take us long down the motorway in the car . . . go up the M55. Be there in no time.
13 PP: Nah I'll remain as I am (Pause of 2.0 secs)
14 PW: Ya can't remain as y'are ya gotta see the doctor . . .

In this stretch of talk, a 'mental welfare officer' (MWO) has called at the house of a 'prospective patient' (PP) and his wife (PW) to try to obtain PP's voluntary admission to a mental hospital.

Although Coulter offers 'a normatively uncommitted or disinterested analysis of this material,'[14] it is plain that substantive descriptions such as 'prospective patient' (rather than 'reluctant victim' for example) are not without their judgmental aspects. For example, the term 'prospective patient' is much more likely to be a term used by the MWO than by the man himself. But this is unremarkable and not the main point. What I argue instead is that even though Coulter is quite correct in his logical-grammatical analysis of the episode, the 'deep' logical-grammatical stratum he locates is *itself* a site of semiosic struggle (rather than a guarantee of consensual understanding).

So I am not arguing that there is just a 'surface' or 'substantive' struggle in the transcribed occasion, underpinned by some kind of logical-grammatical, deep-seated 'agreement' (for example, pace Gadamer, on 'how to struggle'). Rather, I am arguing that how 'the world' is conceptually organized is itself at stake in this event; that a conceptual contestation of the most fundamental order is taking place; and that this has to do with the essentially different community memberships and relevances of at least two of the parties, or with their respective and differential *methods* for producing and understanding spoken indexical particulars.

Although I don't want to repeat Coulter's acute and painstakingly accurate analysis of this transcript, it should be noted that PP's utterances at lines 2, 6, 11, and 13 work to retrospectively 'hear,' and have publicly counted, the prior utterances 1, 5, 9, and 12 by MWO as having been 'offers.' That is, expressions like 'X asked us to call and take you to hospital,' 'X asked us to call and we've got the car,' 'an "appointment" has been made,' and 'it won't take long in the car,' all provide for a multiplicity of readings. As indexical particulars, there are several ways of hearing them. But PP – by his responses to them – tries to have them heard as *offers*, repeatedly and emphatically, across all four instances. Offers characteristically provide options or choices in the slots following them: acceptances and refusals, for example. Now by doing one of these (a polite refusal), PP makes available only one version of himself: as one who has an option or choice in the face of an 'offer.' In doing so he gives a characterization of himself as a particular kind of community member or social subject. For him he is not a 'patient' (a member of the community of the insane, for example, or however this may be expressed), for such community members are not in a position of choice to accept or reject offers of lifts in cars to hospitals. PP offers an account of himself as a member of some kind of roughly democratic public-at-large – a public that offers and accepts (or refuses) on more-or-less equal terms.

Notice then that MWO does not seek to change this reading in the course of the original 'offer' and its several repeats. In fact, he constantly *affirms* PP's understanding of himself as one with options. If anything, MWO's requirements get weaker in the sense that they move away from possible hearings as imperatives. That is, they get more propositional in form, offering 'information' about places, routes, and distances and dropping reference to official authority (Drs. K and S). And they do this progressively. That is, PP's reading of the scene and of himself (of what he is) is the one that tends to gain dominance as the event continues – literally in the face of 'what everyone knows' (and what PW *says*) about asylum admissions.

But not only is PP's verbal strategy (at least partially) successful – at least as far as the fragment we have goes – it also makes acceptable a highly uncommonsensical, 'deviant,' or transgressive conceptual arrangement of things. That is, while the MWO is effectively trying to bring off an incarceration, PP manages to get this very same state of affairs heard as nothing more than 'a lift to the hospital.' To be offered a lift to the hospital is to be given a choice, effectively between being or not being an object of medical and psychiatric practices – a patient. The man in question here is therefore struggling over a very central conceptual point: what or who he is, officially, publicly, and socially. He is either a relatively responsible adult in his own home, merely being offered a lift to a hospital for his own good, at his own behest, and to save him from mere transportation troubles, or else he is a clinical object, an insane person, one to whom the rationality of the 'commonsense' reasonable person cannot be accorded, a subject fit for psychiatric treatment.

What is at stake here is precisely *whether* a putative bedrock (logical-moral rationality) can in fact be extended to all persons and all communities. For it seems to me that there is a plausible counterreading of this transcript: two different community members are in relatively 'deep' contestation as to the 'meaning' of what is being transacted here. What one insists is a quite routine and normal 'offer,' the other uses as a means of getting a hospital admission and, possibly, forever changing this person's community membership.

Coulter is right: PP plays artfully with the presuppositional aspects of MWO's talk. And to support his case that MWO might have a reason for leaving his ultimate 'order' or 'command' tacit, Coulter brings in other evidence:

> MWOs operate with a preference for converting an involuntary admission to mental hospital into a voluntary (or informal) self-admission by the pre-patient wherever possible. In this light, we can discern some discourse-independent grounds for the MWO's recycling of his offer, since he treats it as an offer that cannot ultimately be refused, but as one which nevertheless should be couched *as* an offer rather than, e.g., an order.[15]

Now we can see that there is a tacit connection between the broader institutional concept of an 'informal admission' and the linguistic action of an 'offer,' and a corresponding connection between an 'involuntary admission' and an 'order.' Hence who (or what) one is, one's subject-position, may be contestable only within certain rules of play, and the obvious question of 'strategy' comes to the fore. PP may indeed be seen to be invoking conceptual connections that defeat the dominant logical grammar of the situation in order to save his social identity (as a rational being rather than a madman), but that is always potentially overrulable by a wider array of connections: namely, types of admissions connected with types of linguistic acts.

Put another way: for the MWO, constructing his conjoint and prospective future actions with (or against) PP — that is, an incarceration — as merely an 'offer' acts as a solution to a socio-logical problem. The problem is how to get PP to the hospital at the institution's 'command' without an actual command being issued (since a 'command' would lead, narratively, to a case of involuntary or forced admission)? And the solution to the problem is to modulate the command downwards, to an offer. The problem that then arises is of the order of a catch-22: If the man is in a position to make a rational choice between acceptance and refusal of the offer (if he is one to whom rational choice can be ascribed at all), then he is in no need of psychiatric treatment. Hence PP's pos-

itively strategic uptake of the implied institutional command as a
personal offer.

Either way, MWO and PP are engaging in a struggle at the very
basis of what it is to communicate as particular kinds of social subjects or community members. The interesting thing here is that
they do in fact communicate: but not based on any shared consensus or 'deep common accord.' It is the absence of this very basis
(or the possibility of multiple bases) that is at the core of their conflictual communicational practice here. If one of them is right
about 'who we are' and 'what this occasion is,' then the other is
wrong, and vice versa. Both positions cannot hold at once.

The analysis of this type of contestation might benefit from Lyotard's concept of the *différend*.[16] According to Lyotard, the *différend* exists in any case where a critical difference (for example, a
deep-seated complaint) cannot be properly heard because the idiom
or discourse in which such matters should be properly couched is
not appropriate to it. Lyotard gives the example of a courtroom
situation:

> The plaintiff brings [a] complaint before the tribunal; the ac-
> cused argues in such a way as to show the inanity of the accusa-
> tion. Litigation takes place. I would like to call the *différend* the
> case where the plaintiff is divested of the means to argue and be-
> comes on that account a victim. If the addresser, the addressee,
> and the meaning of the testimony are neutralized, everything
> takes place as if there were no injury. A case of *différend* between
> two parties takes place when the 'regulation' of the conflict
> which opposes them is done in the idiom of one of the parties
> while the injustice suffered by the other is not signified in that
> idiom.[17]

The caller in our first transcript appears to be clearly in this position. The salesperson controls the mode of exchange, *making* this
situation a case of the 'dial-back precall,' a highly economic form
of exchange where complaints (such as 'Why not just sell me a
tape?') cannot be heard. In the classroom example, Rachel is also
to some extent the victim of a *différend*. The idiom of technical geography is relentless to the extent that it hears her attempted complaint ('What's natural?') as not even *being* a complaint. Instead, it

gets to be heard as a request for information – information Rachel is presumed to lack.

But as we have seen in at least three of our transcripts, potential victims are not always without tactics in the face of official forms of conflict regulation. Linda's refusal to take up Karen's Christian idiom and Tony's refusal to take up Kenny's sexism might be cases in point. PP's insistence on a form of conversational address [OFFER + POLITE REFUSAL] in the face of MWO's implicit command appears to be an even stronger case in point.

Such transcripts might therefore be an initial point of departure for establishing a thoroughgoing counterknowledge of how institutional methods operate: a form of knowledge that would be potentially liberating for those who, like PP, might have an interest in transgressive and resistive conceptual schemes, even in the face of overwhelmingly dominant versions. It is interesting that the struggle in this instance occurs not so much within a *given* logical-grammatical domain as between contested versions of what is to count as logical and rational procedure. Working at this sociohistorical level (the contestation of rational grounds themselves) could be a way of building a counterarchive to the official archives, manuals, and tacit techniques of power. But 'empowerment' in the face of a dominant logical-grammatical structure is highly problematic for the simple reason that that structure is not always easily visible. It requires a critical analysis to bring it to public visibility, let alone into tactical contestation.

At the same time, since this type of contestation is not merely technical (linguistic) but technical-ethical (semiotic), the ethical position of the analyst is also imbricated in it. The analyst's ethical question is, For whom and with whom (which communities, which technical-ethical interests) should such counterarchives be built, and to whom should they be distributed? Further, what kinds of control can analysts have over these matters? Bogen and Lynch have put this succinctly, referring to an earlier version of my reanalysis of the PP-MWO transcript:

> In essence, McHoul appears to be advancing a sort of civil (or perhaps 'conversational') libertarianism which would not distinguish between, say, the transgressions of a 'reluctant victim' being shipped off to mental hospital and the transgressions of a

'recalcitrant witness' testifying before Joint Committees of Congress concerning his role in 'U.S. covert operations.'[18] It remains unclear whether or not McHoul is willing to accept the libertarian implications of his own arguments.[19]

These are harsh words indeed, but telling ones. Why write about and distribute strategies for overcoming institutional incarcerations or (as in Hartland's case) for getting desirable outcomes from magistrates?[20] Are there not, after all, persons who *should* be institutionalized, whether in mental hospitals or prisons or other such places? A choice has to be made here between types of 'victims' and the types of regulation they face. The matter is an ethical one through and through, and it cannot easily be shirked. But what kind of positive ethics could an effective semiotics adduce? A discussion of this vexed question forms the substance of the next (and final) chapter.

14. Analytic Ethics

In this investigation I turn, finally, to effective semiotics itself as a social-historical practice, and in particular I attempt to find the limits (or the possibilities) of an ethics for semiotic analysis. So far in this book there has been very little concern with questions of ethics, because effective semiotics has been grounded in the idea of providing empirical *descriptions* of community-based forms of semiosis. I have, precisely, refrained from generalist positions concerning such key concepts as 'meaning' and 'community,' let alone 'the good,' 'the right,' and 'the proper.' However, at the end of the previous chapter a particular problem arose from the analysis of *intercommunitarian* communications. That is, it becomes difficult in such cases not to position oneself as analyst in relation to the radical differences such forms of communication display. Quite clearly, in analyzing Coulter's transcript in which a mental welfare officer attempted to have a prospective patient admitted to a mental hospital against his wishes, I placed myself on the side of the patient, against the welfare officer. Bogen and Lynch, it seems, were quite right to point out that I probably would not have placed myself so easily on the side of a ' "recalcitrant witness" testifying before Joint Committees of Congress concerning his role in "U.S. covert operations." '[1] But on what grounds? How, then, to choose between the anonymous patient and (if that's what he is, as he is for Bogen and Lynch) the infamous Oliver North?

That is, if effective semiotics is to make political interventions (or at least supply an analytic basis for them), can it afford, in Bogen and Lynch's words, to be completely 'libertarian'? Would it, that is, be happy to place itself at the disposal of any forms of transgression and resistance, no matter what? I think not; but I do not yet have any grounds for making the distinction. Intuitively it seems right, good, and proper to see how Coulter's patient might have used tactical forms of talk to resist incarceration, and so for me to disseminate information to others about his strategies; and it seems equally wrong, bad, and improper to align myself with the resistances of such persons as Oliver North and to disseminate information about how *they* might manipulate the semiotics of the courtroom to good advantage. The same problems might occur on a larger political scale. Thus it seems right to me to support Jewish activists who faced (and continue to face) religious oppression from the extreme Right. Yet it seems equally wrong for the Australian, Canadian, and German governments to deny the historian David Irving the right to enter their countries to speak against the historical basis for this oppression. And it seems equally right to support the Palestinian people in their struggles against an invading Israeli state war machine without condoning every action that might be undertaken towards that end. But where, today, are the ethical grounds on which we make such decisions? The problems of an analytic ethics, then, seem to be but a sub-version of general ethics.

If we turn to philosophical ethics today, we find a paradox or a series of them. On the one hand, Caputo reminds us of the dangers and problems surrounding so-called 'postmodern' ethics. Having previously supported such a position, he goes on to construct an argument against philosophical ethics altogether: 'I have up to now always tried to strike a more respectable pose [than being "against ethics"]. Having consorted in the past chiefly with mystics and saints, I have always made it my business to defend ethics, a more originary ethics, an ethics of *Gelassenheit* and letting be, an ethics of dissemination, a veritable postmodern ethics. I have always protested that if I traffic with anarchy, it is a very responsible anarchy.'[2] A 'responsible anarchy'? This is a paradox in itself: what may be called postmodern ethics continually ceases to be a positive ethics. It yo-yos out towards anarchism, letting be, so that anything goes, then pulls itself back in again as it encounters fascism, patriarchy, and a host of other insupportables, realizing that 'anything goes' can also mean that 'everything stays,' realizing that 'responsible anarchy' means conservatism, nonintervention, and a politics of zero transgression. But this paradox in itself is only one side of a larger paradox.

If we turn to the last works of Foucault, we get a historical argument about the positioning of morality and ethics today.[3] Although the first volume of the *History of Sexuality* is quite different from the two volumes that follow it, putting the three together provides a stark contrast between ancient Greek and Roman ethics and post-nineteenth-century morality. Today, and since the nineteenth century at least, Foucault argues, we have been in the grip of an increasing legislation of personal practice. In relation to sexuality in particular, a whole host of legal, social scientific, medical, and criminological discourses have divided bodily acts into categories with values. An array of sexual and perversionary types has come into being in order to define and police our forms of conduct. This is a morality in the true sense, while at the same time its bases are far from absolute or fixed. Instead, the forms of power are distributed and diversified; but all the more to intensify the grip of corporeal control over the most minute of practices and thoughts.

By contrast, there was very little direct legislation in ancient Greece over sexual (and other forms of personal) comportment. At least for 'free men' (as opposed to women and slaves), it seems as if – legislatively at least – all were free to practice sexual acts as they saw fit. However, they did not 'see fit' to act in just any way. A 'culture' of ethics, considered as the relation a man bore towards himself in terms of his relations with others (boys, his wife, the household, and the body politic of the city), grew up. Hence, free men in ancient Greece regulated their conduct in *ethical* ways – there is no need to give the full details here – rather than by the coercion of moral codes. Only with Christianity (which Foucault shows to have misunderstood many of the ancient teachings on chastity, virtue, and so on) did there arise an intense focus on sexual acts themselves. Only then did the catalogs of correct and incorrect behaviors come to be written as moral manuals. In this sense, according to Foucault, today we have perfectly knowable and complex forms of scientific regulation (for example, what Foucault calls the *scientia sexualis*), but we have lost the art of governing ourselves, an *ars erotica*.

If we put this into the picture Caputo draws of philosophical ethics today – a picture that confronts the positive ethical traditions of Kant, Hegel, Heidegger, and Levinas – we can begin to see the larger paradox I mentioned earlier. Everywhere there is (philosophical and pseudophilosophical) ethics, forming mostly as an emergent pluralist-relativist 'responsible anarchy,' a postmodern ethics that celebrates the absence of absolutes and ethical positivities. Yet practical or effective ethics in Foucault's sense (as a positive relation of the self to the self) is almost completely absent and has been displaced by moral legislation forming around highly diverse loci of power and resistances to power. This has led to some peculiar situations, of which I'll mention only two.

At one stage Foucault himself began to embrace a radically liberal ethics, arguing that all forms of criminal legislation (including laws against rape) should be abolished. According to one of his biographers, after 1982 he even entered into regular discussions with the French minister of justice, Robert Badinter, on proposals for officially reforming the penal code along these lines – in fact, proposals for its abolition.[4] Earlier still, he had supported the Iranian revolution as a great popular uprising against the repressions of the shah's regime – and he continued to support the Khomeini government after the revolution despite its own (arguably much more vicious) forms of oppression and genocide.[5] He saw in Iran 'one of the greatest populist explosions in human history.'[6] What these allegiances show is that an ethics that is resistive to moral legislation in all forms, an ethics based on 'the will not to be governed,' runs into all the problems of what Caputo calls *Gelassenheit*.[7] If French rapists and murdering mullahs are included under the general umbrella of such liberal populism, again anything goes and all sorts of barbarity remain. The return to an extreme ethics of individual liberty (which is the logical end of Foucault's investigation) is simply that: a return to an absolute ethics. But to reiterate the paradox, in the absence of absolute canons of action, can any ethics at all (and especially for us here, an ethics of analysis) be constructed?

My second practical instance of ethical paradoxy arises in some fields of feminism. Jane Flax puts the problem succinctly when she asks how it's possible to be both a feminist and a 'postmodernist.'[8] To be a feminist, she argues, requires a positive ethics of opposition to patriarchal forms in all their diversity. It requires something essential in terms of a view of the world that stops short of laissez-faire politics. On the other hand, and as Caputo shows, what is known as postmodernism points in the other direction, towards 'letting be,' tolerance of whatever happens. So can one be a feminist and tolerate everything including patriarchal oppression? No easy solution to the paradox is available, and Flax does not offer us one. However, Rosi Braidotti argues that the feminine (as a positive destiny for women) must be essentialized, against her own better 'philosophical' judgment.[9] It's necessary as a purely practical and pragmatic 'essence,' for without it feminism will be directionless as a political movement for social change. Hence another paradox: this version of feminism uses postmodernist ethics as a first stage to surmount patriarchal forms of normativity and then reinstalls normativity without applying the same ethical critique.

From these two brief examples, we can begin to see a crisis forming in ethics and its relation to that brand of contemporary relativism for which the term 'postmodernism' is but a convenient shorthand.[10] What disturbs me most about this situation is that a complete relativism appears to play into the hands of any form of social control (for example, a church, a legislature, a government, or a father) that is itself arbitrary and relativist.

So, in extremis, absolutist ethics is nothing more than normativity in the form of political-moral legislation; but relativist ethics allows no basis for discerning good from bad conduct and so allows arbitrary and groundless punishments for whatever might, as the situation arises, come to count as a transgression. In ethics, it seems, indeterminacy is just as 'bad' (or as 'good') as certainty.

One possible solution to the paradoxical positions that postmodern ethics seems to entail would be to give up on 'professional' ethics altogether, to argue for the complete unspeakability of ethical positivities. This was Wittgenstein's inclination:

> My whole tendency and I believe the tendency of all men who ever tried to write or talk on Ethics or Religion was to run against the boundaries of language. This running against the walls of our cage is perfectly, absolutely hopeless. Ethics so far as it springs from the desire to say something about the meaning of life, the absolute good, the absolute valuable, can be no science. What it says does not add to our knowledge in any sense. But it is a document of a tendency in the human mind which I personally cannot help respecting deeply and I would not for my life ridicule it.[11]

But again there is a paradox here: any 'tendency in the human mind' that is to be so deeply respected is presumably in itself a good or something very close to it, so that even injunctions against ethics may be read as ethical precepts. By contrast with Wittgenstein then, my own urge – not only to try running against the walls but also to formalize – comes from a distrust of tight oppositions, such as those between philosophy and life (or 'professional' and 'private' ethics), practice and analysis, the speakable and the unspeakable. And it is accompanied by the hope that, in ethics, an analytic failure (necessary failure, if Wittgenstein is to be believed) can show where some important, if unspeakable, limits and possibilities could possibly lie. Not only this, the Wittgensteinian dissolution of ethics leaves us with no way at all of clearing up the practical ethical case in hand, the 'decision' between the cases of the 'mental patient' and Oliver North. In this respect, it is of as little use to me as 'postmodernism.'

Returning then to the term 'postmodernism' and its implication that it should perhaps come 'after' something, Ferenc Feher asks the deceptively simple question, 'After what?'[12] This can be a question about intellectual chronology, or it can ask what postmodernism might be *after*, what it might want to *achieve*. I assume that behind the question is a concern with the forms, or even the very possibility, of social life after the presumed deaths of God, Man, Culture, Economy, Logos, and the rest. That is, for all that these and the other certitudes may have broken down, none of the writers we have looked at so far (Caputo, Foucault, Flax, Braidotti, Wittgenstein) seems to have publicly embraced a total and numbing relativism – none of them has quite given up to the void, 'the swarm of particulars' as philosophers once called it. For all their flirtation with them, radical personalism and, a fortiori, solipsism are by no means popular among these thinkers. This suggests that a space may be left over for some kind of positive ethical thesis, or at least an affirmation. In fact, it suggests that it may be impossible to completely delete all traces of essence, center, and positivity from anything that goes by the name 'ethics,' including counterethics. But it has to be admitted, nevertheless, that the prognosis is not good if we are expecting a postmodern ethics in the traditional sense of a didactic system of moral positivities.

Is it possible that postmodernism's ethical dilemmas stem from its unique ontoepistemological positioning as a general (rather than specifically ethical) philosophy? For postmodernism (along with poststructuralism) appears to want to avoid both objectivism and subjectivism when it comes to the questions of what objects *are* (ontology) and how we can *know* them (epistemology). On the contrary, it has a very different position on the relation between objects and concepts generally.

Let's turn, then, to the case of objectivism. An instance would be the kind of Platonic realism we saw Penrose adopting in chapter 12. If we use x to represent any given concept, the objectivist formula is $x=obj$. Thus the mathematical concept of pi is presumed to map directly onto a really existing entity somewhere in the universe. The concept is a kind of pure crystal through which the world of material or ideal objects can be known. The knowability of objects is ensured through their right and proper concepts, and in turn the knowability of these concepts themselves is undoubtable. On the objectivist account, humans simply are concept-using beings, and the concepts they use (if they use them aright) give unmediated access to the world. If we use brackets to mark out the domain of the fully *knowable*, the objectivist problematic may be represented thus:

$$\{x=obj\}$$

To repeat: the concept is a kind of crystal, and knowledge (including philosophical knowledge) is akin to a kind of optics.

By contrast, the subjectivist view of the concept (for example, the position we encountered in chapter 12 as 'psychological constructionism') sees it as not so much as a crystal as a shuttle, like that used in weaving. That is, it proposes a kind of mutual relation between the concept and its object, with these construed as opposites. Each is held to constitute the other reflexively. However, the object-in-itself is no longer so clearly available to knowledge; for on a subjectivist account the world of objects is always grasped indirectly, through the mediation of subjectively based concepts. And so only the concept, not 'the object' itself, can be fully knowable. The object comes to be referred to in terms of the 'object as presented to consciousness,' the 'phenomenon,' the 'sense datum,' and so on. Using the same formal conventions then, for subjectivism:

$$\{x\} <=> obj$$

These formulations, of course, are caricatures of intellectual struggles, not fixed positions or givens, and presumably no philosopher ever held either of these positions in such simplistic forms. What

I'm referring to as objectivism, then, is a *striving* towards, rather than the achievement of, a clear vision by which objects become absolutely transparent. As we saw in the case of Penrose, it is ultimately a *faith* in the existence of ideal mathematical objects, and in the idea that mathematical concepts directly represent them. By contrast, subjectivism problematizes, or tries to show the mechanics of, what it takes to be the illusory ontological transparency on which objectivism depends. But at the same time, it simply transfers positivity onto the human subject as the proper locus of knowledge. Postmodernism marks itself by a distrust of both these faiths. Following, perhaps, Derrida's critique of the 'metaphysics of presence' and his well-known 'deconstruction' of binary oppositions (such as the opposition between concept and object itself), postmodernism tries to think in a way that deletes both originary objects and primordial subjects as guarantors of concepts. Instead, it asks about the conditions of possibility under which we could come to ask *at all* about concepts and objects. It notices that any concept's conditions of possibility must include that which it is not (so that x always depends on not-x). Additionally, if this is the case, neither a concept (x) nor its negation (not-x) can guarantee full knowability. And this will apply equally to objects. All questions of full, definite, and unmediated 'knowability,' whether subjectively or objectively based, would have to be canceled.

The postmodern radically denies *any* transparency of meaning, whether 'direct' or 'reflexively constituted.' By continually asking what something (concept or object) must be in relation to its negation or absence, positivity comes to be refused. Strong or definite boundaries between positivity and negativity, presence and absence, concept and object, are precisely what come into question in a postmodern view.

Is this the source of postmodernism's specifically ethical dilemmas – that it cannot settle, that it must always hover or flicker between certainty and uncertainty over questions of the good, just as much as over any conceptual domain? Let us see what happens, then, in a case where a critique of binarism is motivated towards overtly ethical ends.

Above I noted that postmodern thinking may work roughly along the lines of Derrida's 'deconstruction' of the metaphysics of presence (hence its positioning outside both sheer objectivism and sheer subjectivism) as well as with his critique of the kinds of bina-ristic thinking that derive from that metaphysics. One ethical problem with binarism (for example, as it operates in structuralist thinking) is that it tends to *equate* both terms in any given opposi-tion. They appear as merely formal-structural inversions of one another. So on a standard view, if something is defined as the nega-tion of its opposite, then the inverse should also be the case. To give an example (one all computers depend on), if 'on' is 'not off,' then 'off' should be 'not on.' Each should be definable as not being its other. But in plenty of actual cases this simply does not work. In the case of gender difference, to follow Irigaray's example, we know that although the feminine is routinely defined as the nega-tion or absence of the masculine, the reverse does not hold.[13] For the present at least, masculinity is not simply the absence of femi-ninity: it is a primary term in a hierarchy. Its primacy, in a sense, *is* patriarchy.

Irigaray's question, however, is not a formal-structural one, but a qualitative and ethical one: How do we think about a feminine quality that is not dependent on its definition as merely the not-masculine? But at the same time, if we *recognize* that the binaries are not simply formal-structural but already contain values and then decide to take *action* against them on the basis of a possible array of countervalues, how can the position thus taken not be an essentialist one? Again, we come across the paradoxes of post-ethics. Ultimately a postmodern ontoepistemology at the formal-structural level (and presumably its related ethics at the level of value) requires positing the very realm of essentials it is opposed to (such that it *defines* itself by that opposition). And this may be one reason the idea of the postethical is so fraught with paradox.

Going back to Bogen and Lynch's ethical dilemma: postmoder-nist relativism will certainly be able to tell us that a particular bi-nary (for example, sane/insane as general categories and regard-less of local practices) involves an opposition that is far from equal. But it will not be able to easily advance a positive ethics of 'support' for the side of the binary that is subordinated to its other (in this case the insane). Equally, unless it is supplemented by a positive feminist ethics, postmodern theory alone cannot produce ethical arguments for a critique of patriarchy and an affirmation of women. There is a crucial difference between identifying victims, and making an ethical argument against their victimization. Otherwise an emancipatory analysis could easily be mobilized on behalf of such figures as, say, Oliver North. But in raising the question of this choice, we return (although the distinction is problematic) from the domain of the theoretical-ethical to practical situations of personal-ethical choice.

Or using the gender example: postmodern theory alone would not be able to distinguish between two counterarchives, one enlisted on behalf of a rape victim and the other on behalf of a rapist facing the legal authorities. To this point, a postmodern ethics could not answer the question, Are there no victims of repression who deserve to be just that? For this would be like asking postmodernism for an originary, definitive, and fixed notion of the pure victim (the victim-in-general, perhaps). And indeed, Foucault himself has been criticized along these lines.[14]

But for all this I think it is possible to locate a definite theoretical-ethical affirmation in recent critical theory, or at least a struggle for one, a struggle that necessarily eschews definite ethical positivities or strict social-moral norms. Gasché argues similarly for the project he calls 'deconstructive interpretation':

> In *Spurs*, Derrida insists that deconstructive interpretation is affirmative interpretation. . . . The affirmative character of deconstructive interpretation, however, is not to be confused with positivity. Deconstructive interpretation is affirmative in a Nietzschean sense. . . . [T]his means that deconstructive interpretation affirms the play of the positive *and* the negative, and thus it wards off the ethical temptation to liquidate negativity and difference.[15]

For Gasché, the only point is to 'ward off' the ethical tendencies of other theoretical positions; it is not to establish any affirmative position in his own right. And in fact Derrida tells us why no ethical decision can ever run completely or perfectly along the lines of a moral program or, that is, run from cause to effect in an efficient and linear manner:

> Above all, no completeness is possible for undecidability. . . . A decision can only come into being in a space that exceeds the calculable program that would destroy all responsibility by trans-

forming it into a programmable effect of determinate causes. There can be no moral or political responsibility without this trial and this passage by way of the undecidable. Even if a decision seems to take only a second and not be preceded by any deliberation, it is structured by this *experience and experiment of the undecidable*.[16]

Staten's position is less cautious than Gasché's or Derrida's in this regard, if more alarming and fraught with risk. He argues for a general, not specifically ethical, affirmation of the accidental against the essential, indeed for a *law* of the possibility of accident. Accident becomes essential. But since 'at the end of the book I only reach the point at which one first picks up one's pen',[17] Staten does not fully explore the ethical dimensions of his affirmation of accidence. Yet it may be worth seeing if his argument can be taken to that point.

If, as Derrida argues throughout his work, originary presences (essences such as 'the good') never simply arrive alone but are always constituted by repetition (accident, what happens to happen), then an ethics along these lines would involve an affirmative ethic-in-struggle, with no guarantee of returning to a fixed origin or arriving at a final destination. For example, this would mean struggling to think *the necessity* of, say, the masculine as the negation (or absence) of a primarily given feminine: that is, a gender politics in which men are considered (and in which we consider *ourselves*) as lacking a femininity and where this 'femininity' is derived without reference to an originary 'baseline' of the masculine. Clearly this theoretical-ethical problem is not without its relations to personal-ethical questions. We seem to have reached a point where the two domains begin to touch. It is no longer clear that there's one rule for philosophy and another for life. For example, for a man in any patriarchal society, 'thinking the necessity of a lacking femininity' would be a type of persistent ontoepistemological-ethical perversity that required, that made essential, the accidental or aleatory *as it actually appears in specific ethical-political techniques, under specific conditions*. For that one side of a pair such as masculine/feminine comes to be negatively valued is in no sense a pure effect of philosophical speculation. It comes about only given the operation of such general ideas within specific conditions, a specific history of gender relations, particular socio-historical communities, the emergence, sedimentation, and stabilization over time of particular institutions, including the apparent 'naturalness' of an unequal relation, and so on.

Accordingly, we might locate a number of sites of the inessential, sites of 'minority communities,' sites to which the accidental is currently confined and that would be affirmed by a postmodern ethics. The list would be long, but it might include writing rather than speech, woman rather than man, sign rather than essential meaning (but also spacing rather than sign), contamination rather than purity, and margin rather than center, where each of these would require an analysis of gender politics, the politics of representation, and so on as a precondition of any affirmative (that is, *tactical*) ethics.[18]

Because this is a precondition of possible counterethical or post-ethical practices rather than an end in itself, it figures as part of a strategy that is more than a mere negation or overturning. The idea of stressing the typically unstressed member of ethical-moral binaries has in view their eventual deconstruction, as a practical political matter and not a merely 'theoretical' one.[19] It acknowledges that the dominant binarism of, say, modernist thought is co-extensive with the whole ethical-political field. Binarism then comes be seen as a 'cryptogrammar' whose terms must be used (initially negated) and analyzed for their intrinsic play (*jeu*) in Derrida's sense, their never being perfectly completable.[20] Binarism will not easily disappear, leaving us with a new ethical field overnight. Inversion, then, could not be the end but would be only the beginning of a counterethics of the post.

However – and here we hit the Wittgensteinian boundaries – the precise point or site at which a particular analyst carried out a particular critique would always be a matter of personal ethics (insofar as it involved a choice at all). It might, for example, have to do with particular community memberships and allegiances. This is the point – the point of personal and community allegiance – where ethical *theory* as such drops out. It is the point where formal ethical language runs up against Wittgenstein's ethical limits. And this is why Bogen and Lynch's questions (Why the helpless madman and not Oliver North? – Why the rape victim and not the rapist?) can never be answered by a single and definitive ethical for-

mula that would be somehow 'built in' to semiotics to keep it ethically 'pure.' If I am asked why I choose the first and not the second, I cannot say. I can only say that my history and my forms of
life make it quite clear to me. And I can *then* point back to the traditional or historical undervaluing of insane persons and rape victims as a secondary – more arguable, more discussable – *support*
for my choice.

Nevertheless, the unmasking of such undervaluings of and by
metaphysical binaries has a certain value. Unmasking or 'psycho-
analyzing' this metaphysics would mean more than simply affirm-
ing what it negates: the possibility of the accidental. It would mean
showing, by a kind of double move, that the conceptual purity of
an absolute boundary *between* a concept (x) and its negation or
absence (not-x) is itself a matter of faith. If the undervalued nega-
tive concept (impurity or contamination, say) is first reaffirmed,
then the boundary between concept and object cannot be an-
chored either *concept*ually or *object*ively. Neither of the terms
alone can secure the boundary between them. The proposition
that the boundary or spacing must not allow contamination is not
self-evidently true. Rather, this ethical requirement of conceptual
purity is itself merely one of the overvalued positivities of the
metaphysics postmodernism opposes.

Let me put this more formally. As we have seen, while objectivist
metaphysics required a positive relation, $\{x=obj\}$, between a concept and its object, and subjectivism required a relation of mutual
constitutivity between them, $\{x\} <=> obj$, a critique of both finds
in them a common formula of *presence* of the general form: $a\ R\ b$.
Here: R is the relation that is always a *difference* even when expressed as 'equals' or 'is' or 'is identical with' or 'mutually constitutes.' Every such realization of R requires a faith in some form of
pure presence. This faith holds that what *is* present (for example,
an 'object') is pres*ented* (for example, to consciousness) in a 'medium' of pres*ence*. As such, then, both objectivism and subjectivism forget difference, the always possible nonrelation (corresponding to any arbitrarily given relation) between a concept and
its other.

The relation R always carries or allows, and sometimes even requires, permeability. The project of a postethics would ideally
show every R to be a perforated membrane as opposed to a water-

tight seal. Under such a 'deconstruction' (if that's what it is), R does not dissolve altogether. The relation of presence is not merely canceled. Instead it is remembered that R can do other than mark identity. For example, it can be the undecidable double of identity-difference, the 'experience and experiment of the undecidable.'

Between *a* and *b* there is a situation of *always possible contingency*: the possibility of leakage, contamination, transfer, the threat of wholesale rupture in some cases. This always possible contingency is the nearest to an affirmative (positive?) thesis that a formal postethics can come. The boundary can, however, in no case whatever be kept ideally intact. Even to imagine such a pure state, we must be able to imagine its transgression. The strongest ethical positions utterly require and contain their opposites. In this sense Staten's law of the *possibility* of accident would never *not* be in play: there could be no pure case that was unregulated by it.

The crunch comes when we must ask whether there is anything to be said from this position with respect to ethics – with respect, that is, to the 'regulation of conduct' as it might be put in the more traditional zones of moralism or the 'moral sciences.' Here we can begin to discern a number of possible pro-ethical 'maxims' that would follow from postmodernism's paradoxical ontoepistemological positioning.

1 Within conceptual doubles, there is an emerging revaluation of the politically undervalued concept: privation, absence, contamination, and so on. This is not so much to instigate a new positivity; rather, it is a first step that shows how such oppositions are always hierarchical in terms of value even though they may appear to have equal logical or structural positions. After this first step, however, there is still work to be done. Derrida writes: 'What must occur then is not merely a suppression of all hierarchy, for an an-archy only consolidates just as surely the established order of a metaphysical hierarchy; nor is it a simple change or reversal in the terms of any given hierarchy. Rather, the *Umdrehung* must be a transformation of the hierarchical structure itself.'[21]

2 Even if the postethical is not anarchic, it takes on the *style* of refusal. 'Athesis,' as refusal, is therefore a definite strategy insofar as it is – and it must be – a material practice at all.[22] A

material practice with the style of refusal remains a material practice. In fact, we can discern in the postethical a positivity of the material in a domain traditionally reserved for intangible 'principles.'

3 A crucial point, as we have seen, is that the accidental-aleatory becomes positive in that it becomes essentially possible. In this sense ethics is a form of *invention*. It is no longer a question of pregiven and selfevident principles or formulas. It no longer conceives of freedom as the freedom to invent *practice* based on given (uninvented) moral principles. The postethical points to a different state of affairs in which we must invent principles (such as Staten's essential aleatoriness?) while cut adrift, as it were, in the domain of practice. The 'post' element of the postethical points to the ethical arriving *after* the practical. The rules are always formulated after the fact. In this sense these are not *dis*coveries or uncoverings of 'natural' facts or principles.

4 The domain of practice itself, however, is not to be thought of as without any constraint or limit. Absence of a definite, watertight R-relation between concepts and their opposites does not mean practice is a swarm of particulars, an infinite celebration of the play of signifiers, a semiotic carnival.[23] Any specific leakage across R, it is important to note, cannot be without its own history and politics, its own customs and conventions, its own techniques and practices, its own relevances to the specific communities or forms of life involved. To this extent we must say it is subject to a constitutive outside, which is always 'there' if only because the accidental is always possible, precisely outside any definite prediction. To return to Wittgenstein: the accidental is thinkable as the 'beyond-the-limit,' for example, of language. This 'beyond' points to *at least one* area of unknowable constraint, an area of possibility-conditions that are not specifiable in advance. And this is precisely why formal or professional ethical inquiry is always different from personal ethics – including the personal ethics of the analyst.

5 Last, then, can a postethics have a strategy or tactics? In *Speech and Phenomena*, Derrida writes of 'a strategy without finality . . . blind tactics [*tactique aveugle*].'[24] We can read this

at least two ways: either as endless accidence as itself a given tactic or as the tactic of making, enforcing aleatoriness upon the supposedly proper and precise. Either way, this can be read affirmatively.

But what is this rather general affirmation in terms of Foucault's idea of ethics as a relation to oneself *in* relation to others? And in particular, what can it mean for the semiotic analyst's relation to himself or herself in relation to the various community-based forms of semiosis being analyzed? By asking these questions we begin to see the limits of the postethics that comes down to *tactique aveugle*: for such a blindness gives us no clear way to proceed in terms of deciding how effective semiotic analyses should position themselves in terms of the communities outside them that they subject to empirical analysis. Let us now, then, try to consolidate what we have learned from our excursion into the terrors of relativism and see what can be done today in the name of a specifically analytic ethics.

All ethical grounds (as absolute grounds) have been shattered, broken into fragmented slabs like a crazy paving. Today, that is, we have a single ethical principle: that all absolute ethics are anathema, since they become normative principles. But if we start to look closely at the shattered remains of those once-firm ethical grounds, we can see that some are so precarious as to forbid all construction upon them while others retain sufficient solidity to allow us at least the idea of a positive analytic ethics. All grounds are shattered – to repeat – yet some remain workable or effective nevertheless, even if there are those who would think they are vestiges of an old positivity that should be cleared away. The ethical project would then be to identify these (and their flaws) empirically. Ethics would then be a method or calculation, one methodic practice that effective semiotics might both analyze and contribute to (as theory and practice). Ethics would be where effective semiotics both *does and* describes methodic practices.

This would mean trying to find a form of empiricism that was not conservative but critical – critical by means of its intervention into the ethical. To this point my effective semiotics has been conservative in simply attempting to describe (without judging) methodic practices. That has left it open to charges of being unable to discriminate between, to return to our paradigm case, Coulter's patient and Oliver North. So effective semiotics could take this move into criticism (into the space of the critical) as the start of 'the good,' its good. Then the ethical question would be, What are the objects of that criticism or critical move? Evidently they would have to be empirical objects, so we could never know their problems in advance. Or their problems could not be given by any general form of normativity. By 'problems' we would then have to mean problem-solutions, except that now effective semiotics would be identifying and proposing them rather than simply describing them. And this would involve intervening in communities or forms of life, with all its attendant risks. Principally, the risk is that such a form of critique would be tendentious in Garfinkel's sense: we would not know its point of application in advance of the investigation.

In important ways, this tendentiousness would fit not only with Derrida's 'experience and experiment of the undecidable' but also with Foucault's idea of the dispersal of power in contemporary society. If Foucault is right, ethics (as a counter to power) is necessarily plural. For effective semiotics, then, this would involve a calculation in two parts, with each part corresponding to the first two 'levels' of semiosis. The first part would mean locating and describing the *intelligibility* of the good in a particular locale. It would mean asking, What counts as the good in this community? The second part of the calculation would move beyond mere intelligibility or identification and towards critique and intervention. It would ask about the *actionability* of the good. That is, it would begin to ask questions about the ways socio-logical problems and their solutions are formed in the community under investigation. It would ask, How is the good this community *sets* as the good carried into action? Then, at both levels of semiosis (intelligibility and actionability), it would reserve the right of disagreement: the right to say that it refuses this idea of the good or that it refuses this idea of its (proper) implementation. Then effective semiotics might begin to realize its own community status – and acknowledge its specific positioning with regard to those other communities it analyses.

This gives us a positioning for the first two semiotic levels, but what of the third: *historicity*? If Foucault is right and a genuine ethics of the self (in relation to itself) has been taken over today by a legislated and normative morality, then an analytic actionability oriented to a return to ethics (in Foucault's sense) is already a historical move. It would already be in the position of arguing for a new 'art' of the self against an old science of government. It would already be arguing for (and attempting to practice) the installation of a return to self-judgment and the 'will not to be governed.'

There are risks involved in such a policy, but the possible outcome is a return to the ethical domain, the installation of an ethics of the self over the dominance of morality (as sociopolitical normativity). And this may in itself be a form of the good – the first good of a positive ethics of analysis.

Such an ethics as a situationally located form of calculation (of the good outcome?) will always be imperfect, since, as Derrida reminds us, the result of the calculation always lies in the future. It leaves itself subject to unknowabilty, to being (potentially) wrong (as Foucault was about Iran and the delegislation of rape). But on this account the good is to calculate despite this – risking being wrong but trying at every step not to be.

An unethical analytics would then involve either the quietism of failing to calculate at all – leaving history as it is, condoning everything – or the retrospectivism of adjusting one's earlier calculations so that they show themselves as having been right all along. In empirical terms this would be the equivalent of fudging the results. Taking the risks involved in such work is a matter of courage or its lack. As with experimentation in the natural sciences, Derrida's 'experience and experiment of the undecidable' means that one has to be prepared for things to turn out wrong. These are the stakes in an empiricist ethics.

How then to choose between Coulter's patient and Oliver North? Why is it that I want to back one and not the other? When I look at the transcript of PP's attempted incarceration, I see just that – an attempted incarceration. But I see the attempt as happening against PP's own relevances and self-positioning (as a free person without obligation to the mental welfare system). This prompts me to describe the intelligibility of the situation from his point of view (a point of view he makes clear to all those involved in the scene and to any analyst). Then I feel obliged to describe his ethnoanalytic strategy, his way of finding an actionable solution to the problem he has been *put* in. But I can't find any equivalents in the case of Oliver North, no matter how closely I read Bogen and Lynch's paper and no matter how much I share (as perhaps an ethnomethodologist) their own community relevances.[25] For it seems that in the end the North case is not an instance of intercommunity dissensus. North has worked for the state, albeit via an agreement that he would (on its behalf) appear to work outside it. The appeals he makes against the judgment against him are appeals based on the fact that the state he worked for allowed him (he would say legally) to act illegally. In whatever way one analyzes this, North has already agreed to his complicity with the moral norms by which he is judged. None of this is true for PP. He has in no way registered himself as a member of any community that is in agreement with the metal health authorities. In the PP transcript we are dealing with a definite, direct, and genuine case of intercommunity difference. A position has to be taken, and I can see no grounds for taking the position of the mental health authorities. North is by no means a victim of such communitarian differences; he is being tried by the very system he has served and has 'subscribed' to. There is no *différend* in his case, and hence no victimization.[26] Ethically we have no choice but to allow others (including North) such choices: everyone has the right to do wrong, and no one has the right to take that right away. By doing it they choose, equally, to be judged by the value system they have chosen to be wrong within. Victims exist only when value systems arrive from other communities to insist that their (exterior) judgments should stand. Then semiotics needs to analyze and disseminate the complex means by which such victims find artful ways of refusing to be governed, legislated, or judged.

Whether this type of analysis can be collected and publicized in ways that can be reused by (or mobilized on behalf of) victims of social injustice remains to be seen. In the end they may only serve to increase the analyst's own understanding of the world and how it operates. What they might change, in this minimal respect, would be who the analyst is, in terms of community positionings and sociohistorical allegiances. But this in itself may not be the worst of outcomes. Effective semiotics would then be only one possible 'art of existence' or 'technique of the self,' to reinvoke Foucault's terms. It would be, at minimum, one way of 'knowing if

one can think differently than one thinks, perceive differently than
one sees.'[27] And though it has been much quoted elsewhere, what
Foucault has to say about such a practice (which he calls 'philosophy') continues to be instructive – one of the few moves towards a
positive ethics arising out of poststructuralist thought:

> People will say, perhaps, that these games with oneself would be
> better left backstage; or, at best, that they might properly be part
> of those preliminary exercises that are forgotten once they have
> served their purpose. But, then, what is philosophy today –
> philosophical activity, I mean – if it is not the critical work that
> thought brings to bear on itself? In what does it consist, if not in
> the endeavor to know how and to what extent it might be possi-
> ble to think differently, instead of legitimating what is already
> known? There is always something ludicrous in philosophical
> discourse when it tries, from the outside, to dictate to others, to
> tell them where their truth is and how to find it, or when it works
> up a case against them in the language of naive positivity. But it
> is entitled to explore what might be changed, in its own thought,
> through the practice of a knowledge that is foreign to it. The 'es-
> say' – which should be understood as the assay or test by which,
> in the game of truth, one undergoes changes, and not as the sim-
> plistic appropriation of others for the purpose of communica-
> tion – is the living substance of philosophy, at least if we assume
> that philosophy is still what it was in times past, i.e., an 'ascesis,'
> *askesis*, an exercise of oneself in the activity of thought.[28]

Perhaps, after all, Wittgenstein found ethical propositions to be in-
expressible in his day (and today) because they *are* currently inex-
pressible, but for historical reasons rather than for reasons that
have to do with the *essential* inexpressibility of ethics. As we saw
in chapter 1, historical thinking was never Wittgenstein's forte.
Perhaps it is only today that the ethical cannot be spoken: because
the relation to the self (*le rapport à soi*), insofar as it exists at all, is
currently overshadowed by legal, juridical, and religious forms of
controlling the self – forms that are better thought of as *moral*
codes than as ethical principles.[29]

In this case the unspeakability of the ethical today is not a fixed
condition. Foucault has shown that things have been quite otherwise and, at least in principle, could be again: 'We have hardly any

remnant of the idea in our society, that the principal work of art which one has to take care of, the main area to which one must apply aesthetic values is one's self, one's life, one's existence.'[30] Perhaps, then, the ethical struggle is no more and no less for a return to ethics itself, against moral legislation. And perhaps one way of securing this struggle would be to turn away from ethics as a branch of philosophy and towards ethics as an empirical, factical, actional, or effective decision. If so, ethics as (and in) effective semiotics may be a contribution to 'genealogico-deconstructive research.'[31] It may even be the first move towards that branch of it that Derrida has tentatively named 'pragrammatology.'[32]

Notes

PREFACE

1. The term 'effective' does not quite capture the German *wirkliche*. Nothing in English quite can. We may therefore need a better term to approximate the combined senses of 'working,' 'practical,' 'everyday,' 'actual,' 'mutable' and 'plastic,' along with the idea of 'serviceability' – but one that does not (as does 'effective') appear causalist. A further matter of terminology: I use the noun 'semiosis' and the adjective 'semiosic' for what is analyzed and reserve the noun 'semiotics' and the adjective 'semiotic' for the discipline(s) that do that analysis.

2. Foucault, 'Politics,' 14.

3. See, for example, Bennett, 'Foreword.'

4. Quoted in Gadet, *Saussure*, 19.

5. Saussure, *Cours*.

6. There is still a question whether Saussure's late concern with anagrams might be one instance of the picturesque. See Starobinski, *Words*.

7. In particular I'm thinking of the work of Michael Halliday and post-Hallidayan versions of social semiotics. See, for example, Hodge and Kress, *Social Semiotics*.

8. Nietzsche, *Basic Writings*, 381.

9. *Chambers Dictionary* gives the following definition of 'paralogia': 'impairment of reasoning power characterized by difficulty in expressing logical ideas in speech.'

10. Foucault, *Histoire*, 7–8. This translation is by Betsy Wing; quoted in Eribon, *Foucault*, 124.

11. Garfinkel, *Studies*.

12. Rhees, 'Private Language,' 268.

13. This is a feature of them I was completely unaware of until Bob Hodge pointed it out to me.

CHAPTER ONE

1. The early Marx refers to *consciousness* as the fundamentally human property that marks this inheritance. See Marx, 'Extract,' 51.

2. Here I am questioning not so much Derrida's own uses of the idea that there is nothing outside the text (*il n'y a pas de hors-texte*) as those of some of his interpreters. See Derrida, *Grammatology*, 158–59.

3. See Gleick, *Chaos*, 27.

4. The term 'fixed laws' (*lois fixes*) is from Taine's positivist philosophy of art and literature. See Taine, *Philosophie*, 47.

5. In a lecture broadcast on ABC's *Science Show*, Gould illustrated this by relating Mark Twain's moral tale that goes roughly as follows: At the top of the Eiffel Tower, there is a layer of paint one-tenth of an inch thick. Everyone knows, of course, that the rest of the structure was built to make this layer possible!

6. Foucault, 'Questions,' 6.

7. Derrida, 'Structure, Sign.'

8. Foucault, 'Questions,' 6–7.

9. Foucault writes: 'A total description draws all phenomena around a single centre – a principle, a meaning, a spirit, a world view, an overall shape; a general history, on the contrary, would deploy the space of a dispersion.' *Archaeology*, 10.

10. Or to invoke Harvey Sacks's notion of a 'sequence grammar,' history may be more like a conversation – something with rules, to be sure, but not the sorts of rules that will utterly predict the exact contents of the next turn. See Sacks, *Aspects*.

11. Derrida, *Signéponge*.

12. Wittgenstein, *Investigations*, par. 38.

13. Horgan, 'Profile,' 17.

14. Gleick, *Chaos*, 24.

15. Nietzsche, *Use and Abuse*, 8.

16. See Winspur, 'Wittgenstein's Semiotic.'

17. Monk, *Wittgenstein*, 322. Monk's source is Wittgenstein, *Lectures*, 97.

18. Wittgenstein, *Lectures*, 98.

19. Wittgenstein, *Grammar*, 130, 131.

20. Wittgenstein, *Grammar*, 86–87.

21. Wittgenstein, *Grammar*, 87.

22. See, for example, Hodge and Kress, *Social Semiotics*. Or in a more traditional vein, Barthes, *Image Music Text*. For a recent and radical re-evaluation of the relations between visual and verbal production (and analysis), see Maras, 'Hermeneutics.'

23. See Coward and Ellis, *Language*.

CHAPTER TWO

1. See Derrida, 'Parergon,' in *Truth*, 15–147. Derrida makes the following observation that is highly pertinent to the centrality of the parergon for effective semiotics: 'No "theory," no "practice," no "theoretic practice" can intervene effectively [*effectivement*] in this field if it does not weigh up and bear on the frame, which is the decisive structure of what is at stake, at

the invisible limit to (between) the interiority of meaning (put under shelter [*mise à l'abri*] by the whole hermeneuticist, semioticist, phenomenologicalist, and formalist tradition) *and* (to) all the empiricisms [*empirismes*] of the extrinsic which, incapable of either seeing or reading, miss the question completely.' *Truth*, 61, with added terms from Derrida, *Vérité*, 71.

2. Barthes, *Camera Lucida*.

3. See Jayyusi, 'Reflexive Nexus.'

4. Jacques Derrida, '"Genesis and Structure" and Phenomenology,' in *Writing*, 154–68.

5. For a further discussion see Foucault, 'Nietzsche, Genealogy, History,' in *Language Counter-memory*, 139–64, and Hassan, 'Pluralism.'

6. Tagg, 'Power.' Revised in Tagg, *Burden*, 66–102.

7. On the connections between these factors, see Hunter, 'Culture, Bureaucracy.' On the relations between these historical changes and photography, see Donald, 'Beacons.'

8. Sanders, 'Notes.'

9. This is by no means to deny the massive contribution of nineteenth-century women photographers. As with other social practices and labor formations, it is only to say that there is an implicit set of gender *expectations* governing nineteenth-century notions of who was to take photographs and who was to be taken by them.

10. Wittgenstein, *Investigations*, 178e. See also his *Culture*, 49e.

11. Wagner and Lloyd, *Camera*, 4.

12. Wagner and Lloyd, *Camera*, 4.

13. Wagner and Lloyd report that by 1905 Barnardo's had eight thousand children in its homes and four thousand boarded out, and it had sent eighteen thousand to Canada and Australia. *Camera*, 6.

14. Wagner and Lloyd, *Camera*, 14.

15. Wagner and Lloyd, *Camera*, 11.

16. See Tagg, 'Power,' and Donald, 'Beacons.'

17. Hacking, 'History of Statistics' and 'Biopower.'

18. Foucault, *Discipline and Punish*.

19. T. J. Barnardo, quoted in Wagner and Lloyd, *Camera*, 14. See Tagg, 'Power,' 43–44, and Donald, 'Beacons,' 235.

20. Wagner and Lloyd, *Camera*, 39.

21. Wagner and Lloyd, *Camera*, 5.

22. Indeed, a number of charges were laid against Barnardo during the late 1870s. Among these were that he ran his charity for personal monetary advantage; that he consorted with women of dubious morals (the 'Mrs. Johnson' affair); that he was not legally entitled to call himself 'Doctor' and had forged a letter of reference from the University of Giessen

(though he was *later* admitted as an FRCS in 1879); that he was the author of the 'Clerical Junius' letters criticizing George Reynolds and Frederick Charrington, Barnardo's main critics; that he used faked photographs to 'prove' the effectiveness of his work; that his missions extended to both the 'deserving' and the 'undeserving' poor and thus encouraged mendicancy and subverted the Poor Laws; that he was guilty of cruelty and neglect towards the children in his homes. The nearest I have been able to get to the detail is chapters 8 and 9 of Wagner, *Barnardo*, 21–155.

23. The Rev. George Reynolds, charges against Barnardo, in Wagner and Lloyd, *Camera*, 12.

24. Wagner and Lloyd, *Camera*, 5 and 14.

25. T. J. Barnardo, in Wagner and Lloyd, *Camera*, 14.

26. John Lee, personal communication. John offered these comments to me after I presented an earlier form of this chapter at the University of Manchester in September 1989.

27. Wagner and Lloyd, *Camera*, 20.

28. Charity card verso, ca. 1874, reproduced in Wagner and Lloyd, *Camera*, 21.

29. See Stallybrass and White, *Politics and Poetics*.

30. If literary history is any guide in this matter, it seems that the *problem* of the orphan is a specifically nineteenth-century one. This is not to say there were no fictional orphans before the nineteenth century. Instead – and *Moll Flanders* and *Tom Jones* are paradigm cases – the foundling (rather than the orphan as such) was a positive central character who was cast as the person without connections or obligations and who was therefore free to *make* himself or herself through enterprising actions. By the nineteenth century, orphans are rarely central characters. The novel by then is much more centered on the family – though, to be sure, it often focuses on figures who are out of line with their family situations. When the orphan does appear, then, he or she is cast outside the normal structures, to be pitied, to be an object of charity. By the nineteenth century, that is, the orphan becomes a problem that demands local solutions. Barnardo simply institutionalized those solutions by creating the homes and their manifold technologies. None of this would have been possible a century earlier.

31. Proust, *Search*, 29.

32. Proust, *Search*, 6.

33. Proust, *Search*, 41, 46–47.

34. Wagner and Lloyd, *Camera*, 15.

35. Wagner and Lloyd, *Camera*, 16.

36. Indeed, there is a deeply striking resemblance between Sarah and the

gamine figure used as the logo for the popular 1990s stage play *Les Misér-ables*.

37. Barthes, *Camera Lucida*, 96.

38. Berger, *Ways*, 118.

39. On the highly paradoxical position of history in 'postmodern' thinking, see Frow, *What Was Postmodernism?*

40. Eagleton, 'Capitalism,' 67.

41. Huyssen, 'Search,' 35.

42. Hutcheon, 'Beginning,' 14.

43. Williamson, *Authorship*.

CHAPTER THREE

1. Natanson, 'History as a Finite Province of Meaning,' in *Literature*, 172.

2. Wittgenstein, *Blue and Brown Books*, 18.

3. Greenblatt, 'Towards a Poetics.'

4. One antiessentialist treatment of the idea of a cultural object is Hatch, 'Analysis.'

5. And indeed, some 'conservative' critics of American English studies have almost completely conflated cultural studies with the 'New Historicism.' See, for example, Schwarz, 'Review Essay.'

6. See Hunter, 'Learning.' Hunter has shown how the CCCS critique of normative aesthetics shares many of its features in terms of the technologies for producing certain kinds of historical subjects. His argument needs to be looked at in detail in conjunction with the present remarks.

7. Emmison and McHoul, 'Drawing.'

8. Williams, 'Base and Superstructure.'

9. Hall, 'Toad in the Garden,' 46.

10. By this I mean, of course, a quack remedy; but on a strictly etymological reading, 'nostrum' could also remind us of cultural studies' (as opposed to anthropology's) avowed attempt to explicate 'our own' culture.

11. Grant and Reeve, *Observations*, quoted in Monk, *Wittgenstein*, 452.

12. Stratton, 'Sociology.'

13. Kuhn, *Structure*; Latour, *Science in Action*.

14. Fabian, *Time*. Unlike me, however, Fabian is critical of anthropology's noncoevalist version of its 'object' communities.

15. Derrida, *Spectres*.

16. Nancy, 'Finite History,' 150.

17. Nancy, 'Finite History,' 149; my italics.

18. See also Pratt, 'Linguistic Utopias,' and Anderson, *Communities*.

19. Nancy, 'Finite History,' 149.

20. Nancy, 'Finite History,' 162.

21. Remarks by Harold Garfinkel in Hill and Crittenden, *Proceedings*, 119, 121.

22. Said, *Culture and Imperialism*, 403.

CHAPTER FOUR

1. Part of my thinking in this case has been guided by Anne Freadman's concept of not-statements. See Freadman, 'Untitled,' 79, 77.

2. To use Foucault's term, the adoption of attitudes towards oneself is properly the domain of ethics. See Foucault, *Care of the Self*.

3. Vico, *New Science*, 137.

4. Wittgenstein, *Blue and Brown Books*, 18. Note that although I want to locate signs' internal relations in the space of *coscienza* – of particularity – this does not mean that their *external* relations will be relations-in-general and therefore available to *scienza*. They too will be material particulars.

5. On this question see Derrida, 'Some Statements,' and see especially 74–76 on the use/mention distinction as it is used in speech-act theory.

6. See Schutz, *Collected Papers*, vol. 1.

7. I thank my colleague Horst Ruthrof for this wording. For his own position on these matters, see Ruthrof, *Pandora*.

8. Derrida, 'White Mythology: Metaphor in the Text of Philosophy,' in *Margins*, 211.

9. I take the notion of pertinent absences from Harvey Sacks. He mentions this idea in his lecture for 6 February 1970 (typescript). In his unpublished manuscript, 'Aspects of the Sequential Organization of Conservation' (which may also be from 1970), Sacks refers to utterances that are 'noticeably absent' and to an analyst's 'trivializable assertion that X is absent.' See Sacks, 'Aspects,' chap. 2, 26. In particular, he is referring to such things as 'He didn't even say hello' – where one person complains that a greeting was expectable but turned out to be absent. See also Sacks, *Lectures*.

CHAPTER FIVE

1. Donald, 'Beacons,' 214.

2. On this project see Henriques et al., *Changing*.

3. Staten, *Wittgenstein*, 84 ff.

4. Wittgenstein, *Investigations*, par. 167.

5. Wittgenstein, *Investigations*, par. 167.

6. One disastrous and soon abandoned wave of spelling reform, the Initial Teaching Alphabet, was designed precisely to *remove* the familiarity of

the printed page from the classroom. For examples, see Diringer, *Alphabet*, 425–26.

7. Staten, *Wittgenstein*, 85.

8. Staten, *Wittgenstein*, 103.

9. Derrida, *Grammatology*.

10. Coulter, *Social Construction*, 69 ff.

11. Chomsky, 'Empirical Assumptions,' 280.

12. This difficulty led Chomsky to distinguish between (ordinary) cases of knowing and (special) cases of 'cognizing.' See Chomsky, *Rules*, 97–98.

13. See Heap, 'What Counts.'

14. Coulter, *Social Construction*, 74.

15. Freadman, 'Untitled.'

16. See Halliday, *Social Semiotic* and *Spoken and Written Language*.

17. Freadman, 'Untitled,' 71.

18. Freadman, 'Untitled,' 71–72; my italics.

19. Freadman, 'Untitled,' 72.

20. Wittgenstein, *Investigations*, par. 71.

21. Freadman, 'Untitled,' 92.

22. Cf. Heap, 'What Counts.'

23. See, for example, the 'Definitions of Standards by the Revised Code, 1862,' in Maclure, *Documents*, 80; cited in Donald, 'Beacons,' 234.

24. Foucault, *Discipline and Punish*, 172. See also Donald's treatment of this passage in 'Beacons,' 227 ff.

25. See chapter 2 above. T. J. Barnardo, quoted in Wagner and Lloyd, *Camera*, 14.

26. Donzelot, *Policing*, 47.

27. Tagg, 'Power,' 21.

28. That, in British English at least, the term 'reading book' is not a pleonasm might indicate that a rather special sense of 'reading' is intended.

29. Hunter, 'English,' 730, 734.

30. Again, I rely here and below mainly on Hunter's work but also on historical material from Donald. See Hunter, 'Culture, Bureaucracy' and 'English,' and Donald, 'Beacons.'

31. Toby Miller has investigated this dichotomy (and the necessary ethical incompleteness of the subject it produces) at length. See Miller, *Well-Tempered Self*.

32. Aspects of its characterization can be found in Foucault's discussion of 'man' as an 'empirico-transcendental doublet' in the final chapters of *Order of Things*.

33. These terms are variations on Hunter's. He writes of 'reciprocating tactics within a single pedagogical strategy.' See 'Culture, Bureaucracy,' 30.

34. See Hunter, 'Learning.'

35. Hunter, 'English,' 730. English is 'the discipline in which children found themselves and found themselves wanting.'

36. Hunter, 'English,' 730.

37. Again the phrase is from Hunter, 'Culture, Bureaucracy,' 30.

CHAPTER SIX

1. The mistaken picture that formalism routinely uses is also summarized by Wittgenstein in terms of the 'life' of signs: 'Every sign *by itself* seems dead. *What* gives it life? – In use it is *alive*. Is life breathed into it there? – Or is the *use* its life?' Wittgenstein, *Investigations*, par. 432. I read the passage this way: Against logicist and formalist versions of meaning that believe one can treat signs *by themselves* (such that, later, they have to have life breathed into them), one can say instead that signs are always in use, in life. There is no need to account for them as 'dead' objects and therefore no need to find out how they come to be revived, 'in use.' Situations of use are signs' primary substance; one cannot go back 'before' that.

2. Garfinkel, *Studies*, 28.

3. See Hartland, 'Discourse Analysis.' This section on methods/activities (R1) and methodic activities/socio-logical problems (R2) owes a great deal to Hartland's elaboration of some of my work on socio-logics. Hartland argues that such an approach obviates any and every sign-based analysis of discourse, but I suspect our differences on this point are largely terminological. That is, he is correct if the concept of sign is a traditional semiotic one, but not (tautologically perhaps) if that concept is reconstructed in terms of methodic activities.

4. Later we will see that it will be more appropriate to use the term 'the *historical* meaning of the sign' for R3, since R1 and R2 can also be seen to be sites of meaning ('intelligibility' and 'actionability' respectively).

5. Hartland, 'Discourse Analysis'; Garfinkel, *Studies*; Garfinkel and Sacks, 'Formal Structures.'

6. Wieder, *Language*.

7. For a more detailed treatment, see Ashmore, *Reflexivity Thesis*.

8. One exception is the study of 'formulations' (where participants say, in so many words, what it is they are doing in and as the activities they are producing). See Heritage and Watson, 'Aspects' and 'Formulations.'

9. Garfinkel 'solves' this problem by saying, after Schutz, that it is social members themselves who construct and use typifications. However, it may be equally true that communities use *specifications*. Then 'to see as typical' and 'to see as specific' would simply be distinct practices available to particular communities, and their use (comparative to one another *or not*) could not be guaranteed by relying upon the *essential givenness* of typifica-

tory practices for all sense making; rather, it could be guaranteed only by situationally specific relevances. 'Typification,' then, seems to be an unfortunate hangover in ethnomethodology of one of Schutz's anthropological constants. See Schutz, *Phenomenology*, and Schutz and Luckman, *Structures*.

10. Garfinkel and Sacks, 'Formal Structures.' Again, as with typification, the theoretical postulate is asserted to be *extra*theoretical; that is, it is apparently grounded (prior to theory) in the theory's own object: everyday methodic accomplishments. But what are the grounds of that assertion?

11. Hartland gives a meticulous analysis of the many and varied methods magistrates use for describing accused persons. Just one of these is the use of membership categorization devices, a major subdomain of ethnomethodological inquiry. See Sacks, 'Initial Investigation' and 'Analysability.'

12. Sacks, 'Aspects.'

13. A collection of exemplars can be found in Knorr-Cetina and Cicourel, *Advances*.

CHAPTER SEVEN

1. In the next chapter these three points on the range of semiosis will be formalized as 'intelligibility,' 'actionability,' and 'historicity.'

2. Marx, *Theses on Feuerbach*, in Marx and Engels, *Selected Works*, 29.

3. See Lodge and Law, 'Structure.'

4. Turner, *Body*; Armstrong, *Political Anatomy*; Short and Bird, 'Incorporation.'

5. Foucault, *Madness*; *Order of Things*; 'Orders'; *Archaeology*; and *Birth of the Clinic*.

6. Pollner, 'Mundane Reasoning'; '"Very Coinage"'; and *Mundane Reason*.

7. Foucault, 'Questions'; Garfinkel, *Studies*, 33.

8. Foucault, 'Questions,' 8.

9. Garfinkel, *Studies*, 32–33.

10. Foucault, 'Le souci.'

11. Heritage, *Garfinkel*.

12. See Foucault, *Archaeology*, 81–87.

13. Garfinkel, *Studies*, 28–29.

14. Sacks, 'Analysis.'

15. Foucault, *Pierre Rivière* and *Order of Things*.

16. Garfinkel, *Studies*, 116–85; Garfinkel, Lynch, and Livingston, 'Discovering Science.'

17. Garfinkel, *Studies*, 32.

18. Garfinkel and Sacks, 'Formal Structures.'

19. Foucault, *Power/Knowledge*, 212.

20. Heritage, *Garfinkel*, 227.

21. This question (the moral grounds of ethnomethodology's moral 're-fusal') is superbly handled by Lena Jayyusi. See Jayyusi, 'Values.'

22. Foucault, *Order of Things*, xiv.

23. Garfinkel is on record as saying that there is nothing of interest to be found beneath the skull. See Garfinkel, 'Sociological Concepts.'

24. See his contribution to Hinkle, 'Phenomenology.'

25. Foucault, *History of Sexuality*, vol. 1.

26. Dreyfus, 'Heidegger's Critique,' 33.

27. Dreyfus, 'Heidegger's Critique,' 31.

28. Dreyfus, 'Heidegger's Critique,' 31–32.

29. Garfinkel, *Studies*, 104–15.

30. Garfinkel, *Studies*, 116–85; Heritage, *Garfinkel*, 186.

31. See the review of these in Strong, 'Doing Sex.'

32. Source: Victorian AIDS Council poster, 'When you say yes . . . say yes to safe sex' (1990).

33. Sacks, 'Analysis.'

34. For a different view of sex education's social positioning, see Hunter, 'Laughter.'

35. For details of the terms 'membership category' and 'category-bound activity,' see Sacks, 'Initial Investigation' and 'Analysability.' Put formally: if f and v are both logical and necessary functions (attributes) of A, the observation of f in A will mean that v is also present (though unobserved).

36. Sykes, cited in Strong, 'Doing Sex,' 36–37.

37. Willis, *Learning*, 36.

38. See Tolson, *Limits*, and Metcalf and Humphries, *Sexuality*.

39. The standard forms of transcript notation, devised by Gail Jefferson, were not observed by the original transcriber; however, I have replaced his or her ellipses by the conventional sign for the untimed pause: '(.),' since ellipses can appear to be omissions rather than pauses. See the 'Transcript Notation' section in Atkinson and Heritage, *Social Action*, ix–xvi.

40. Payne and Hustler, 'Teaching,' 49–66.

41. Schegloff and Sacks, 'Opening up Closings.'

42. Prince, *Narratology*, 4.

43. For a remarkable reading of everyday utterances (such as 'Boys will be boys') as logical tautologies (!), see Ward and Hirschberg, 'Pragmatic Analysis.'

44. Some readers will hear in this an echo of a very famous Monty Python comedy sketch.

45. Foucault, 'Rituals,' 65–66.

CHAPTER EIGHT

1. A case in point would be Mehan and Wood, *Reality*.

2. Maturana and Varela, *Tree*, 253.

3. See in particular Gleick, *Chaos*.

4. See Penrose, *Emperor's New Mind*. So far I have relied on Penrose's notion of recursive enumerability. However, although it should not concern us, Penrose asks whether there are some (rather strange) sets that are recursively enumerable but are not strictly recursive in the sense that for them, once algorithmically generated, 'there is no general algorithmic way of deciding whether or not an element (or "point") belongs to the set.' Penrose, *Emperor's New Mind*, 161. One case he considers is the Mandelbrot set and its complementary not-set (that which lies outside the set).

5. The term 'actionability' is a first approximation and may need to be replaced by a term that better represents the longer term 'acting as a problem-solution.'

CHAPTER NINE

1. On the various opposites of context-dependence and context-sensitivity, see Frawley, 'Review Article,' especially 364.

2. On the audiovisuality of methodic activities' intelligibility, see Sharrock and Anderson, *Ethnomethodologists*.

3. This makes the ethnomethodological concept of indexicality almost the exact opposite of Peirce's and comes closer to his idea of the 'symbolic' sign. For Peirce, 'An indexical sign is a sign that is actually connected to its object. A symbolic sign is an arbitrary and conventional (in the sense of socially determined) representation of whatever it represents.' McNeill, *Conceptual Basis*, 5.

4. Derrida, *Grammatology*. Some readers may find the attribution of the term 'critical theory' to Derrida problematic since, in sociology at least, it is sometimes thought that the Frankfurt school has a copyright on the term. However, I intend 'critical theory' to refer to *the theory of textual criticism* in its broadest sense and to the Derridean inflection of it in particular. For a basic introduction, see Orr, *Dictionary*.

5. On this score see Ulmer, *Applied Grammatology*.

6. In some of his recent work, Derrida has returned to using the term 'deconstruction.' Although the term can, Derrida says, be used to describe a scholarly or philosophical activity, it is better thought of as a process in 'what one might call history (all of the geopolitical earthquakes: the 1917 revolution, the two world wars, psychoanalysis, the Third World, the techno-economico-scientific and military mutations, etc., etc., etc.).' Derrida, 'Politics and Friendship,' 226. See also Derrida, *Spectres*.

7. On this possibility within EM, see Silverman, *Reading*.

8. Heritage, *Garfinkel*, 144.

9. Wittgenstein, *Investigations*, 71.

10. See Pollner, *Mundane Reason*, 69.

11. Mehan and Wood, *Reality*, 95.

12. I mark this point 'po' because at this point all indexical potential would be null, the sign henceforth having a single meaning in perpetuity.

13. Here the expression would become indexical in *Peirce's* sense (see note 3 above).

14. Derrida, '*Origins of Geometry*,' 72.

15. See Derrida, '*Origins of Geometry*,' 101–2, and Ulmer, 'Post-age,' especially 48.

16. I mark this point 'p1' because at this point the expression would have preserved its full indexical potential – it could mean anything and so would be a kind of semiotic plenum in its own right.

17. Cf. Eco, *Limits*, 32–34.

18. Wittgenstein says, concerning an uncontexted and therefore highly 'entropic' expression: 'A multitude of familiar paths lead off . . . in every direction.' Wittgenstein, *Investigations*, par. 525.

19. This is shown most clearly in Garfinkel's rewriting experiment, where students were able to proliferate descriptions of what they had said earlier (in a conversation), to proliferate descriptions of those descriptions, and so on, potentially infinitely – but precisely 'in the name of' trying to say, definitively, what it is they had 'meant.' Hence, even in a very strange community (Garfinkel's seminar) that attempts indexical proliferation, Garfinkel finds the tendency to want to find relatively singular or definitive meanings. It was based on experiments like these that Garfinkel was able to conclude that indexicality (difference) was the basis of homogeneous social order. See Garfinkel, *Studies*, 38–42.

20. For example, the attempt of the pre-Socratics to find an ideal language that adhered to the law of *unum nomen, unum nominatum* (one name for each thing named).

21. Schutz, *Collected Papers*, vol. 1.

22. For an imaginary version of the latter, see Borges, 'Tlön, Uqbar.'

23. I will use the terms 'closing' and 'opening' henceforth to refer to the *tendencies* towards po and p1, respectively. In this sense my use of the terms is markedly different from the notion of 'closed' versus 'open' texts in the work of Eco and others.

24. Latour, *Science in Action*.

25. The matter of 'opening' methods or strategies will be discussed in the next investigation, chapter 10.

26. Cf. de Certeau, *Practice*. One problem with de Certeau's analysis of the 'resignification' of everyday texts and objects is that it ignores the possibility (raised here) that certain kinds of popular texts may in fact be *re-*

cipient-designed in order to be corruptible or 'resignifiable' – in which case assumptions about 'resistance' will be problematic.

CHAPTER TEN

1. Another interesting account of cinephilia, from within that community, is Martin, 'No Flowers.'

2. Kelly and Donen, *Singin' in the Rain*; Masson, 'Promenade.' Whereas Masson's 'data' are filmic signs, my 'data,' which I describe by repeating them here, are Masson-as-cineast's readings of them.

3. Masson, 'Promenade,' 52 (French), 162 (English).

4. Masson, 'Promenade,' 53 (French), 164 (English).

5. The documentary method and prospectivity-retrospectivity are methods Garfinkel isolates as classical ways definite sense can be made of indexical expressions. See Garfinkel, *Studies.*

6. Masson, 'Promenade,' 52 (French), 162 (English). Lynn Davis has discovered a similar spatial indefiniteness operating in Peter Greenaway's *The Cook, the Thief, His Wife and Her Lover.* Although Greenaway's films are sometimes thought of as 'making no sense,' the obvious possibility here is that they make *more than one* sense but provide no obvious resources for choosing between the contenders. See Davis, 'Greenaway.'

7. On reality disjunctures, see Pollner, *Mundane Reason.*

8. Masson, 'Promenade,' 54 (French), 165 (English).

9. Masson, 'Promenade,' 50 (French), 159 (English).

CHAPTER ELEVEN

1. Gibson, 'Introduction,' 3.

2. On the distinction between opacity and transparency of community descriptions, see Quine, *Word and Object*, and Coulter, *Rethinking.*

3. Fabian, *Time.*

4. For example, readers of DC's recent *Star Trek* comics have been informed, following quibbles about continuities between the comics and other generic versions of *Star Trek*, that there is a canon (inside which continuity takes place) and also an apocrypha (which may formally depart from it). In issue 13 (October 1990), comics editor Ron Greenberger announced that 'Gene Roddenberry [the originator of *Star Trek*] prefers to consider the filmed episodes and films *Star Trek* fact and everything else *Star Trek* fiction. That is the one reason few, if any, of the comics and novels refer to previous novels or comics – that is by Gene's and Paramount's request.' A similar reading condition appears in issue 15, and Greenberger suggests that readers who are unhappy with it should 'drop Paramount Licensing a line.'

5. The concept of recipient design is again attributable to Garfinkel.

6. *Groo the Wanderer*, no. 68 (August 1990): 31.

7. Rather paradoxically, this allows Mark Evanier (the writer of Groo and the one who replies to readers' letters) the unique luxury of occasional 'literal,' and therefore irreverent, readings. He frequently takes his readers to task for not seeing how obviously predictable the stories are, how obviously similar they are from month to month, how obviously stupid Groo is, how they are obviously being conned out of their money, and so on.

8. Bennett, 'Foreword,' ix.

9. See Larry Feldman's letter in *Detective Comics*, no. 624 (December 1990): 23. For a quickly digestible instance of the changes in *Batman* from 1939 to the present, see *Detective Comics*, no. 627, a special anniversary issue, celebrating Batman's six hundredth appearance in *Detective* and collecting rewritings of 'The Case of the Chemical Syndicate' from various periods.

10. Burton, *Batman*. On the specific qualities of this production in relation to the comic, see Marriott, *Batman*, 8–13.

11. Stock *Batman* print versions also include a range of one-offs in hardcover (*Arkham Asylum*, *Batman 3-D*, *Batman Archives*, *Batman Bride of Demon*, *Batman Dailies*, *Batman Digital Justice*) and paperback (*Batman Murders*).

12. Although the legend and the list were included in almost every publication, this particular version is from *Skreemer*, no. 4 (August 1989), which is itself marked 'Suggested for Mature Readers.'

13. See *Batman*, no. 457 (December 1990), for Tim's formal emergence as the revamped (third) Robin who later became the main hero of the new *Robin* comic (DC Comics, January–May 1991). In *Batman*, no. 466 (August 1991), the third Robin formally rejoined Batman in Gotham City in an episode ironically titled 'No More Heroes.'

14. A distorted version of Batman as detective sometimes remains in the *Detective Comics* variation. And occasionally there is a reasonably straightforward use of the detective story genre: see *Detective Comics*, no. 630 (June 1991), titled 'And the Executioner Wore Stiletto Heels.'

15. *Batman*, no. 454 (September 1990) includes references to Thomas Pynchon's *The Crying of Lot 49*, and the *Detective* sequence nos. 622–24 (October–December 1990) examines the effects on Batman when a *Batman* comic begins to appear in Gotham City.

16. This is particularly problematic for non-American readers – and parallels the confusions of the offshore Hollywood cinephile. See Martin, 'No Flowers.'

17. The four-part *Detective* series 'Rite of Passage' involved Batman in a trip to the Carribean to hunt out the voodoo leader called the Obeah Man.

18. *Batman* writer Alan Grant said, 'I find it easier to write Batman than

any other figure, probably because I like him so much. It's not hard because you don't have to make him the center of every story, he's more of a presence. To me the stories are as much about Gotham City as they are about him.' Nutman, 'Psychotics,' 20.

19. The Slasher sets up a classic ambiguity for the new Batman. His aim is to carve up the city's 'vermin,' but when Batman comes to inflict justice on him, the Slasher himself is referred to (directly, by Batman) as 'vermin.'

20. Cf. a parallel use of this theme in the first *Terminator* movie. There the villain is utterly without human features and is merely set on his mission of destruction. Even though SF-horror moviegoers know he is a cyborg, there is, I think, a constant tension in the movie arising from the expectation that this villain will somehow crack, become more 'human,' be somehow pushed into a position where he has to be bargained with. No such thing, of course, is allowed to happen.

21. The flyleaf to Pearson and Uricchio's *Many Lives* informs the reader that no original graphics from the comic have been reproduced in the book. DC Comics withheld permission, since the cultural studies readings of Batman in the book did not correspond with 'their' Batman.

22. It would be interesting, for example, to see how relativist cultural studies could square the Demon's prayer with the following discussion of the complexities of political targets for comics writers: 'There is a great deal of mind control which is coming from the liberal rather than the conservative camp. It's very easy to do the usual corporate villains, dyed-in-the-wool Reaganites. It's a very easy target, but it has been done to death. I have a basic reflex action that when I see a sacred cow I shoot, and having had a few run-ins with censors, discovering that most of them declare themselves liberal, I found a whole new area that hadn't been tapped.' Frank Miller (originator of the Dark Knight version of Batman), interviewed in Nutman, 'Miller's Crossing,' 24.

23. See Wittgenstein, *Certainty.*

24. Although ethnomethodology, for example, has discovered the commonsense embargo on stating the obvious, it has not considered the possibility that what constitutes the obvious, in some cases, can be normatively indeterminate.

CHAPTER TWELVE

1. Latour, *Science in Action.*

2. Penrose, *Emperor's New Mind*, 114.

3. Penrose, *Emperor's New Mind*, 124; my italics.

4. Brouwer's actual argument was highly influential on Wittgenstein's shift from a calculus-based semantics to a 'form of life' theory of signification.

5. Penrose, *Emperor's New Mind*, 125–26; my italics except for 'there.'

6. Penrose, *Emperor's New Mind*, 126–27; my italics.

7. Perhaps Penrose's argument does *not* require the principle of external definability: but then his problem is an ontological rather than a merely logical one. He would then have to be saying that mathematical truth is absolute because *E* and *C* are absolute, not mere conventions of logic.

CHAPTER THIRTEEN

1. Gadamer, 'Universality,' 131.

2. Habermas, cited in Bleicher, *Hermeneutics*, 203.

3. Habermas, 'Universal Pragmatics,' 1.

4. See Coulter, *Social Construction*.

5. Auster, *Leviathan*, 29.

6. I am very grateful to Heather Davies, Julie Hemmett, and Alison Lee for giving me access to their transcripts. I have altered only the personally identifying details. Unless otherwise specified, the transcription conventions are those devised by Gail Jefferson. See the 'Transcript Notation' section in Atkinson and Heritage, *Social Action*, ix–xvi.

7. Sacks, Schegloff, and Jefferson, 'Simplest Systematics.'

8. One other option that is technically possible (though for Linda it may not be morally possible) is what Jefferson calls the 'nyem' – a half-agreement, half-disagreement. See Jefferson, 'What's in a "Nyem"?'

9. See Schegloff and Sacks, 'Opening up Closings.'

10. Jefferson's conventions have not been used for this transcription.

11. Lee, 'Gender.'

12. McHoul, 'No Guarantees.'

13. Coulter, *Social Construction*, 26. The transcription is copied verbatim from Coulter. Its conventions are different from those currently used in conversation analysis. The symbol '//' marks the point at which overlap commences.

14. Coulter, *Social Construction*, 27.

15. Coulter, *Social Construction*, 30.

16. Lyotard, '*Différend.*'

17. Lyotard, '*Différend,*' 5.

18. See Bogen and Lynch, 'Taking Account.'

19. Bogen and Lynch, 'Social Critique.'

20. See Hartland, 'Discourse Analysis.'

CHAPTER FOURTEEN

1. See Bogen and Lynch, 'Taking Account.'

2. Caputo, *Against Ethics*, 1.

3. Foucault, *History of Sexuality*, vol. 1; *Use of Pleasure*; *Care of the Self*.

4. Miller, *Passion*, 328–34.

5. Miller, *Passion*, 306–9.

6. Miller, *Passion*, 307, quoting Cottam, 'Inside,' 3.

7. 'The will not to be governed' is Miller's paraphrase of Foucault's position; *Passion*, 310. It amounts to an inversion of the Kantian imperative and could be expressed as follows: Act in such a way that the grounds of your action defy all principles of general legislation.

8. Flax, 'End of Innocence.'

9. Braidotti, *Patterns*.

10. See Frow, *What Was Postmodernism?*

11. Wittgenstein, 'Ethics,' 11–12.

12. Feher, 'Being After.'

13. My argument here is informed by a (perhaps idiosyncratic) reading of the work of Luce Irigaray. See Irigaray, *That Sex* and *Speculum*.

14. See de Lauretis, *Alice*, 94, regarding Foucault's 'paradoxical conservatism.'

15. Gasché, *Tain of the Mirror*, 154.

16. Derrida, 'Afterword,' 116.

17. Staten, *Wittgenstein*, xvi.

18. For a list of such countervalues, see Hassan, *Postmodern Turn*, 91–92.

19. On Derrida's turn towards deconstruction as a practical-political formation (as opposed to a merely analytic strategy in philosophy), see Derrida, *Spectres*.

20. The term 'cryptogrammar' is taken from Threadgold, 'Postmodernism.'

21. Derrida, *Spurs*, 81.

22. On athesis and the athetical, see McHoul and Wills, *Writing Pynchon*, 90 ff.

23. See Coulter, 'Contextualising,' 690.

24. Derrida, *Speech*, 135.

25. Bogen and Lynch, 'Taking Account.'

26. Lyotard's concept of the *différend* is briefly explained in chapter 13.

27. Foucault, *Use of Pleasure*, 11, 8.

28. Foucault, *Use of Pleasure*, 8–9.

29. If so, it is ironic that the nearest imaginable society to ancient Greece in recent times (where 'free men,' old and young, composed their own ethics relatively unhindered by legal restraint) was, arguably, Wittgenstein's Cambridge.

30. Foucault, 'Genealogy of Ethics,' 245.

31. Derrida, 'Politics and Friendship,' 231.

32. Derrida, 'My Chances,' 27.

Works Cited

Anderson, Benedict. *Imagined Communities: Reflections on the Origin and Spread of Nationalism*. London: Verso, 1983; 2d ed., London: Verso, 1991.

Armstrong, David. *The Political Anatomy of the Body: Medical Knowledge in Britain in the Twentieth Century*. London: Cambridge University Press, 1983.

Ashmore, Malcolm. *The Reflexivity Thesis*. Chicago: University of Chicago Press, 1989.

Atkinson, J. Maxwell, and John Heritage, eds. *Structures of Social Action: Studies in Conversation Analysis*. London: Cambridge University Press, 1984.

Auster, Paul. *Leviathan*. London: Faber & Faber, 1992.

Barthes, Roland. *Camera Lucida*. Translated by R. Howard. New York: Hill & Wang, 1981.

———. *Image Music Text*. Edited and translated by S. Heath. London: Fontana, 1977.

Bennett, Tony. 'Foreword.' In *The Many Lives of the Batman*, edited by R. A. Pearson and W. Uricchio, i–ix. New York: Routledge, Chapman & Hall, 1991.

Berger, John. *Ways of Seeing*. London: BBC/Penguin, 1972.

Bleicher, Joseph. *Contemporary Hermeneutics*. London: Routledge & Kegan Paul, 1980.

Bogen, David, and Michael Lynch. 'Social Critique and the Logic of Description.' *Journal of Pragmatics* 14, no. 3 (1990): 505–21.

———. 'Taking Account of the Hostile Native: Plausible Deniability and the Production of Conventional History in the Iran-Contra Hearings.' *Social Problems* 36, no. 3 (1989): 197–224.

Borges, Jorge Luis. 'Tlön, Uqbar, Orbis Tertius.' Translated by A. Reid. In *Ficciones*, 17–35. New York: Grove, 1962.

Braidotti, Rosi. *Patterns of Dissonance*. Cambridge: Polity, 1991.

Burton, Tim, director. *Batman*. Los Angeles: Warner Brothers, 1989. Motion picture.

Caputo, John D. *Against Ethics: Contributions to a Poetics of Obligation with Constant Reference to Deconstruction*. Bloomington: Indiana University Press, 1993.

Chomsky, Noam. *Rules and Representations*. Oxford: Blackwell, 1980.

————. 'Some Empirical Assumptions in Modern Philosophy of Language.' In *Philosophy, Science and Method: Essays in Honor of Ernest Nagel*, edited by S. Morgenbesser, P. Suppes, and M. White, 260–85. New York: St. Martin's, 1969.

Cottam, Richard. 'Inside Revolutionary Iran.' In *Iran's Revolution*, edited by R. K. Ramazani, 3–26. Bloomington: Indiana University Press, 1990.

Coulter, Jeff. 'Is Contextualising Necessarily Interpretive?' *Journal of Pramatics* 21, no. 6 (1994): 689–98.

————. *Rethinking Cognitive Theory*. London: Macmillan, 1983.

————. *The Social Construction of Mind: Studies in Ethnomethodology and Linguistic Philosophy*. London: Macmillan, 1979.

Coward, Rosalind, and John Ellis. *Language and Materialism*. London: Routledge & Kegan Paul, 1977.

Davis, Lynn. 'Greenaway in Writing.' B.A. honours diss., Murdoch University, 1991.

de Certeau, Michel. *The Practice of Everyday Life*. Translated by S. Rendell. Berkeley: University of California Press, 1984.

de Lauretis, Teresa. *Alice Doesn't: Feminism, Semiotics, Cinema*. Bloomington: Indiana University Press, 1984.

Derrida, Jacques. 'Afterword: Toward an Ethic of Discussion.' Translated by S. Weber. In *Limited Inc*, 111–60. Evanston IL: Northwestern University Press, 1988.

————. *Edmund Husserl's 'Origins of Geometry': An Introduction*. Translated by J. Leavey. Stony Brook NY: Nicolas Hays, 1978.

————. *Margins of Philosophy*. Translated by A. Bass. Chicago: University of Chicago Press, 1982.

————. 'My Chances/Mes Chances: A Rendezvous with Some Epicurean Stereophonies.' In *Taking Chances: Derrida, Psychoanalysis, and Literature*, edited by J. H. Smith and W. Kerrigan, 1–32. Baltimore: Johns Hopkins University Press, 1984.

————. *Of Grammatology*. Translated by G. C. Spivak. Baltimore: Johns Hopkins University Press, 1976.

————. 'Politics and Friendship: An Interview with Jacques Derrida.' In *The Althusserian Legacy*, edited by E. A. Kaplan and M. Sprinker, 183–231. London: Verso, 1993.

————. *Signéponge/Signsponge*. Translated by R. Rand. New York: Columbia University Press, 1984.

————. 'Some Statements and Truisms about Neologisms, Newisms, Postisms, Parasitism, and Other Small Seismisms.' In *The States of 'Theory,'* edited by D. Carroll, 63–94. Bloomington: Indiana University Press, 1993.

————. *Spectres de Marx: L'état de la dette, le travail du dueil et al nouvelle Internationale.* Paris: Galilée, 1993.

————. *Speech and Phenomena.* Translated by D. B. Allison. Evanston IL: Northwestern University Press, 1973.

————. *Spurs/Eperons: Nietzsche's Styles.* Translated by B. Harlow. Chicago: University of Chicago Press, 1978.

————. 'Structure, Sign, and Play in the Discourse of the Human Sciences.' In *The Structuralist Controversy*, edited by R. Macksey and E. Donato, 247–72. Baltimore: Johns Hopkins University Press.

————. *The Truth in Painting.* Translated by G. Bennington and I. McLeod. Chicago: University of Chicago Press, 1987.

————. *La vérité en peinture.* Paris: Flammarion, 1978.

————. *Writing and Difference.* Translated by A. Bass. London: Routledge & Kegan Paul, 1978.

Diringer, David. *The Alphabet: A Key to the History of Mankind*, vol. 2. 3d ed. London: Hutchinson, 1968.

Donald James. 'Beacons of the Future: Schooling, Subjection and Subjectification.' In *Subjectivity and Social Relations*, edited by V. Beechey and J. Donald, 214–49. Milton Keynes: Open University Press, 1985.

Donzelot, Jacques. *The Policing of Families.* Translated by R. Hurley. London: Hutchinson, 1979.

Dreyfus, Hubert L. 'Heidegger's Critique of the Husserl/Searle Account of Intentionality.' *Social Research* 60, no. 1 (1993): 17–38.

Eagleton, Terry. 'Capitalism, Modernism and Postmodernism.' *New Left Review* 152 (1985): 60–76.

Eco, Umberto. *The Limits of Interpretation.* Bloomington: Indiana University Press, 1990.

Emmison, Mike, and Alec McHoul. 'Drawing on the Economy: Cartoon Discourse and the Production of a Category.' *Cultural Studies* 1, no. 1 (1987): 93–112.

Eribon Didier. *Michel Foucault.* London: Faber & Faber, 1992.

Fabian, Johannes. *Time and the Other: How Anthropology Makes Its Object.* New York: Columbia University Press, 1983.

Feher, Ferenc. 'Being After: The Condition of Postmodernity.' *Age Monthly Review* 7, no. 5 (1987): 8–9.

Flax, Jane. 'The End of Innocence.' In *Feminists Theorize the Political*, edited by J. Butler and J. W. Scott, 445–63. New York: Routledge, 1992.

Foucault, Michel. *The Archaeology of Knowledge.* Translated by A. M. Sheridan Smith. London: Tavistock, 1972.

————. *The Birth of the Clinic: An Archaeology of Medical Perception.* Translated by A. M. Sheridan. London: Tavistock, 1973.

————. *The Care of the Self.* Vol. 3 of *The History of Sexuality.* Translated by R. Hurley. London: Allen Lane/ Penguin, 1988.

————. *Discipline and Punish: The Birth of the Prison.* Translated by A. Sheridan. London: Allen Lane, 1977.

————. ed. *Herculine Barbin: Being the Recently Discovered Memoirs of a Nineteenth-Century French Hermaphrodite.* Translated by R. McDougall. Brighton: Harvester, 1980.

————. *Histoire de la folie à l'âge classique.* Paris: Gallimard, 1972.

————. *The History of Sexuality.* Vol. 1, *An Introduction.* Translated by R. Hurley. London: Allen Lane, 1979.

————. *I Pierre Rivière, Having Slaughtered My Mother, My Sister, and My Brother. . . . : A Case of Parricide in the 19th Century.* No translator credited. London: Peregrine, 1978.

————. *Language Counter-memory, Practice.* Translated by D. Bouchard. Oxford: Blackwell, 1977.

————. *Madness and Civilisation.* Translated by R. Howard. London: Tavistock, 1967.

————. 'On the Genealogy of Ethics: An Overview of Work in Progress.' In *Michel Foucault: Beyond Structuralism and Hermeneutics,* edited by H. L. Dreyfus and P. Rabinow, 229–64. Chicago: University of Chicago Press, 1982.

————. *The Order of Things: An Archaeology of the Human Sciences.* No translator credited. London: Tavistock, 1970.

————. 'Orders of Discourse.' Translated by R. Swyer. *Social Science Information* 10 (1972): 7–30.

————. 'Politics and the Study of Discourse.' Translated by C. Gordon. *Ideology and Consciousness* 3 (spring 1978): 7–26.

————. *Power/Knowledge: Selected Interviews and Other Writings, 1972–1977.* Edited by C. Gordon. Translated by C. Gordon, L. Marshall, J. Mepham, and K. Soper. London: Harvester, 1980.

————. 'Questions of Method: An Interview with Michel Foucault.' Translated by C. Gordon. *I&C* 8 (spring 1981): 3–14.

————. 'Rituals of Exclusion.' Translated by J. Johnston. In *Foucault Live: Interviews, 1966–84,* edited by S. Lotringer, 63–72. New York: Semiotext(e) Foreign Agents Series, 1989.

————. 'Le souci de la vérité: Propos receuillis par François Ewald.' *Magazine Littéraire* 207 (1984): 18–23.

————. *The Use of Pleasure.* Vol. 2 of *The History of Sexuality.* Translated by R. Hurley. London: Viking, 1986.

Frawley, William. 'Review Article: *Handbook of Discourse Analysis.*' *Language* 63, no. 2 (1987): 361–97.

Freadman, Anne. 'Untitled (On Genre).' *Cultural Studies* 2, no. 1 (1988): 67–99.

Frow, John. *What Was Postmodernism?* Sydney: Local Consumption Publications, 1991.

Gadamer, Hans Georg. 'The Universality of the Hermeneutic Problem.' In *Contemporary Hermeneutics*, by J. Bleicher, 128–40. London: Routledge & Kegan Paul, 1980.

Gadet, Françoise. *Saussure and Contemporary Culture*. Translated by G. Elliott. London: Century Hutchinson, 1989.

Garfinkel, Harold. 'Some Sociological Concepts and Methods for Psychiatrists.' *Psychiatric Research Reports* 6 (1956): 181–95.

———. *Studies in Ethnomethodology*. Englewood Cliffs NJ: Prentice-Hall, 1967.

Garfinkel, Harold, Michael Lynch, and Eric Livingston. 'The Work of a Discovering Science Construed with Materials from the Optically Discovered Pulsar.' *Philosophy of the Social Sciences* 11 (1981): 131–58.

Garfinkel, Harold, and Harvey Sacks. 'On Formal Structures of Practical Actions.' In *Theoretical Sociology: Perspectives and Developments*, edited by J. C. McKinney and E. A. Tiryakian, 338–66. New York: Appleton-Century-Crofts, 1970.

Gasché, Rudolph. *The Tain of the Mirror: Derrida and the Philosophy of Reflection*. Cambridge: Harvard University Press, 1986.

Gibson, William. 'Introduction.' In *William Gibson's Neuromancer: The Graphic Novel*, Vol. 1, by Tom de Haven and Bruce Jensen, 3. New York: Berkley Books, 1989.

Gleick, James. *Chaos: Making a New Science*. London: Cardinal/Sphere, 1987.

Grant, R. T., and E. B. Reeve. *Observations of the General Effects of Injury in Man*. London: HMSO, 1951.

Greenblatt, Stephen. 'Towards a Poetics of Culture.' In *The New Historicism*, edited by H. Aram Veeser, 1–14. New York: Routledge, 1989.

Habermas, Jürgen. 'What Is Universal Pragmatics?' Translated by T. McCarthy. In *Communication and the Evolution of Society*, 1–68. London: Heineman, 1979.

Hacking, Ian. 'Biopower and the Avalanche of Printed Numbers.' *Humanities in Society* 5, nos. 3–4 (1982): 279–95.

———. 'How Should We Do the History of Statistics?' *I&C* 8 (spring 1981): 15–26.

Hall, Stuart. 'The Toad in the Garden: Thatcher among the Theorists.' In *Marxism and the Interpretation of Culture*, edited by C. Nelson and L. Grossberg, 35–74. Urbana: University of Illinois Press, 1988.

Halliday, Michael. *Language as Social Semiotic*. London: Arnold, 1978.

————. *Spoken and Written Language*. Geelong: Deakin University Press, 1985.

Hartland, Nicholas. 'A Discourse Analysis of the Magistrate's Court.' Ph.D. diss., University of Melbourne, 1991.

Hassan, Ihab. 'Pluralism in Postmodern Perspective.' *Critical Inquiry* 12, no. 3 (1986): 503–20.

————. *The Postmodern Turn: Essays in Postmodern Theory and Culture*. Columbus: Ohio State University Press, 1987.

Hatch, David. "The Analysis of Cultural Objects: Organizational Parameters of Utterance Design." *Analytic Sociology* (microfiche) 1 (1978): n.p.

Heap, James. "What Counts as Reading When Reading Counts: Toward a Sociology of Reading." Paper presented at the Canadian Sociological and Anthropological Association, Fredericton, New Brunswick, June 1977.

Henriques, Julian, Wendy Hollway, Cathy Urwin, Couze Venn, and Valerie Walkerdine. *Changing the Subject: Psychology, Social Regulation and Subjectivity*. London: Methuen, 1984.

Heritage, John. *Garfinkel and Ethnomethodology*. Cambridge: Polity, 1984.

Heritage, John, and D. Rodney Watson. "Aspects of the Properties of Formulations in Natural Conversations: Some Instances Analysed." *Semiotica* 30, nos. 3–4 (1980): 245–62.

————. "Formulations as Conversational Objects." In *Everyday Language*, edited by G. Psathas, 123–62. New York: Irvington, 1979.

Hill, Richard J., and Kathleen Stones Crittenden, eds. *Proceedings of the Purdue Symposium on Ethnomethodology*. Institute Monograph Series, no. 1. Lafayette, IN: Purdue Institute for the Study of Social Change, Department of Sociology, 1968.

Hinkle, Gisela J., ed. "When Is Phenomenology Sociological?" *Annals of Phenomenological Sociology* 2 (1972): 1–40.

Hodge, Robert, and Gunther Kress. *Social Semiotics*. Cambridge: Polity, 1988.

Horgan, John. "Profile: Physicist John A. Wheeler." *Scientific American* 264, no. 6 (June 1991): 16–17.

Hunter, Ian. 'Culture, Bureaucracy and the History of Popular Education.' In *Child and Citizen: Genealogies of Schooling and Subjectivity*, edited by D. Meredith and D. Tyler, 11–34. Brisbane: Institute for Cultural Policy Studies, 1991.

————. 'English in Australia.' *Meanjin* 47, no. 4 (1988): 723–38.

————. 'Laughter and Warmth: Sex Education in Victorian Secondary Schools.' *Local Consumption*, ser. 5 (1984): 52–81.

————. 'Learning the Literature Lesson: The Limits of the Aesthetic Personality.' In *Towards a Critical Sociology of Reading Pedagogy: Papers of the XII World Congress on Reading*, edited by C. Baker and A. Luke, 49–82. Amsterdam: Benjamins, 1991.

Hutcheon, Linda. 'Beginning to Theorize Postmodernism.' *Textual Practice* 1, no. 1 (1987): 10–31.

Huyssen, Andreas. 'The Search for Tradition: Avant-Garde and Postmodernism in the 1970s.' *New German Critique* 22 (winter 1981): 23–40

Irigaray, Luce. *Speculum: Of the Other Woman*. Ithaca: Cornell University Press, 1985.

————. *That Sex Which Is Not One*. Ithaca: Cornell University Press, 1985.

Jayyusi, Lena. 'The Reflexive Nexus: Photo-Practice and Natural History.' *Continuum: The Australian Journal of Media and Culture* 6, no. 2 (1993): 25–52.

————. 'Values and Moral Judgement: Communicative Praxis as a Moral Order.' In *Ethnomethodology and the Human Sciences*, edited by G. Button, 227–51. Cambridge: Cambridge University Press, 1991.

Jefferson, Gail. 'What's in a "Nyem"?' *Sociology* 12, no. 1 (1978): 135–39.

Kelly, Gene, and Stanley Donen, directors and choreographers. *Singin' in the Rain*. Los Angeles: Metro-Goldwyn-Mayer, 1951. Motion picture.

Knorr-Cetina, Karen, and Aaron Cicourel, eds. *Advances in Social Theory and Methodology: Towards an Integration of Micro- and Macro-sociologies*. Boston: Routledge & Kegan Paul, 1981.

Kuhn, Thomas. *The Structure of Scientific Revolutions*. 2d ed. Chicago: University of Chicago Press, 1970.

Latour, Bruno. *Science in Action: How to Follow Scientists and Engineers through Society*. Cambridge: Harvard University Press, 1987.

Lee, Alison. 'Gender and Geography: Literacy Pedagogy and Curriculum Politics.' Ph.D. diss., Murdoch University, 1993.

Lodge, John, and Peter Law. 'Structure as Process and Environmental Constraint: A Note on Ethnomethodology.' *Theory and Society* 5 (1978): 373–86.

Lyotard, Jean-François. 'The *Différend*, the Referent, and the Proper Name.' *Diacritics* 14, no. 3 (1984): 4–14.

Maclure, J. Stuart. *Educational Documents: England and Wales 1816 to the Present Day*. London: Chapman & Hall, 1965.

Maras, Steven. 'The Hermeneutics of Production: Extensions of the Return to Bergson.' Ph.D. diss., Murdoch University, 1993.

Marriott, John. *Batman: The Official Book of the Movie*. London: Hamlyn/Octopus, 1989.

Martin, Adrian. 'No Flowers for the Cinéphile: The Fates of Cultural Populism, 1960–1988.' In *Island in the Stream: Myths of Place in Australian Culture*, edited by P. Foss, 117–38. Leichhardt: Pluto, 1988.

Marx, Karl. 'Extract from the *Economic and Philosophic Manuscripts of 1844*.' In *Marx and Engels on Literature and Art: A Selection of Writings*, edited by L. Baxandall and S. Morawski, 51–52. St. Louis MO: Telos, 1973.

Marx, Karl, and Friedrich Engels, *Selected Works*. Moscow: Progress, 1970.

Masson, Alain. 'An Architectural Promenade.' Translated by A.-M. Medcalf and A. McHoul. *Continuum: The Australian Journal of Media and Culture* 5, no. 2 (1992): 159–66.

———. 'Une promenade architecturale.' *Positif* 331 (1988): 50–54.

Maturana, Humberto R., and Francisco J. Varela. *The Tree of Knowledge: The Biological Roots of Human Understanding*. Translated by Robert Paolucci. Boston: New Science Library, 1988.

McHoul, Alec. 'Why There Are No Guarantees for Interrogators.' *Journal of Pragmatics* 11, no. 4 (1987): 455–71.

McHoul, Alec, and David Wills, *Writing Pynchon: Strategies in Fictional Analysis*. London: Macmillan, 1990.

McNeill, David. *The Conceptual Basis of Language*. Hillsdale NJ: Erlbaum, 1979.

Mehan, Hugh, and Houston Wood. *The Reality of Ethnomethodology*. New York: Wiley, 1975.

Metcalf, Andy, and Martin Humphries, eds. *The Sexuality of Men*. London: Pluto, 1985.

Miller, James. *The Passion of Michel Foucault*. London: HarperCollins, 1993.

Miller, Toby. *The Well-Tempered Self: Citizenship, Culture and the Postmodern Subject*. Baltimore: Johns Hopkins University Press, 1993.

Monk, Ray. *Ludwig Wittgenstein: The Duty of Genius*. London: Cape, 1990.

Nancy, Jean-Luc. 'Finite History.' In *The States of 'Theory,'* edited by D. Carroll, 149–72. Bloomington: Indiana University Press, 1993.

Natanson, Maurice. *Literature, Philosophy and the Social Sciences: Essays in Existentialism and Phenomenology*. The Hague: Nijhoff, 1968.

Nietzsche, Friedrich. *Basic Writings of Nietzsche*. Edited by W. Kaufmann. New York: Modern Library, 1968.

———. *The Use and Abuse of History*. Translated by A. Collins. Indianapolis: Bobbs-Merrill, 1949.

Nutman, Philip. 'Miller's Crossing.' *Comics Scene* 17 (February 1991): 9–12, 24.

———. 'One Man's Psychotics.' *Comics Scene* 17 (February 1991): 19–23, 60.

Orr, Leonard. *A Dictionary of Critical Theory.* Westport CN: Greenwood, 1991.

Payne, George, and David Hustler. 'Teaching the Class: The Practical Management of a Cohort.' *British Journal of Sociology of Education* 1 (1980): 49–66.

Pearson, R. A., and W. Uricchio, eds., *The Many Lives of the Batman.* New York: Routledge, Chapman & Hall, 1991.

Penrose, Roger. *The Emperor's New Mind: Concerning Computers, Minds, and the Laws of Physics.* London: Vintage, 1991.

Pollner, Melvin. 'Mundane Reasoning.' *Philosophy of the Social Sciences* 4 (1974): 35–54.

———. *Mundane Reason: Reality in Everyday and Sociological Discourse.* Cambridge: Cambridge University Press, 1987.

———. '"The Very Coinage of Your Brain": The Anatomy of Reality Disjunctures.' *Philosophy of the Social Sciences* 5 (1975): 411–30.

Pratt, Mary Louise. 'Linguistic Utopias.' In *The Linguistics of Writing: Arguments between Language and Literature*, edited by N. Fabb, D. Attridge, A. Durant, and C. MacCabe, 48–66. New York: Methuen, 1987.

Prince, Gerald. *Narratology: The Form and Functioning of Narrative.* Berlin: Mouton, 1982.

Proust, Marcel. *A Search for Lost Time.* Translated by J. Grieve. Canberra: Australian National University Press, 1982.

Pynchon, Thomas. *The Crying of Lot 49.* Philadelphia: Lippincott, 1966.

Quine, W. V. *Word and Object.* Cambridge: MIT Press, 1960.

Rhees, Rush. 'Can There Be a Private Language?' In *Wittgenstein: The Philosophical Investigations*, edited by G. Pitcher, 267–85. London: Macmillan, 1968.

Ruthrof, Horst. *Pandora and Occam: On the Limits of Language and Literature.* Bloomington: Indiana University Press, 1992.

Sacks, Harvey. 'An Analysis of the Course of a Joke's Telling in Conversation.' In *Explorations in the Ethnography of Speaking*, edited by R. Bauman and J. Sherzer, 337–53. London: Cambridge University Press, 1974.

———. 'Aspects of the Sequential Organization of Conversation.' Draft manuscript, n.d.

———. 'An Initial Investigation of the Usability of Conversational Data for Doing Sociology.' In *Studies in Social Interaction*, edited by D. Sudnow, 3–74. New York: Free Press, 1972.

———. *Lectures on Conversation.* Edited by G. Jefferson. Oxford: Blackwell, 1992.

———. 'On the Analysability of Stories by Children.' In *Directions in Sociolinguistics*, edited by J. Gumperz and D. Hymes, 325–45. New York: Holt, Rinehart & Winston, 1972.

Sacks, Harvey, Emanuel Schegloff, and Gail Jefferson. 'A Simplest Systematics for the Organization of Turn-Taking for Conversation.' *Language* 50, no. 4 (1976): 696–735.

Said, Edward. *Culture and Imperialism.* London: Chatto & Windus, 1993.

Sanders, Noel. 'Notes on Photoportraiture.' In *Photo Discourse*, edited by K. Brereton, 116–21. Sydney: Sydney College of the Arts, 1981.

Saussure, Ferdinand de. *Edition critique du Cours de linguistique générale.* Edited by R. Engler. Wiesbaden: Otto Harrassowitz, 1967–74.

Schegloff, Emanuel, and Harvey Sacks, 'Opening up Closings.' *Semiotica* 8, no. 4 (1973): 289–327.

Schutz, Alfred. *Collected Papers.* Vol. 1, *The Problem of Social Reality.* Edited by M. Natanson. The Hague: Nijhoff, 1962.

———. *The Phenomenology of the Social World.* Evanston IL: Northwestern University Press, 1970.

Schutz, Alfred, and Thomas Luckman, *The Structures of the Lifeworld.* Evanston IL: Northwestern University Press, 1973.

Schwarz, Daniel R. 'Review Essay: Canonicity, Culture, and Pluralism – a Humanistic Perspective on Professing English.' *Texas Studies in Literature and Language* 34, no. 1 (1992): 149–75.

Sharrock, Wes, and Bob Anderson. *The Ethnomethodologists.* London: Tavistock, 1986.

Short, Stephanie, and John Bird. 'The Incorporation of the Works of Michel Foucault into Sociology: An Evaluation of the Strategies of Armstrong and Turner.' Paper presented at the annual meeting of the Sociological Association of Australia and New Zealand, Brisbane, August 1985.

Silverman, David. *Reading Castaneda: A Prologue to the Social Sciences.* London: Routledge & Kegan Paul, 1975.

Stallybrass, Peter, and Allon White. *The Politics and Poetics of Transgression.* London: Methuen, 1986.

Starobinski, Jean. *Words upon Words: The Anagrams of Ferdinand de Saussure.* New Haven: Yale University Press, 1979.

Staten, Henry. *Wittgenstein and Derrida.* Lincoln: University of Nebraska Press, 1986.

Stratton, Jon. 'Sociology and the Category of Culture: The Problem of

Specificity.' *Australian and New Zealand Journal of Sociology* 23, no. 2 (1987): 246–60.

Strong, Philip. 'Doing Sex: Some Notes on the Management of Sexual Action.' Paper presented at the annual meeting of the British Sociological Association, 1974.

Tagg, John. *The Burden of Representation*. London: Macmillan, 1988.

———. 'Power and Photography: Part One – a Means of Surveillance: The Photograph as Evidence in Law.' *Screen Education* 36 (autumn 1980): 17–55.

Taine, Hippolyte. *Philosophie de l'art, Voyage en Italie, Essais de critique et d'histoire*. Paris: Hermann, 1966.

Threadgold, Terry. 'Postmodernism, Systemic-Functional Linguistics as Metalanguage and the Practice of Cultural Critique.' Paper presented at the Inaugural Australian Systemics Workshop, Deakin University, January 1990.

Tolson, Andrew. *The Limits of Masculinity*. London: Tavistock, 1976.

Turner, Brian. *The Body and Society*. London: Heineman, 1984.

Ulmer, Gregory. *Applied Grammatology: Post(e)-pedagogy from Jacques Derrida to Joseph Beuys*. Baltimore: Johns Hopkins University Press, 1985.

———. 'The Post-age.' *Diacritics* 11 (1981): 39–56.

Vico, Giambattista. *Principles of New Science of Giambattista Vico concerning the Common Nature of the Nations*. Edited and translated by T. Bergin and M. Fisch. Ithaca: Cornell University Press, 1968. Originally published 1725.

Wagner, Gillian. *Barnardo*. London: Weidenfeld & Nicolson, 1979.

Wagner, Gillian, and Valerie Lloyd. *The Camera and Dr Barnardo* (exhibition catalog). London: National Portrait Gallery, July–November 1974.

Ward, Gregory L., and Julia Hirschberg. 'A Pragmatic Analysis of Tautological Utterances.' *Journal of Pragmatics* 15, no. 6 (1991): 507–20.

Wieder, D. Lawrence. *Language and Social Reality: The Case of Telling the Convict Code*. The Hague: Mouton, 1974.

Williams, Raymond. 'Base and Superstructure in Marxist Cultural Theory.' *New Left Review* 82 (December 1973): 2–16.

Williamson, Dugald. *Authorship and Criticism*. Sydney: Local Consumption Publications, 1989.

Willis, Paul. *Learning to Labour: How Working Class Kids Get Working Class Jobs*. Farnborough: Saxon House, 1977.

Winspur, Steven. 'Wittgenstein's Semiotic *Investigations*.' *American Journal of Semiotics* 3, no. 2 (1984): 33–57.

Wittgenstein, Ludwig. *The Blue and Brown Books*. 2d ed. Oxford: Blackwell, 1969.

————. *Culture and Value.* 2d ed. Translated by P. Winch. Oxford: Blackwell, 1980.

————. 'A Lecture on Ethics.' *Philosophical Review* 74 (1965): 3–12.

————. *On Certainty.* Edited by G. E. M. Anscombe and G. H. von Wright. Translated by D. Paul and G. E. M. Anscombe Oxford: Blackwell, 1974.

————. *Philosophical Grammar.* Edited by R. Rhees. Translated by A. Kenny. Oxford: Blackwell, 1974.

————. *Philosophical Investigations.* 3d ed. Translated by G. E. M. Anscombe. Oxford: Blackwell, 1968.

————. *Tractatus Logico-philosophicus.* 2d ed. Translated by D. F. Pears and B. F. McGuinness. London: Routledge & Kegan Paul, 1961.

————. *Wittgenstein's Lectures: Cambridge, 1930–1932.* Edited by D. Lee. Oxford: Blackwell, 1980.

Index

accident (as law), 201, 205–6
actionability (semiosic relation R2), xi–xvi, 129, 131–36, 146, 150–51, 207
Agnes (case study by Garfinkel and Stoller), 111
agreement vs. understanding, 171
archaeology/genealogy, x, 8, 85–87, 100–108, 211
architecture (film sets), 148–51
Aristotle, 45
ars erotica, 193
art of existence, 209–11
asides (in talk), 122–24
as-structure, 79
athesis/athetics, 204
Auster, Paul, 175–76
authenticity, 44
author function, 39

background, taken-for-granted, xv, 175
Badinter, Robert (French minister), 194
Barnardo, Thomas J., 16, 24–35; accusations against, 30–31
Barnardo's Homes, viii, 16, 24–35
Barnes, Thomas (photographer), 16, 26
Barthes, Roland, 20, 36–37, 57
basal readers, 76–82
Batman (comic), 155–63
battle shock, 46–47
Beatles (musical group), 170–71
Bennett, Tony, 155
Berger, John, 37
binarism, 201–2, 204
blind tactics, 205–6
Bogen, David, 188–89, 191, 199, 202, 209
Braidotti, Rosi, 194–96
Brouwer, L. E. J., 166–67, 169

Burge, Sarah, 16, 18, 22–23, 26–29, 36–38

capitalism, 33, 99
Caputo, John, 192–94, 196
Cartesian linguistics, 4
category-bound activities, 124
cause, 13–14
cautionary work, 121–23
center, 7
ceremony/game, 71–73
chaos, 5–6, 163
charity, 31–33
chess, 110
Chomsky, Noam, 69–70
choreography, 148–49
Christianity, 193
classrooms, ix, 64, 73–85
classroom talk, 181–82
closing/opening talk, 123
closure (semiosic), 153–63
coevalness, 49
comics/comic books, xiii, 151, 153–63; history of, 156
community, viii–ix, xv, 15–16, 40, 48–53, 92, 102, 125, 135, 151; consensus, 173–75; membership differences, 178, 184, 209
concept/object relations, 197–98, 203–4
consciousness, 58, 99, 108
consensus/dissensus, xv, 145–46, 173–75, 185–89; deep common accord, 174, 177–78, 187
conservatism, position on sex of, 116
constitutive theorizing, 129
constructionism, 173–74
context-sensitivity, 137. *See also* indexicality/indexical potential
contingency, 204
contradiction (logical), 168–70
control, 96–97
conversation, 175–88

conversational strategy, 186
convict code, 94–95
coscienza, 58–59
Coulter, Jeff, 69–71, 183–87, 191,
    207–8
criteria, 70–71
critical theory, 138–39
cryptogrammar, 202
cultural function, 47
culturalism, 44
cultural poetics, 42
cultural studies, xiii, 42–46, 57
culture, viii, xxi, 41–48
current-selects-next technique, 178

death, 36–37
debate, civil vs. theoretical, 139
de Certeau, Michel, 224 n.26
deconstruction, 198–201, 204, 211
Deleuze, Gilles, 52
deriving, 67–68
Derrida, Jacques, xii, 7, 9, 19, 49,
    52, 61, 69, 139, 198, 200–202,
    204–8, 211, 213 n.2
Descartes, René, 4
determinacy/indeterminacy, x
diachrony/synchrony, 11–12, 14,
    55–56, 59, 93, 96, 105
dial-back precall, 177, 187
Diamond, Hugh (psychiatrist), 26
différance, xii, 138–39
différend, xvi, 146, 187, 209
discourse, x
discourse analysis, 100–108, 176
dissensus/consensus, xv, 145–46,
    173–75, 185–89
distorted communication, 171
Donald, James, 28–29, 66, 80
Donzelot, Jacques, 77
Dreyfus, Hubert, 110–11
Dumézil, Georges, 108
dynamics/statics, 9

Eagleton, Terry, 38–39
economy, 43
education, 73–85
educational housekeeping, 121–23
effective/*wirkliche*/effectivity, vii, ix,
    xvii–xviii, 7, 12

Enlightenment, 45–46
entropy, 143–44, 163
epistemology/ontology, 197
Escher, Maurits, 141
ethical strategy/tactics, 205–6
ethics, xv–xvi, 8–9, 80, 107, 188–
    89; of analysis, 191–211
ethnogenealogy, 101–29
ethnomethodological indifference,
    107
ethnomethodology, x–xii, xv, xx,
    85–87, 91–100, 175–76; com-
    pared with Foucault, 100–108;
    compared with critical theory,
    138–46
ethnopolitics, 146
Euclid, 142
Evanier, Mark, 226 n.7
eventalization, 7, 103
evolution, 6
excluded middle, 168–70
external definability, 168–70

Fabian, Johannes, 49, 154
fact/value, 48, 107
family, 77
fans, xiii, 147–51
Feher, Ferenc, 196
feminism, 194–95
film, xiii, 147–51
film sets, architecture of, 148–51
Flax, Jane, 194–96
forgetting/remembering, 11, 14
formalism, x, 40, 86, 91–100; in ef-
    fective semiotics, 93–94
Foucault, Michel, x–xi, xix, 6, 29,
    85–87, 100, 127–28, 214 n.9;
    compared with ethnomethodol-
    ogy, 100–108; on/and ethics,
    192–94, 196, 200, 206–11
framing, ix, 19–40, 71, 85
Frankfurt school, 223 n.4
Freadman, Anne, 71–73
Frege, Gottlob, 57
Freudian repression, 109

Gadamer, Hans-Georg, 174, 184
Galtonianism, 26
game/ceremony, 71–73

gap, conversational, 180
gaps/filling, 141–42
Gardner, Alexander (photographer), 36
Garfinkel, Harold, xii, xv, xx, 91–96, 100, 101–11, 115, 129, 138–39, 207, 224 n.19, 225 n.5
gatekeeping, xiv, 165–71
Gelassenheit, 192, 194
Gemeinschaft, 50
gender(ing), 23, 199–200, 202, 215 n; in talk, 180–81
genealogy/archaeology, x, 8, 85–87, 100–108, 211
geography (in schools), 181–83, 187
Gibson, William, 153
God, 132
Gorbachev, Mikhail, 158–60
Gould, Stephen Jay, 6
governing, 208
graffiti, 98, 113–14, 170
Grant, Alan, 226 n.18
Grant, R. T. (medical researcher), 46–47
Greece, ancient, 193
Greenaway, Peter, 225 n.6
Greenberger, Ron, 225 n.4
Greenblatt, Stephen, 42
Guattari, Félix, 52

Habermas, Jürgen, 174
Hall, Stuart, 43–45
Halliday, Michael, 71, 213 n.7
Hartland, Nick, 94–99, 131–33, 189, 220 n.3
Hatch, David, 217 n.4
health, 84
Hegel, G. W. F., 7–8, 11, 41, 193
Heidegger, Martin, 50, 79, 110, 193
Heritage, John, 105, 107, 111, 115, 140
historicity (semiosic relation R3), xi–xvi, 125, 129, 131–36, 150–51, 207
history, vii, xi, 3–16, 22, 41, 50–51, 132, 136
HIV, public campaigns to halt, 112
Hobbes, Thomas, 45

Hunter, Ian, 79, 82–85, 217 n.6, 219 n.33
Hussein, Saddam, 158
Husserl, Edmund, 142
Hutcheon, Linda, 38–39
Huyssen, Andreas, 38

ideology, 45, 99, 104
ID-photographs, 27
imperatives vs. offers (in conversation), 184–85
indexicality/indexical potential, xii, 9, 136, 137–46, 149–50, 163, 175, 184; formalized version of, 142–46
intelligibility (semiosic relation R1), xi–xvi, 128–29, 131–36, 150–51, 207
intentionality, 110
intercommunitarian communications, 173–89
intimism, 150
intuitionism, 166–67, 173–74
invariance, 103
Iran, 194
Irigaray, Luce, 119
ironic stance, 106

Jameson, Fredric, 42
Jayyusi, Lena, 222 n.21
Jefferson, Gail, 178, 222 n.39, 228 n.8
Johnstone, Roderick (photographer), 16, 26
jokes, 114–16

Kane, Bob, 157
Kant, Immanuel, 193
Keynes, Maynard, 43
Khomeini, 194
Kuhn, Thomas, 48, 52

langue/paroles, 105
lantern slides, 35–36
Latour, Bruno, 48, 52, 145, 165
law. *See* accident
Leavis, F. R., 44
lecturing, 119–27
Lee, John, 31

Lenin, V. I., 160
letter pages (comics), 154–55, 161–62
Levinas, Emmanuel, 193
limits of ethics, 191–211
limits of semiosis, xiii–xiv, 153–63, 205
Lloyd, Valerie, 26–35
locality/historicality, x, 63
logic (propositional), 168–70
logical grammar, 175, 184, 188
logicism, 57
Lynch, Michael, 188–89, 191, 199, 202, 209
Lyotard, Jean-François, xvi, 42, 187

macro/micro, 98–99
magistrates' courts, 96–97, 132
Mandelbrot, Benoit, 223 n.4
Marx, Karl, 43, 102, 213 n.1
Marxism, 39, 43–44, 102, 161; boy-meets-tractor variety, 159
Masson, Alain, 147–50
mathematics, 163, 165–71, 197
Mead, Margaret, 109
media (of semiosis), vii
Mehan, Hugh, 141
membership categorization, 117–18
mental welfare officers, 186
Merkmal, 68
metaphysics, 198–200, 203
method, xvi–xvii
methodicity, 51, 206
micro/macro, 98–99
Miller, Frank, 227 n.22
Miller, Toby, 219 n.31
minority communities, 202
mise en abyme, 61
mise-en-scène, 149
Monk, Ray, 12
monologism, 121
Monty Python, 222 n.44
Moore, G. E., 13
moral vs. technical choice, 179
musical comedy, 147–51

Nancy, Jean-Luc, 50–52, 59, 138
narrative, 122, 125
Natanson, Maurice, 41, 43

New Historicism, 42
New International, 49
New Wave (comics), 154
Nietzsche, Friedrich, vii, xviii, 6–16, 22, 50
normalization, 29, 128
normativity, 206
North, Oliver, 191–92, 196, 200, 202, 207–9
not-doubting, 161
not-signs, viii–ix, 22, 39–40, 52–53, 55–64
noumenon/phenomenon, 52, 64, 197

object/concept relations, 197–98, 203–4
objectivism/subjectivism, 196–98
offers vs. imperatives (in conversation), 184–85
Ogden, C. K., 57
ontology/epistemology, 197
opening (semiosic), 153–63
opening/closing talk, 123
ordinary language philosophy, x
orphans, 216 n.30

paralogics, xix
parergon, 19, 214 n.1
Parsons, Talcott, 47
Pearson, R. A., 227 n.21
Peirce, Charles Sanders, 56–57, 61, 223 n.3, 224 n.13
Penrose, Roger, xiv, 165–71, 173, 175, 197–98, 223 n.4, 228 n.7
phenomenology, x, 99, 107–8, 111
phenomenon/noumenon, 52, 64, 197
photography, viii, 19–40
physics, 165–71
Platonism/Platonic realism, 144, 165–71, 197
plausibility (vs. truth), 170–71, 173, 176
poesis, 8
political ethics, 192
politicism/realism, 19–22, 34–40, 161–63
Pollner, Melvin, 103

polyvalency (of signs), 151
popular, the, 41, 135
popular science, xiv, 163, 165–71
populism, 194
pornography, 30, 32
postcards, 32
postethics, 203–6
postmodern ethics, 192–200
postmodernism, 38–39, 217 n.39
power, 99, 128
pragrammatology, 211
pre-Socratics, 5
print, 67
prison, 97, 117–18
professional control (of indexical expressions), 165–71
professionality vs. voyeurism, 121–26
Proust, Marcel, 34–35
psychological constructionism, 173–74, 197
psychologism, 66, 78–79
p-values, 142–44
punctum, 36–37
Pythagorean theorem, 142

questioning, 182–83
Q- vs. N-type questions, 182–83

radio talkback, 179–81
rationality, 104
reading, ix, 64, 65–87; in classrooms, 74–85
realism/politicism, 19–22, 34–40, 161–63. *See also* Platonism/Platonic realism
real numbers, 166
recursivity, 133–34
Reeve, E. B. (medical researcher), 46–47
referent, viii, 56–57
reflexivity, x, xxi, 87, 91–100, 115, 124; of semiosic relations, 131–36
relations (semiosic), 59–61, 93–94, 135, 137, 150–51, 220 n.3
relation to oneself, 210
relativism, 21, 39, 144, 162–63, 199
religious affiliation, 178–79, 188

remembering/forgetting, 11, 14
representation, 77
responsible anarchy, 192–93
Reynolds, Rev. George, 216 n
Richards, I. A., 57
Roddenberry, Gene, 225 n.4
Rousseau, Jean-Jacques, 139
rules, xxi, 13, 68–70
Rushdie, Salman, 151
Ruthrof, Horst, 218 n.7

Sacks, Harvey, 31, 94–97, 102, 106, 114–15, 123, 178, 214 n.10, 218 n.9, 221 n.10, 222 n.35
Said, Edward, 51–52
Sanders, Noel, 23
Saussure, Ferdinand de, xvi–xx, 57, 61, 139
Schegloff, Emanuel, 123, 178
Schutz, Alfred, 60, 95, 108, 144, 220 n.9
Schwartz, Daniel, 217 n.5
scientia sexualis, 193
scienza, 58–59
secondary systems of elaboration, 113–19, 135
second-order constructs, 144
semantics, 3, 163, 170
sexism (in talk), 180–81, 188
sexuality, xi, 97–98, 108–27, 193
sexual learning, 111–19
sexual talk, clinical vs. dirty, 126
Shaftesbury, Lord, 24–25, 31
signifier/signified, xvii
social constructionism, 173–74
social semiotics, xviii–xix
socio-logical problems/solutions, xi–xii, 97–99, 102, 128, 132–34, 145, 220 n.3; regarding sex, 108–27
song-and-dance routine, 147–51
spelling reform, 218 n.6
Starobinski, Jean, 213 n.6
Staten, Henry, 67–69, 71, 201, 205
statics/dynamics, 9
Stratton, Jon, 47
student (social position), 127
subjectivism/objectivism, 196–98

surveillance, 29, 128
synchrony/diachrony, 11–12, 14,
  55–56, 59, 93, 96, 105

Tagg, John, 26, 28–29
Taine, Hippolyte, 214 n.4
taken-for-granted background, xv,
  175
talkback radio, 179–81
teaching, 65
techniques of the self, 209–11
telephone talk, 176–77
telos, 56, 61
tendentiousness, 207
tennis, 72
textualism, 20
Threadgold, Terry, 229 n.20
touched-off topics, 123–24
transcribed talk: hospital admission,
  183–87, 208–9; psychiatric admission, 183–87, 208–9
transition relevance place, 178
translation, 153
Turing, Alan, 168
turn-pause, 179
twenty questions (game), 10
typification, 122, 220 n.9

undecidability, 201, 204, 208
understanding, 173–75; vs. agreement, 171

Uricchio, W., 227 n.21
USA/America, 157–62
usage (in Garfinkel), 91–92, 115, 137
USSR/Soviet Union/Russia, 158–62

value/fact, 48, 107
Vico, Giambattista, 58–59
victim(ization), 188–89, 199–200,
  202–3, 209. See also *différend*
voyeurism, 115–16. *See also* professionality vs. voyeurism

Wagner, Gillian, 26–35
Weber, Max, 49
welfare reform, 82–84
Wheeler, John, 10
Wieder, D. Lawrence, 94–95
Williams, Raymond, 43
wirkliche. See effective/*wirkliche*/ef-
  fectivity
Wittgenstein, Ludwig, vii, x, 9, 23,
  42, 46–47, 58, 73, 91, 102,
  138, 141–42, 175, 224 n.18; on
  grammar, 12–14; on reading,
  67–71; on/and ethics, 195–96,
  202, 210
Wood, Houston, 141
writing-in-general, 69

youth, xxi; learning reading, 74–85;
  learning sex, 108–27

In the *Stages* series

Volume 1
The Rushdie Letters: Freedom to Speak,
Freedom to Write
Edited by Steve MacDonogh in Associa-
tion with Article 19

Volume 2
Mimologics
By Gérard Genette
Edited and translated by Thaïs Morgan

Volume 3
Playtexts: Ludics in Contemporary
Literature
By Warren Motte

Volume 4
New Novel, New Wave, New Politics:
Fiction and the Representation of History
in Postwar France
By Lynn A. Higgins

Volume 5
Art for Art's Sake and Literary Life:
How Politics and Markets Helped Shape
the Ideology and Culture of Aestheticism,
1790–1990
By Gene H. Bell-Villada

Volume 6
Semiotic Investigations: Towards an
Effective Semiotics
By Alec McHoul

DATE DUE
